School

School

Why Would
Anyone Do That to Kids?

Jeff Gregg

HAMILTON BOOKS
Lanham • Boulder • New York • London

Published by Hamilton Books
An imprint of The Rowman & Littlefield Publishing Group, Inc.
4501 Forbes Boulevard, Suite 200, Lanham, Maryland 20706
www.rowman.com

6 Tinworth Street, London SE11 5AL, United Kingdom

Copyright © 2021 The Rowman & Littlefield Publishing Group, Inc.

British Library Cataloguing in Publication Information Available

Library of Congress Control Number: 2020952186

ISBN: 9780761872030 (pbk: alk. paper)
ISBN: 9780761872047 (electronic)

∞™ The paper used in this publication meets the minimum requirements of American National Standard for Information Sciences—Permanence of Paper for Printed Library Materials, ANSI/NISO Z39.48-1992.

Contents

Acknowledgments

To Aidan and Anne, with love and pride

With gratitude to
Diana, for her love, support, and insight
Jane, for her artistic magic
Saul, for forwarding all those articles on education
John Holt and John Nicholls, for their wise and gentle spirits

The author would like to thank Diana Underwood, Jane Bentz, and Saul Lerner for their helpful comments on a previous version of the manuscript.

Cover Art: Marshall Memorial School, by Jane Bentz

Preface

As a graduate student in the late 1980s and early 1990s, I fell under the spell of constructivism. Knowledge cannot be transmitted; individuals construct knowledge on the basis of their experiences. Further, we cannot know if our knowledge is the truth in a correspondence sense. We negotiate meanings that we take to be shared with others. We act *as if* their interpretations are the same as our interpretations. This theory helped me explain so many of my prior experiences as a student and a teacher. Armed with this theory and an almost missionary zeal, my peers and I prepared to go out and save the world of education. We had seen classes where students worked in pairs on challenging tasks, developing strategies and solutions that made sense to them. We had seen teachers orchestrate class discussions where students explained and justified their thinking, questioned each other, and negotiated meaning as members of a classroom community. These classes seemed so much more energized, interesting, and humane than those we had experienced as students. Soon, we believed, all classrooms, everywhere, would look like this. We know now what a fanciful vision that was. How naïve we were to believe it would be so easy.

The Standards movement followed on the heels of the constructivist surge in the 80s. Initially, the Standards in various fields tried to incorporate constructivist principles. In an effort to push the Standards and expand their influence, the educators who developed and supported them may have cast their lot too easily with others who didn't understand or care about the underlying principles and who had different motivations. Ultimately, the Standards became a political object. Educators' initial goals were overrun by politicians' quest for accountability via high-stakes standardized tests.

The corruption of the Standards and their lack of impact as originally intended serves as a recent example of the difficulty of reforming school practice. There have been prior "progressive" attempts at school reform. But as David Tyack and Larry Cuban showed in their book, *Tinkering toward Utopia*, these reform efforts also had little impact on classroom practices. Why are schools and, in particular, classroom practices so resistant to change? My thinking about this has been influenced by Seymour Sarason's writings about school change and the failure of reform efforts. In addition to indicting the structure of schools and the power relationships within schools, he argues that reformers ignore the overarching purpose of schools. The overarching aim of this book is to encourage readers to think about and discuss the purpose of education.

This book is formatted as a roundtable discussion about educational issues among a group of fictional characters. The participants in the discussion include teachers, school administrators, state politicians and bureaucrats, parents, community members, and businesspeople. Though the characters are fictional, the majority of the dialogue consists of direct quotes or paraphrases of actual statements about education that have been made by those involved in education and education reform in this country. Some characters' statements were made to me in the course of interviews I conducted. Pseudonyms are used to refer to these interviewees in the notes. The format of the book is shamelessly stolen from Imre Lakatos' *Proofs and Refutations*. In that book, a teacher and students carry out a dialogue that reconstructs the historical development of one of Euler's mathematical theorems. The notes that accompany the dialogue trace out the history and identify the mathematicians who made the arguments that students put forth in the dialogue. The accompanying notes also form an important part of this book, not only to identify the source of participants' statements, but also to provide context and elaboration of arguments. Because the cast of characters is large, readers may find keeping track of who's who to be difficult. For some inexplicable reason, my publisher was unwilling to create a fold-out of the character list attached to the front or back cover. To remedy this, I suggest that readers simply take a picture of the character list with their smartphone for ease of reference. The list may also be accessed via the following Google link: https://drive.google .com/file/d/1bZddLR1BIPMcggHhhfE9d0CMubNutXk7/view?usp=sharing.

My original intent for the book's format was that there would be a chapter of dialogue centered around a particular topic, followed by a chapter of most insightful analysis provided by me. That seems quite arrogant, but not atypical. However, it soon became clear that if the goal was to promote discussions, there was no need for my commentary telling readers what they should have gotten from the dialogue. (How constructivist is that?) Not having to play the role of analyst proved quite freeing for my role as—I find it difficult to say "author"—perhaps "editor" would be more appropriate. I am not claiming that the book presents some sort of objective or unbiased dialogue. It does not. I chose who got to speak and what they said. The dialogue presented plays out as I imagined it in my mind. I am trying to shift the focus of discussions about education, but I don't have any panaceas to offer. In the words of George Counts, "although college professors, if not too numerous, perform a valuable social function, society requires great numbers of persons who, while capable of gathering and digesting facts, are at the same time able to think in terms of life, make decisions, and act. From such persons will come our real social leaders."

I am ambivalent about the depth of the dialogue presented. Some may find it superficial. There are no new ideas. If anything, the book is an attempt to highlight the ideas of other writers that I believe are neglected in current conversations about education. There are several places in the dialogue where an idea could have (should have?) been explored in more depth. If this book is used in education courses, I am confident that instructors and students can pursue in more depth those ideas that pique their interest or raise questions. Is teaching a science or an art? Is the notion of objective educational research a fallacy? Why does it seem that the same educational ideas are continually recycled in different packaging? What is an appropriate relationship between education and the state? For members of the general public reading the book, I hope that you have friends or colleagues who will engage in discussions of educational issues the book raises. Organize a reading group with this book as your first selection!

Finally, I confess that this book is an outgrowth of my frustration, both with the lack of impact of reform efforts mentioned in the opening paragraphs and with the insular nature of the educational research community. I had happily played the publication game several times when one of my journal article submissions was rejected and the accompanying reviewer comments included this: "At the end, the manuscript degenerates into social and political analysis." Of course, my first reaction was anger—I assume that is common—but after cleaning up the shards of broken glass from the floor and calming down a bit, I thought, "You know, that's the point!" Journals have their standards, which is fine, but when the attempt to situate research in social and political context is deemed "out-of-bounds," then what are we doing? It is no wonder that educational research has so little impact on classroom practice. If we are not willing to consider how research will be perceived in the prevailing social and political climate and we are not willing to attempt to influence that climate, then all we are doing is playing an artificial game that enables people to pad their resumes and obtain tenure. I am not optimistic that this book will have any better luck promoting alternative educational practices, but at least it was a somewhat healthy way for me to vent my frustration.

Chapter One

What's the Matter Here?

INTRODUCTION

The Setting: A school cafeteria. Rectangular tables have been arranged to form a large square. Twenty-six people are seated at the tables. They have come to participate in a "roundtable" discussion about issues facing K–12 schools in their community, their state, and the United States.

The Participants:

- Anderson—governor's policy director for education
- Blanchard—parent of a third grader and a seventh grader
- Carpenter—sociology professor
- Druley—high school English teacher
- Easton—school board member and small business owner
- Foster—state senator and chair of the state senate's education committee
- Grable—middle school social studies teacher
- Harris—vice president of a venture capital firm interested in improving K–12 education in the state
- Inglehart—a vice chancellor at a state university and the lead university administrator for a statewide middle school STEM initiative.
- Johnson—director of curriculum and instruction for the school district
- Karch—educational researcher
- Lawrence—teacher educator
- Moderator—recently retired school superintendent
- Newcomer—associate director for mathematics curriculum at the state department of education
- Oates—parent of a fifth grader, eighth grader, and tenth grader

- Peterson—educational psychologist
- Quinn—retired elementary school teacher
- Ross—high school chemistry teacher
- Snepp—middle school math and science teacher
- Taylor—elementary school principal
- Ulrich—local reporter who writes about education issues
- Van Houten—fifth-grade teacher
- Walter—local religious leader
- Xander—education professor
- Yann—history professor
- Zeigler—second-grade teacher

Moderator: Welcome. Thank you for coming to this education roundtable. We're here to discuss K–12 education in the United States. It has been 35 years since the publication of *A Nation at Risk*, a report that set in motion a series of seemingly unending attempts to fix American education. "In August 1981, Education Secretary T. H. Bell created a National Commission on Excellence in Education to examine, in the report's words, 'the widespread public perception that something is seriously remiss in our educational system.' Secretary Bell's expectation, he later said, was that the report would paint a rosy picture of American education and correct all those widespread negative perceptions. Instead, on April 26, 1983, the commission released a sweeping 65-page indictment of the quality of teaching and learning in American primary and secondary schools couched in a style of apocalyptic rhetoric rarely found in blue-ribbon commission reports. 'The educational foundations of our society are presently being eroded by a rising tide of mediocrity that threatens our very future as a nation and as a people,' it warned. 'If an unfriendly foreign power had attempted to impose on America the mediocre educational performance that exists today, we might well have viewed it as an act of war.' . . . *A Nation at Risk* resonated with Americans, who seemingly agreed that there was indeed something 'seriously remiss' in their schools. . . . The most important legacy of *A Nation at Risk* was to put the quality of education on the national political agenda—where it has remained ever since."[1] During the past 35 years, there have been numerous other reports decrying the state of education in the U.S. Calls for reform have emanated from the business community, politicians, academics, and education practitioners. We have witnessed "math wars," debates about "standards-based" reform, and pushback over the use of "high-stakes" tests. The George W. Bush and Obama administrations have promoted their educational policies through federal legislation: No Child Left Behind and Race to the Top. Recently, many states and the federal government are pushing for more choice in education through the expansion of vouchers and charter schools.

Anderson: I think one of the most important influences of *A Nation at Risk* is that it tied the quality of schooling to the country's economic competitiveness. In other words, in order for the United States to maintain its standing in the world and remain competitive with other countries, we must have a strong education system.[2]

Yann: There is no doubt that the report suggested a link between the quality of schooling and the strength of the economy. However, that link has not been supported by recent history. At the time, Americans marveled at Japan's economy and noted that their students always scored at the top of international comparative tests. We assumed the strength of their education system was responsible for their economic growth. But then their economy went through a prolonged downturn and our economy rebounded. Each country still had the same education system it had had before the reversal in fortunes of their economies. "With the wisdom of hindsight, it is clear that the link between educational excellence and economic security is not as simple as *A Nation at Risk* made it seem. . . . Indeed, a consensus seems to be emerging among educational experts around the world that American schools operate within the context of an enabling environment—an open economy, strong legal and banking systems, an entrepreneurial culture—conducive to economic progress."[3] [4]

Harris: The relationship between schooling and the economy may not be as direct as *A Nation at Risk* made it seem, but I believe the ominous language in the report is still justified today. According to international comparisons, nearly one-third of young people in the United States do not possess the knowledge and skills needed to function as citizens and workers. "This is particularly distressing news at a time when the baby boomers are aging and a growing proportion of the future work force comes from groups—members of ethnic and racial minorities, students from low-income families, recent immigrants—that have been ill served by our education system. The challenge today is to build access as well as excellence. That's the new definition of 'a nation at risk'—and ample reason for a new commission to awaken the nation to the need to educate all our young people."[5]

Inglehart: While there have been many reports that identify the well-documented problems with contemporary U.S. education, they contain no recommendations or proposals for action. I fear clucking about the sad state of affairs avoids confronting some obvious issues and challenging reorganization of the way education is done in this country. The disheartening conditions produced by our current system are partly vested in misguided and inadequate parenting, a long series of systemic flaws in the recruitment and training of teachers—as educators we are accomplices in that crime, hopeless failure to act forcefully on the part of docile and litigation sensitized school administrations, and allowing local community politics to control teaching content thereby allowing nonsense like "intelligent" design to be taught as legitimate biology. Only a draconian and revolutionary reversal of teaching approach and substance can save our children's future. Mathematics, reading, and writing have to be restored to a preeminent place in the primary and secondary school curriculum. We cannot let a girl's swim coach teach algebra and someone who never read Shakespeare teach literature. Teachers must demonstrate proficiency in their instructional topic and be given absolute control over their classroom with the attendant authority to act in a fashion that clearly rewards student learning and punishes failure to respond to learning responsibilities. Administrators must back teachers committed to extracting the best out of their students, rather than cautioning them to coddle the students or placate protective parents. Parents bringing a lawyer to school should immediately face the expulsion of their child. All children entering the school, regardless of their race, sex, religious orientation, or weight automatically lose their individual rights, allowing the school's personnel to teach rather than worry about their students' self-esteem. If we want change in the system, we will have to discard any misguided applications of progressive education and go back to teaching competence in the basic skills that compel all emerging cohorts of our new barbarians to become competitive and civilized.[6]

Grable: What about a boot-camp-style school?[7]

Easton: Used to be called a Catholic boys' school in my day. An interesting concept that should not be rejected out of hand. Why should education be fun?[8]

Druley: As a culture we don't value education. That would be clear from the statements recommending boot camps and Catholic boys' schools that we just heard, if it were not already abundantly clear from the behavior of so many of my students. You gentlemen seem to have bought completely into the concept of education as "teaching them to behave." My students know how to behave. What they are absolutely guaranteed to come into my class without knowing is how to learn. By focusing on inadequately and improperly standardized tests in the pursuit of funding opportunities and blaming the victims of such a policy—the students—when we cannot make it work, we have taught our young people to pursue the devil's bargain of "Show up and shut up and they owe you an A." Learning plays only a minor part in the modern high school curriculum and our students have learned that, should any occur, it will not be valued. I don't think you're going to solve this one with discipline.[9]

Inglehart: I'm not certain that you can separate "learning how to behave" from "learning how to learn." Is there a disconnect between behavior and learning? My comments are based in experiences with youth caught up in the messy and disorganized environment of urban public schools. Discipline has become anathema to so-called progressive education because it smacks of caning, dunce caps, paddling, and sitting in the corner. That's not the discipline I referenced. The discipline needed is the school's ability to control early learning experiences without allowing the taught to assume control of the direction their education takes. If they know it already, why even bother teaching them to behave or learn? Why do we need a formal education system that legally requires attendance through 16 years of age? Our children's shabby performance in numeracy, literacy, and science should not be addressed directly because they find the topics uninteresting or not enough fun? Where is the solution to this problem?[10]

Blanchard: How do you know our students are performing poorly?

Inglehart: "Education policymakers and analysts express great concern about the performance of U.S. students on international tests. Education reformers frequently invoke the relatively poor performance of U.S. students to justify school policy changes."[11] In 2009, when the Program for International Student Assessment (PISA) results were released, and again in 2012, when the Third International Mathematics and Science Study (TIMSS) results were released, Secretary of Education Arne Duncan called the results "unacceptable," bemoaned U.S. students lack of preparation for participating in a "knowledge economy," and warned that other countries' students were better prepared for "economic leadership."[12]

Johnson: The shabby performance should be addressed. But perhaps it is shabby because they find the topics uninteresting. Maybe a different approach to these topics is needed.

Peterson: In response to Inglehart's criticism, I would like to say that progressive education does not eschew the discipline of learning; rather it opposes the disrespect for persons implied in caning, dunce caps, paddling and corner sitting. Progressive education asserts that children are born seeking to learn and looking for respectful social relationships. All children have the potential to learn. If supported and encouraged as individuals, they can learn to be productive and critically aware participants in society. To do that, they need opportunities and encouragement to investigate material on their own and in depth. Such opportunities allow children to develop the academic and social discipline that comes from struggling to answer genuine questions and to solve real problems encountered in those investigations. Children need teachers who have the knowledge and authority to support and extend those explorations. Standardized tests do not, in themselves, contribute to children's learning. If designed and used properly, they can assist in finding ways to assist children who need more specific support. Too often, currently, they are used to identify and punish those children and their teachers who are most vulnerable, narrowing the curriculum in ways that ignore the broad reaches of culture, and cut off many possible approaches to engaging children's learning. Though teachers and parents are central to children's learning, they are not the only essential contributors. Children must also have appropriate access to food, shelter and appropriate health care and other social supports. These conditions are deteriorating in the United States, making parenting and teaching more difficult.[13]

Grable: As one of the younger members of this group, I have a not-too-distant memory of high school. I can tell you that the collective attention span of my generation is short. We learn differently from the generation that raised us. We were raised in front of televisions that never were turned off and computers that would deliver whatever information we desired at any moment. If you ask us to read, we almost certainly won't. If you ask us to watch a video of the same material, we would likely oblige. As for the disciplinarian approach, when it is successful at getting students to do what is asked of them, it breeds an attitude of "pass the test and forget it" and doing exactly what is required to pass and no more. If a genuine interest is not generated, genuine learning will not occur.[14]

Ross: I suggest that if you want to build a boot camp, its first inhabitants should be teachers. To say that students aren't learning or can't learn or that high school has somehow made them defective or that they now need some sort of boot camp to have knowledge magically infused into their heads illustrates an interesting general ignorance of (and perhaps frustration with) how this current generation learns and processes information. Are most students today learning? Probably not, but that's due, to a large degree, to the fact that many teachers simply don't understand how to teach them. Do students want to learn? Of course, and plenty examples exist outside the classroom of students doing just that, many times in conflict with and in spite of what happens in the classroom. What might faculty learn at boot camp? Perhaps they might learn something about quite a bit of research conducted in the past 10 years or so about this current generation of students (sometimes referred to as the "Net Generation" because they represent the first generation of students to grow up in a digital world) who value learning as a collaborative and cooperative venture, in which technology plays a major role. Perhaps they might learn that while this generation of students interacts with the world through multimedia and online social networking, routinely multitasking, their teachers tend to approach learning linearly, one task at a time, as an individual activity centered largely around printed text. Perhaps they might learn of recent national surveys of colleges and universities that found 80 percent of these institutions equate "good teaching" with lecturing, yet other studies have found that an average college student retains less than 10 percent of information delivered via a lecture. Perhaps they might learn that many students don't read their textbooks because they aren't written in a way that students read or value information. Perhaps they might learn that the educational landscape is changing. Perhaps boot camp isn't the answer. It could simply just be a question of teaching teachers how to learn.[15]

Druley: I had thought that the Internet would be a great tool of learning. No more hearing, "I couldn't get to the library"; no more making mental excuses for my students who didn't have easy access or time to exercise their intellectual curiosity or fill in the quite obvious gaps in their earlier education. I also looked forward to answering student emails and queries if they had difficulty with a reading assignment and furthering classroom discussion among students with messaging. Even after many and varied ways of telling them that it is their responsibility and that their success in my class and in others, and in life, depends on this intellectual curiosity, they still do not avail themselves of the wealth of information that is, quite literally, at their fingertips. Very few exhibit any intellectual curiosity at all. They seem to have what I term a consumerist mentality towards education—"I've paid for it, I'll occupy a seat, and that's all I need to do." It occurs to me that this is the same passive mode that occurs with media interaction. So to respond to Grable's comments, while I can see more media in some disciplines, I think there are some in which there is simply no substitute for grappling with understanding the written word, but I'd like to hear some specifics on what methods you think would be useful and feasible. In my experience, Plato and Aristotle simply cannot be reduced to a PowerPoint presentation.[16]

Grable: I don't think the problem is curiosity specifically, although I can see how it would appear that way. If students were interested in the material and there was no other way to get the material, they would go to the library. I remember once when the Internet was down at my house, my sister (who lacked a car) walked to the library to use the Internet. I have friends who surf Wikipedia from one article to another following the links in the articles to fill in the gaps in understanding that disallow the understanding of the first article. I have had to stop reading not because I was not interested, but because my reading had led to an infinite regress. When I talk to some teachers about Wikipedia, they scoff at the idea that Wikipedia could even be a useful or accurate source of information. After all, the truth is not democratically determined. I agree that it is wildly unintuitive. It does something, however, that a book does not. It engages. It doesn't know anything. It asks what you know, so you can share it. I guess what I am trying to say is that we are not as good at being passive recipients of information. We prefer to be engaged in a conversation instead of a lecture, and in multimedia communication at that. On the second point, if a presentation is done well, it isn't a reduction at all. Most PowerPoint presentations are the bullet points of a lecture. Most of the time, when I see the Internet used to educate, the book has been put online, or the syllabus has been posted for download. It is true that the Internet is better at being a book than a book is. However, its real strength lies in hypertext and multimedia. Why explain Plato's cave, when you could show it to students?[17]

Carpenter: The "entitlement" attitude of many (not all) youth did not spontaneously come from the youth, nor can it be explained by simplistic explanations about how "social welfare programs created a culture of dependency." The whole economy, from the top on down, has been moving at an accelerated pace towards "immediate profits taking precedence over long-term stability and socially-constructive production for society." We all want accountability, but sometimes "immediate payoffs" is mistakenly seen as genuine accountability. In the past thirty years this has accelerated in the economy, financial markets, and in our institutions, including schools demanding high-stakes testing, and, obviously, in our "immediate gratification" popular culture. Youth are not stupid. They are simply "playing the game" put before them. I'm not making excuses for unmotivated students—on my recent trip I saw students from incredibly distressed backgrounds struggling against huge obstacles because they believed that an education could help them. Many youth in the USA don't have that drive not because they are lazy but because they are cynical. These appear to be the same, and they do overlap, but they are fundamentally not the same. As teachers, one of our main responsibilities is fighting against that cynicism—not with simplistic cheerleading but rather by helping students understand that they will be weaker if they just want to drift through life rather than doing the work which can give them more power over their lives. And maybe even get them a better job.[18]

Druley (to Grable): Your generation has been trained to have a short attention span by the mass media. For example, magazines now publish much shorter articles and stories than they did when I was leaving high school. I do not just refer to *Seventeen*—that, too—but to the *New York Times Sunday Magazine* as well. Articles are short so that they can fit on one or two computer screens, even if they are projected to appear only in print. To those who wish to hide behind the notion that I blame the students for this—shame on you! The students are much too young to have made this mess, and generally do not have access to the means to correct or change it; a finding of which I and a great many others have been aware for a very long time. The question is now what to do about it and, by the way, the students are entitled to our leadership in education issues, not our blame. Unfortunately, leadership in this area may sometimes mean taking a tough stance on both student and administrative baloney. I do not equate progressive education with letting the young run wild, nor do any of its serious proponents. But progressive education is expensive. Moreover, learning may take place! Our society does not value education enough to pay the piper. Then we cry when the children run away through the mountains.[19]

Johnson: In my view, education is about learning how to think critically about the world we live in, while at the same time helping students to form some level of expertise in a subject area. Getting back to the point though, what we thirst for is information. The teacher is tasked with the responsibility of helping her or his students learn where, when, and how to take in that information and how to filter it for truth and value. Sometimes the value isn't truth at all. A poem doesn't have to have anything truthful about it to be a valuable piece of literature, to exemplify a style of writing or storytelling. The source of information has long been in the spoken and written word. Written works have been compiled into books, for obvious reasons, and therefore have long been the source of our information. Computing, networking, and multimedia have changed the way we can deliver information. We have more options, more to filter, more responsibility to present information in a useful and insightful way in whatever medium we use. For better or worse, the Internet and the Web, in particular, has allowed the spread of information without the censorship of reviewers, editors, publishers, librarians, and so on. This has led to a tremendous influx of junk information, as well as an infusion of truly genuine, valuable, and beautiful works by individuals of all walks of life. Some love it, and some dislike it. We all need to learn to deal with it and to use what works, while filtering out what doesn't. Teachers need to help students learn this process, so that they emerge as productive, insightful, and intelligent members of society who don't suffer from the stereotyping, racism, and misbeliefs that disinformation can entangle us in.

I like to use analogies. Sometimes I'm not very good at it. So, please forgive this if you think it's a bad one. I see this discussion much the same way as talking about the history of water use. We need water to survive, in much the same way that we yearn to gain informative insight into the world around us. In the days before piped and treated water, this meant something very different from what it means now. By the way, these days still exist in many "third world" locales. Today, water is something that comes from the tap, cooler, or bottle. We may take for granted how it got there; what we don't have to do is get it or ensure that it's safe for us. In some cases, it's not safe at all. Bottled water still lacks the regulation that most municipalities put on treated drinking water. Most of us drink it anyway. An outsider might say, "You're crazy to drink something that you don't know the history of." There's a level of truth to that. We need to be critical thinkers—to examine to the best of our ability what we consume and think about how we obtained it. Information is no different. Even going to the library to read Britannica doesn't ensure that what we read isn't junk. I personally find a lot of useful information in Wikipedia. There is a real sense of ownership that authors there take in their work, and this is offset in most cases by critical review by others with a shared sense of ownership in the area of a given topic. The key is to be vigilant of what you consume. Know, as best you can, where it comes from. Keep track of that and pass it on (by referencing) when you pass on this information. The rules are the same as they've always been. We just need to learn how to properly apply them, every time, in this new age.[20]

Carpenter: To follow up on Druley's comment about a consumerist mentality, part of the problem comes from a college culture that is currently rampant throughout the United States, where students are referred to as "customers." I even heard of one administrator complimenting some faculty by saying that they "added value" to the university as if they offered an extra Ginsu knife or special paint job to the "product" that students are "buying." I understand that public school K–12 students don't pay for their education in the same way that college students or their families do. But this culture of "customers" and "value adders" (no snake pun intended) reinforces the idea of trying to get the most for the least and has seeped into all aspects of our lives. I do understand that there has to be accountability and some way to measure competency of the teachers. That is not an easy task. But education should not be finitely measured, like weighing grain on a scale in a store. That leads to students wanting to do only "exactly" what is "required" (and no more) for "certification." And that leads to cutting corners and a general sense of alienation that one should not care about the subject matter, but only about the certification of completion. Most of our students are not even conscious that this culture may be at work in schools because they are already saturated with it from the society at large. As to why so many students don't seem to want to learn and aren't enthusiastic about learning the tools to be able to keep on learning when they leave the classroom? That's a much longer, deeper discussion that relates to general alienation and sense of powerlessness in society leading many to "take what they can as fast as they can and live for the moment" and the rise of a culture that has separated "reward" from "effort," because despite our culture's claim that it is the best system in the history of the world for linking "reward" and "effort" and therefore produces the most and best for all, the reality is that there are many, many ways to "beat the system," especially if one has money, such that the goal is to make money without working. This culture extends all the way from Wall Street to the streets of our depopulated, deindustrialized, demoralized cities. And into the classroom as well.[21]

Easton: You can lead a horse to water, but you can't make him drink. You can color the water, warm it, cool it, make it smell like a female horse or a male horse, but it may still die of dehydration. Most people want happiness. Knowledge is power, but ignorance is bliss.[22]

Grable: I didn't know Yogi Berra was here. How many aphorisms can you pack into one statement?

Snepp: If students start seeing themselves as "customers" of our educational system, it won't be long until they ply the old adage, "The customer is always right." Heaven help us then.

Ulrich: Treating the student as a customer is not quite correct. At a public school, the customer is society. The school receives money from the government (ideally, society's representative). This society buys educated citizens who, in turn, enrich society. Schools create productive workers, informed citizens, and (sometimes) capable leaders, who are all the lifeblood of a modern democratic society. When students do not perform as promised, society has a tendency to stop paying for those students, as any rational paying customer should.[23]

Quinn: Who is making a promise of student performance? And on what basis? The reason students do not perform as promised may be due to the students, their teachers, their schools, but it also may not be due to any of these. It may be due to socioeconomic factors or ill-advised education policy forced upon students, teachers, and schools.

Foster: Perhaps students simply need to be reminded of their primary and most important role/responsibility in school—to learn. I am not advocating or suggesting that we not provide students a voice to express concerns or opinions. Doing so would be totalitarian and against the core democratic principles of education in this country. But I believe this responsibility has simply been lost among most students and we are now seeing the results firsthand.[24]

Druley: At this point, I would settle for students simply being respectful. I had a guest speaker come in today, at the request of the students, and had to nudge a young lady in the *front* row to stop texting on her phone during the speaker's presentation. I would be happy to modify my teaching style, but students still have the minimal responsibility to be respectful.[25]

Easton: I agree with Foster. Students do not deserve a say in how a school operates. However, students should have a voice to express relevant concerns in an *advisory* manner through proper channels. The actual responsibility (and authority) for the way a school is operated should fall only to the faculty, staff, administration, and governing school board who have the relevant real-world professional and life experience that qualifies them to make critical decisions regarding matters centric to the school's success.[26]

Ulrich: What about parents?

Carpenter: Well, since I helped start this discussion thread about so-called "customers," allow me to reiterate. The question is not "Who is the customer?" but rather, why do we have to use the culture of "immediate exchange for money, immediate reward for spending cash," etc.? It corrupts the whole process of learning. Students should not have absolute authority, but certainly students should have some input. Think of it this way: "You should not live every moment of your life trying to please whoever it is that is standing immediately in front of you, because then, you have no life and besides, you might not be pleasing the right people." But on the other hand, "If nobody anywhere likes you, then you probably are doing something wrong." Student (and parent) input is an important component in the educational process, but not because they might be paying part of the bills.[27]

Grable: Can we get an interpreter for some of these analogies that people are making?

Quinn: I would just like to say that students today are faced with enormous challenges. Dysfunctional homes, single parent, and no parent homes. They are inundated with sex, crime, drugs, and disillusionment in their communities and the media. The list is long. They get a daily barrage of marketing telling them they are inferior if they don't own this or that, wear this or that, drink this or that. They are constantly called inferior compared to students in other countries. They are told to be honorable and respectful and to follow the rules, but heroes from Rambo to whomever are the people who are idolized because they make their own rules and respect nothing. Our political process is one of personal destruction. The promises of equality, jobs, opportunity, even social security, are seen slipping away every day, except to only the most privileged. And now there may not even be enough affordable fuel or food for their future. One thing is for sure. They all have hopes and dreams for the future. And at least some still hold out hope that school will help make that possible.[28]

Newcomer: While almost everyone agrees that the country has serious problems with its educational system, there is little consensus about solutions, despite all the money spent on research. There is at least one thing that we should do, and I do not think we've done enough, which is to set aside our ideological differences and empirically study the successful models around the world. What kind of system do they have? How do they recruit and train their teachers? How much funding do they have for education and how is the funding allocated? How do they determine curriculum? How do they determine what kinds of textbooks to use? How are learning materials distributed, sequenced, and articulated from grade to grade? What kind of quality control mechanism do they have? How are their children raised? What kinds of messages are parents giving to their children? What is the prevalent attitude the society has about hard work? When things are going so wrong, it's time to have a dose of humility and question our basic assumptions. The best place to start is to stop looking into the mirror where we can only see our own face and stop arguing with each other endlessly based on our preconceptions. Look around and learn from other people who are doing better.[29]

Foster: I like that idea. I am starting to get a sense already that we are spinning our wheels and we haven't yet started talking about how to fix education.

Taylor (to Newcomer): By what criteria will you determine that a certain country's educational system is successful? Ranking via the international tests? Are there other criteria besides test performance that we should consider? Also, I think it would be important to know what different countries value about education. How do their values align with what we value in the United States?

Moderator: Excellent questions Taylor. I am happy to see that our discussion is off and rolling along.

Grable: Rolling off the rails maybe.

Moderator (chuckles): I would like to structure our discussion a little as we proceed. I can tell that Foster and Inglehart and others are anxious to get to solutions, but before we discuss those ideas, I think it is important to establish some historical, social, and philosophical context so that we can understand how we got to where we are today. I would like to begin by posing a question that Taylor has just alluded to in asking what other countries value about education. Thus, my question is, "What is the purpose of education?"

THE PURPOSE OF EDUCATION

Anderson: Education is the soul of society, passed from one generation to another.[30] The purpose of education is to transmit civilization.[31] Through education, students become culturally literate—they are given a common fund of knowledge that allows them to participate as citizens in public discourse.[32] [33] [34] [35] [36] [37] [38] [39] [40] [41] [42]

Blanchard: Yes, I agree, but I think it is more than that. It is not just "a common fund of knowledge" that students need. They need to be taught skills that will prepare them to participate as responsible citizens in a democratic society.[43] [44] [45] [46] [47] "The aim [of education] must be the training of independently acting and thinking individuals who, however, see in the service to the community their highest life problem"[48]. In this way our democracy will be maintained.[49]

Easton: By creating a harmonious relationship between man (body, intellect, and spirit) and God and nature, education will produce individuals of good character and thus promote civic virtue and social harmony.[50]

Carpenter: I think education has more than just a maintenance function. It should preserve, but it should also provide for change.[51] Education should equip people with the skills needed to participate in the social life of the community and to change the social order as needed.[52]

Druley: "Education is the fundamental method of social progress and reform."[53] It is through education that we can address social ills such as crime, poverty, and unemployment.[54][55][56][57][58] Education can promote equality and provide equal opportunity.[59] So I agree that education should have a change function. It is through education that we can shape society in the direction of goodness[60] and promote progress as a nation.[61]

Carpenter: Education should promote "the fullest development of human potentialities, the fullest development of group welfare."[62] If students develop a sense of responsibility to society and are encouraged to apply their talents to solving social problems, they will help build a better world.[63][64][65]

Foster: The purposes stated so far are all quite noble sounding. A cynic might say they are pie-in-the-sky fantasies. I suppose schools do contribute to citizenship development in some way, but I prefer to be practical. I think the purpose of K–12 education should be to prepare students for college.

Grable: Not every student is going to go on to college.

Foster: Good point. Let me elaborate. I think the purpose of K–12 education should be to prepare students for college or jobs.[66][67][68][69][70][71][72][73][74][75][76][77][78][79][80][81] In both cases, there is an overriding purpose—to ultimately produce students useful to an employer. Education should provide the knowledge and skills so that graduates can compete in the job market.

Inglehart: I believe the quality of education will determine the nation's economic success.[82] Education will help us create a highly skilled workforce and build a strong economic future for the U.S.[83]

Easton: "Students must 'learn so they can earn' in [the] global economy."[84]

Yann: "College and career ready." That's the message I hear from my kids' school.

Carpenter: That's the slogan we hear, but is that really what schools are doing? The focus seems to be on helping students prepare an attractive college application, but that is not the same thing as preparing them for college. And for all the talk about career readiness, I see little serious consideration given to this.[85]

Harris: Well, we need to bring student levels of achievement in line with the needs of business and industry in order for the U.S. to maintain global economic competitiveness.[86] [87] We need to make sure that schools are producing workers with communication skills, mathematical literacy, and the ability to use technology. Improving math and science education is especially important in order to improve the workforce by producing more engineers and technically-prepared workers. [88] This is necessary for the U.S. to maintain its technological advantage and lead the world in innovation.[89]

Ziegler: Our state recently passed a law that requires teachers to obtain 15 out of the 90 professional growth points needed for license renewal by participating in 1) an externship with a company; 2) professional development provided by the state, a local business, or a community partner that provides opportunities for school and employers to partner in promoting career navigation; or 3) professional development provided by the state, a local business, or a community partner that outlines 'current and future economic needs of the community, state, nation, and globe and ways in which current and future economic needs . . . can be disseminated to students.'"[90] If that doesn't say the purpose of education is to support the business community and the economy, I don't know what does.

Walter: To what grade levels does that requirement apply?

Ziegler: All. K through 12.

Johnson: Such requirements do not just support the business community and the economy. "Education has a market value; that it is so far an article of merchandise, that it can be turned to pecuniary account; it may be minted and will yield a larger amount of statutable coin than common bullion."[91]

Grable: What?!

Foster: I think he is saying that education provides knowledge and skills that can be "cashed in" for a good job that will enable one to make a successful living.

Oates: "If the aim of education is to gain money and power, where can we turn for help in knowing what to do with that money and power? Only a disordered mind thinks that these are ends in themselves."[92]

Lawrence: Is it knowledge and skills that education provides or credentials— grades, credits, degrees—that give those who possess them an edge in competing for jobs?[93]

Harris: Isn't it the same thing? Those with the most knowledge and greatest skills get the best grades and obtain the highest degrees.

Karch: That's the assumption the educational system operates under. The belief that education promotes social mobility by providing individual students with educational advantages in the competition for the best social positions is what ensures "buy in" to the educational system. The lower classes especially pin their hopes on the social mobility function of education.

Lawrence: There is also a social efficiency function of education. By providing different groups of students with different skill sets necessary for different kinds of jobs, the educational system sorts people into their appropriate positions in the social order.[94] [95]

Grable: Appropriate?

Karch: So, the system accepts all students, but through practices such as tracking it tends to maintain the prestige of the upper- and middle-class students by providing them with more valued credentials. These are the students who are most likely to go on to college.[96]

Blanchard: Why is it that the upper- and middle-class students get the more valued credentials?

Easton: They're the ones in the higher tracks. They must be smarter.

Ulrich: Is the purpose of school to help students develop their talents and abilities or to rank them against each other? From what I have seen, schools are consumed with ranking students, not developing their potential. And, to make matters worse, that ranking is based on knowledge and skills of questionable importance. Not only that, but the ranking criteria are biased toward children from wealthier backgrounds.[97]

Anderson: How are the ranking criteria biased?

Ulrich: Well, standardized tests, one common means of ranking, tend to emphasize the cultural knowledge deemed important by those at the upper end of the socioeconomic strata. Beyond that, children from more affluent backgrounds enter school having had more and richer conversational experiences in their homes and communities that promote language development. This head start gives them an advantage in playing the school learning game that schools in poorer communities, lacking resources, can seldom overcome.

Moderator: Lawrence's, Karch's, and Ulrich's comments suggest that some purposes of education may be entangled in social class issues. This is an important point to which we should return. But for now, does anyone else have a purpose of education they would like to add?

Anderson: I'm not sure this is a new purpose. Rather it is a summary of what we have discussed so far. The purpose of education is to produce employable citizens. It should prepare students both for occupations and for the specific adult roles they will have in society.[98] [99]

Newcomer: Why not say that the purpose of education is, simply put, to prepare children for life?[100]

Oates: I disagree. Education "is not . . . to prepare students to live a useful life, but to teach them how to live pragmatically and immediately in their current environment."[101] "The business of education is not, for the presumable usefulness of his future, to rob the child of the intrinsic joy of childhood . . ."[102]

Harris: So, you reject the social sorting function of education?

Oates: I don't deny that it occurs. But it should not be the purpose, or even a purpose, of education. Education is life, not preparation for life, so the aims of education must reflect the aims of life and growth.[103] [104]

Grable: Social sorting occurs in life so students should be prepared to deal with it.

Peterson: I think his point is that social sorting is a consequence of education, but it should not be a purpose of education.

Carpenter: We should be careful to distinguish between purposes of education and consequences of education.

Harris: I'm not sure the distinction is as clear-cut as you may think. Sorting of individuals into different occupational and social positions is necessary for businesses and society itself to function smoothly. So, I, for one, think that social sorting is an important purpose of education that promotes social efficiency.[105] It is not just a consequence of education.

Quinn: It seems we are on the verge of wandering into social class issues again. I would like to try to shift the focus by suggesting another purpose of education. The purpose of education should be to learn to learn.[106] It should prepare the young to educate themselves[107], develop the habit of continually asking questions[108], and promote a love of learning[109] and a lifelong desire to know.[110] It should realize that even before entering school children are curious and full of questions about themselves and the world around them. They have an innate desire to seek out experiences that will promote growth and develop their identity and sense of self-worth. Without such an attitude toward learning, school, and ultimately life, becomes dull and pointless.[111] In sum, I think the ultimate aim of education should be the development of intellectual autonomy.[112]

Peterson: I like that. Such an attitude of intellectual curiosity provides an opportunity for self-fulfillment[113] by enabling individuals to develop their skills and talents, pursue their interests,[114] and fulfill their potential.[115]

Grable: Fulfill their potential?

Ross: I think the purpose of education is to develop critical thinking skills.[116] [117] [118] [119]

Snepp: To teach students how to think rather than what to think.[120]

Taylor: To replace an empty mind with an open one.[121]

Quinn (to Snepp): Wait a minute. How should students think? Should they all think the way you do? Should they all think the way I do?

Snepp: I mean they should learn to think rationally.[122] I agree with Ross that they should learn critical thinking skills.

Foster: What exactly are "critical thinking skills"?

Ross: "Critical thinking is the intellectually disciplined process of actively and skillfully conceptualizing, applying, analyzing, synthesizing, and/or evaluating information gathered from, or generated by, observation, experience, reflection, reasoning, or communication, as a guide to belief and action. In its exemplary form, it is based on universal intellectual values that transcend subject matter divisions: clarity, accuracy, precision, consistency, relevance, sound evidence, good reasons, depth, breadth, and fairness. It entails the examination of those structures or elements of thought implicit in all reasoning: purpose, problem, or question-at-issue; assumptions; concepts; empirical grounding; reasoning leading to conclusions; implications and consequences; objections from alternative viewpoints; and frame of reference. Critical thinking—in being responsive to variable subject matter, issues, and purposes—is incorporated in a family of interwoven modes of thinking, among them: scientific thinking, mathematical thinking, historical thinking, anthropological thinking, economic thinking, moral thinking, and philosophical thinking."[123]

Taylor: Whoa!

Grable: Ross's very thorough description of critical thinking focuses primarily on a set of cognitive skills. "But beyond those skills, learning how to think requires the development of a set of intellectual virtues that make good students, good professionals, and good citizens." These virtues include love of truth, honesty, fair-mindedness, humility, perseverance, courage, good listening, perspective-taking and empathy, and wisdom.[124]

Peterson: Unfortunately, I believe that "critical thinking has been abandoned as a cultural value" in our society. "What Americans rarely acknowledge is that many of their social problems are rooted in the rejection of critical thinking or, conversely, the glorification of the emotional and irrational. . . . Corporate influence on climate and environmental policy, [for example], is . . . more evidence of anti-intellectualism in action, for corporate domination of American society is another result of a public that is not thinking critically. Americans have allowed democracy to slip away, their culture overtaken by enormous corporations that effectively control both the governmental apparatus and the media, thus shaping life around materialism and consumption. Indeed, these corporate interests encourage anti-intellectualism, conditioning Americans into conformity and passive acceptance of institutional dominance. . . . They are the ones who stand to gain from consumers who spend money they don't have on goods and services they don't need. They are the ones who want a public that is largely uninformed and distracted, thus allowing government policy to be crafted by corporate lawyers and lobbyists."[125]

Xander: The purpose of education "is not to make children fit for tomorrow's job market. Nor is it to make them capable of voting well and serving on a jury. It is to help people escape a life of vapid consumerism by giving them capacities to appreciate richer pursuits and to produce their own complex meanings. . . . To teach students that it is a pleasure to use one's mind and to encourage critical thought and intellectual opposition are our most important tasks as educators."[126]

Ulrich: I think education should promote freedom of the mind; anything that needs an adjective (for example, "civics education") is not education, but tyranny.[127] Freedom of thought and freedom of expression should be the main goal of education.[128]

Karch: The purpose of education is to develop the "muscle of thoughtfulness, the use of which will be the greatest pleasure in life and will also show what it means to be fully human."[129]

Oates: Education should liberate individuals' capacities.[130]

Grable: Capacities? Are you suggesting that everyone has an innate level of ability that cannot be surpassed?

Anderson: Are you suggesting that everyone's potential is unlimited?

Van Houten: Limited or unlimited, education should lead out what is already in the pupil's soul.[131] It should help students develop their own voice.[132]

Walter: In addition to critical thinking, education should promote ethical reasoning, compassion,[133] and the right set of values.[134]

Quinn: I like the first two, but what is "the right set of values"?

Easton: Christian values.

Foster: That is a rabbit hole we should not go down.

Grable: Not all students are Christian.

Ulrich: What about separation of church and state?

Karch: Saying "the right set of values" seems too vague. We could spend hours discussing that and not come to an agreement. Perhaps we should move on.

Van Houten: What about the "intellectual virtues" that Grable suggested? Can't we at least agree on those?

Harris: What bothers me about purposes such as learning to learn, promoting freedom of the mind, and developing the muscle of thoughtfulness is that "many people—most people—don't have the luxury of thinking that way."[135] Students from wealthy backgrounds, perhaps, but middle- and lower-class students need to be concerned with getting a good job.

Quinn: It's not clear to me how learning to learn and developing the muscle of thoughtfulness preclude students from getting a good job. Those qualities should help students get a job.

Lawrence: A recent survey of employers found that "93 percent of the employers surveyed said that 'a demonstrated capacity to think critically, communicate clearly, and solve complex problems is more important than [a candidate's] undergraduate major.' They were not saying that a student's major does not matter, but that, overwhelmingly, the thinking, problem-solving, and communication skills a job candidate has acquired in college are more important than the specific field in which the applicant earned a degree. Looking at successful leaders in business and in the nonprofit sector, you find that they have majored in everything under the sun."[136]

Easton: I read recently that "the economic return to pure technical skills has flattened, and the highest return now goes to those who combine soft skills—excellence at communicating and working with people—with technical skills."[137]

Yann: My purpose for education is broad, but I hope not vague. I believe the purpose of education is intellectual development.[138]

Xander: If by intellectual development you mean not only the growth of knowledge, but also the development of wisdom, then I agree.[139]

Foster: That still seems vague to me. Intellectual development of what? Intellectual development in what direction?

Yann: Intellectual development means the development of tools to communicate, reason, and solve problems and the acquisition of knowledge of reading, writing, science, art, economics, etc.[140]

Ziegler: I believe the "main aim of education should be to produce competent, caring, loving and lovable people."[141]

Anderson: You don't care if students learn anything?

Ziegler: I said competent and caring. In learning to care for themselves, other people, animals, the environment, and ideas, they will develop many competencies.

Taylor: Another fine purpose Ziegler. Our group has made many excellent, albeit quite different, suggestions as to the purpose of education. In most cases, each person has suggested a single purpose. I think the diversity of responses indicates that there is more than one purpose of education. Earlier, Anderson offered a summary. I would like to do the same and propose an all-encompassing statement of purpose: The purpose of education is to prepare individuals for citizenship, work, life, and personal growth.[142] [143] Not only should it prepare students to become experts in a particular vocation, but also experts in the general art of the free man and citizen.[144]

Grable: Encompassing, but perhaps not all-encompassing.

Anderson: That does not include my cultural transmission purpose.

Druley: Nor my social progress and reform purpose.

Karch: Nor the social sorting purpose.

Oates: The purpose of education is not to *prepare* students for anything.

Ulrich: We have named many purposes. But are our schools achieving any of them? In the past few years, I have visited many schools. I made two columns in a notebook to keep track of my observations. Column one was for learning activities relevant to preparation for life. Column two was for those activities that were irrelevant. Column two filled up quickly. In fact, it required several additional pages. Among its entries: factoring polynomials, memorizing the chemical composition of sugar, the different classifications of species, or the different soil horizons, knowing about the encomienda system or the 3/5 compromise, knowing the difference between gerunds and infinitives. When are these ever used in life? But students had to cram all of these facts into their heads for tests. It seemed that the more prestigious the school or the higher the academic track within the school, the more there was to memorize. None of these facts was related to something important in life. This is not to say that students don't learn anything in school that is important for life. In elementary school, they learn to read and write and do basic math operations. In higher grades, they may learn how to write an essay. But the majority of life preparation occurs through social interactions and activities outside of the classroom—after-school clubs, athletics, part-time jobs. My column one, school learning activities that prepare students for life, was close to empty. The pressure on schools to cover state-mandated standards, to raise scores on standardized tests, to push kids to jump through a set of meaningless hoops so they can repeat the process next year, to raise graduation rates and college placements, to deal with overbearing parents and AWOL parents creates an environment that makes it difficult for schools to try to achieve *any* meaningful purpose. In short, I have observed "creative expansive thinking turning into narrow, prescriptive 'right answers,' inquisitiveness shriveling up into 'will this be on the test?', a joy for learning worn down into time-efficient hoop-jumping, a willingness to take intellectual risks morphing into formulaic responses without risk of embarrassment, making your world better becoming a dreary requirement to pick up trash." And what do kids learn? "If there's one thing I learned, it's that they're not learning. Practically anything. . . . The holy grail in our high schools is the Advanced Placement (AP) track. Pioneered 50 years ago by elite private schools to demonstrate the superior student progress, AP courses now pervade mainstream public schools. Over and over, well-intentioned people call for improving U.S. education by getting more of our kids—especially in poor communities—into AP courses. But do our kids learn in AP courses? In an experiment conducted by Dartmouth College, entering students with a 5 on their AP Psychology exam took the final exam from the college's introductory Psych course. A pitiful 10 percent passed. Worse, when the AP superstars did enroll in intro Psych, they performed no better than classmates with no prior coursework in the subject area. It's as though the AP students had learned nothing about psychology. And that's the point"[145]

Blanchard: A sobering analysis.

Ulrich: Yes. The United States was once the world leader in innovation. And yet, with the explosion of technological innovation, our education system seems structured to inhibit innovation. Instead of fostering creativity, we are preparing students for the dull and pointless life Quinn alluded to earlier.[146]

Walter: "Without a transcendent and honorable purpose schooling must reach its finish, and the sooner we are done with it, the better. With such a purpose, schooling becomes the central institution through which the young may find reasons for continuing to educate themselves. . . . Without a narrative, life has no meaning. Without meaning, learning has no purpose. Without a purpose, schools are houses of detention, not attention."[147]

HISTORICAL AND SOCIAL CONTEXT

Moderator: Taylor should be congratulated for her attempt to summarize the varied purposes that have been proposed even if her statement is not all-encompassing. I would like to offer two observations about the purposes you have suggested. The first is related to the comments Anderson, Druley, and Karch just made. Some of the stated purposes are individual in nature. For example, "to prepare students for college or a job," "to prepare students for citizenship," "to develop critical thinking skills," and "to learn to learn" all state outcomes for individuals. These are the types of purposes Taylor included in her summary. But some of the stated purposes are social in nature. "Helping the U.S. compete in the global economy," "transmitting civilization," and "solving social problems" are examples of social purposes. These were the types of purposes Anderson, Druley, and Karch were referencing. Of course, we could just extend Taylor's summary to include social purposes as well. But what I would like you to think about is the compatibility of these purposes. Does it make sense for education to have both individual and social purposes? And more than that, are some of the stated purposes, either individual or social, at odds with some other stated purposes, either individual or social? My second observation is that many, if not all, of the stated purposes are not new. They have been offered by others at various points in the history of education. Finally, as Ulrich pointed out, stating purposes is one thing; achieving them is quite another. So as a prelude to discussing *today's* educational issues, I would like us to think about how these purposes you stated may be tied to social and historical contexts. This will help us make sense of how we got to where we are, where we might be going, and the difficulties we face.

Karch: "In the beginning, for hundreds of thousands of years, children educated themselves through self-directed play and exploration. In relation to the biological history of our species, schools are very recent institutions. . . . With the rise of agriculture, and later of industry, children became forced laborers. Play and exploration were suppressed. Willfulness, which had been a virtue, became a vice that had to be beaten out of children. . . . In sum, for several thousand years after the advent of agriculture, the education of children was, to a considerable degree, a matter of squashing their willfulness in order to make them good laborers. A good child was an obedient child, who suppressed his or her urge to play and explore and dutifully carried out the orders of adult masters."[148]

Anderson: "For various reasons, some religious and some secular, the idea of universal, compulsory education arose and gradually spread. Education was understood as inculcation. . . . The idea began to spread that childhood should be a time for learning, and schools for children were developed as places of learning. . . . Much of the impetus for universal education came from the emerging Protestant religions. . . . In America, in the mid-17th century, Massachusetts became the first colony to mandate schooling, the clearly stated purpose of which was to turn children into good Puritans. . . . *The New England Primer* . . . [contained] various lessons designed to instill in children a fear of God and a sense of duty to their elders."[149]

Walter: Yes. During the early years of our nation, moral development and education for citizenship in a democratic society were primary purposes of education.[150] [151] [152] In many of the colonies, life was organized around religion; after all, religious freedom was the primary motivation for coming to America. Also, in a newly formed country, it was crucial for children to learn the tenets on which the country was based.[153] People need education because it is the people that control the powers of society.[154]

Easton: Good manners and service to God and country.[155]

Johnson: As the country grew and became more heterogeneous, the religious purpose of education waned.[156] Horace Mann advocated a non-sectarian "common school," that is, a school common to all people.[157] Citizenship education and learning skills for a livelihood were the primary purposes of education.[158] Mann believed that education could be "the great equalizer of the conditions of men—the balance-wheel of the social machinery."[159]

Karch: The first change Johnson mentions can be seen in the change in content of the McGuffey Readers, one of the most widely used schoolbooks in the mid- to late-1800s. "McGuffey was remembered as a theological and conservative teacher. He understood the goals of public schooling in terms of moral and spiritual education and attempted to give schools a curriculum that would instill Presbyterian Calvinist beliefs and manners in their students. These goals were suitable for early 19th century America, but not for the nation's later need for unified pluralism. The content of the readers changed drastically between McGuffey's 1836–1837 editions and the 1879 edition. The revised Readers were compiled to meet the needs of national unity and the dream of an American 'melting pot' for the world's oppressed masses. The Calvinist values of salvation, righteousness and piety, so prominent in the early Readers, were entirely missing in the later versions. The content of the books was secularized and replaced by middle-class civil religion, morality and values."[160]

Newcomer: In the late 19th and early 20th centuries, there was another influx of immigrants, which led to an increase in school enrollments. There was also an increase in technology, which meant fewer jobs for lower-class youth.[161] Additionally, children in the labor force were driving down wages so there was a push to put them in school.[162] As a result of these changes, the purpose of secondary education shifted from near exclusive focus on preparation for college to education for life.[163] Schools focused on moral development and job training.[164]

Inglehart: Employers in industry saw schooling as a way to create better workers. To them, the most crucial lessons were punctuality, following directions, tolerance for long hours of tedious work, and a minimal ability to read and write.[165]

Lawrence: And here's where the social sorting purpose enters. "As democratic equality and social efficiency opened access to education for larger groups of people, upper middle-class parents sought to maintain prestige in the credentials their children were attaining. . . . The compromise was the comprehensive high school with its vocational and academic tracks."[166]

Karch: So, the purpose of education had changed from preserving the republic to sorting people into their appropriate positions in the social order.[167]

Van Houten: "Into this mix we must add reformers who truly cared about children, whose messages may ring sympathetically in our ears today. These are people who saw schools as places for protecting children from the damaging forces of the outside world and for providing children with the moral and intellectual grounding needed to develop into upstanding, competent adults. But they too had their agenda for what children should learn. Children should learn moral lessons and disciplines, such as Latin and mathematics, that would exercise their minds and turn them into scholars."[168]

Ulrich: This is also where business ideas began to influence education or at least educational administration. As schools grew, administrators drew upon Frederick Taylor's model of "scientific management," which was developed for businesses, to manage resources efficiently and reduce school expenditures.[169] The top-down organizational structure of school systems, separating students into grade levels, and within grade levels, separating them into upper and lower academic tracks were the result of efforts to increase schools' efficiency. These efforts mirrored similar attempts to promote productivity and efficiency in industry.[170]

Walter: "School has gradually replaced fieldwork, factory work, and domestic chores as the child's primary job. . . . Over time, children's lives have become increasingly defined and structured by the school curriculum. Children now are almost universally identified by their grade in school, much as adults are identified by their job or career. Schools today are much less harsh than they were, but certain premises about the nature of learning remain unchanged: Learning is hard work; it is something that children must be forced to do, not something that will happen naturally through children's self-chosen activities. The specific lessons that children must learn are determined by professional educators, not by children, so education today is still, as much as ever, a matter of inculcation (though educators tend to avoid that term and use, falsely, terms like 'discovery'). . . . Children's own play is certainly understood as inadequate as a foundation for education. . . . School today is the place where all children learn the distinction that hunter-gatherers never knew—the distinction between work and play. . . . That, perhaps, is the leading lesson of our method of schooling. If children learn nothing else in school, they learn the difference between work and play and that learning is work, not play."[171]

Easton: And that is as it should be. Play is too unstructured to promote learning.

Van Houten: Well then how did children learn before there were schools? Even after there were schools, not all children attended them, but they still learned.

Easton: I think many learned through a master-apprentice model. But I should have said that play is too unstructured to promote efficient learning.

Oates: It seems that for most of the 20th century, the primary goal of education was to efficiently prepare the majority of students to fit smoothly into a mass production economy.[172]

Quinn: Not only that but schooling itself operated like a mass production economy.[173]

Karch: As a result of the large number of immigrants entering public schools during the late 19th and early 20th century, class sizes were so large that teachers could not attend to or promote students' individuality.[174] By necessity, the mode of operation resembled mass production.

Blanchard: Excuse me. I'm a little puzzled by the turn our discussion has taken. We started by expressing what we felt should be the purpose of education. Fine. Now we are talking about the purpose of education from a historical perspective. But are we talking about purposes that people have stated in the past or are we inferring purposes based on documented past educational practices?

Oates: I have to say that my statement was more along the lines of "the educational system performed *as if* the primary goal was . . ."

Blanchard: Yes, it seems somewhat callous for one to say that the purpose of education was to prepare most students for factory work.

Carpenter: Again, it is the difference between the purposes of education and the consequences of education. The purposes were preparation for citizenship and jobs; the consequence was that the majority of students were prepared for a mass production economy.

Peterson: This shows the influence that capital was starting to have on schooling.[175] [176] In other words, industry looked to schools to produce workers that would keep industry going.

Harris: And again Carpenter, I don't think we can separate purposes and consequences that easily. If consequences aren't at all related to purposes, then the educational system is just careening randomly. Perhaps we could talk about intended purposes and enacted purposes, but there is some connection between the two.

Johnson: Yes, the citizenship education was for assimilation into American society and the job preparation was for an industrial economy.

Van Houten: How could anyone do that to kids?

Foster: Do what to kids?

Van Houten: Well, it seems like we are saying that the purpose of education was to prepare students for a life of obedience and drudgery.

Inglehart: Children should be obedient.

Druley: We should note that during the early and middle parts of the 20th century, the Progressive movement did offer an alternative to the assimilation and job preparation purposes. John Dewey rejected the goal of preparing students for different slots in the manufacturing process. He thought school should be integrated with society in the sense that learning could emerge from applying the principles and practices of democracy to the actual problems of life.[177]

Karch: Schools in the late 1800s were focused on assimilating immigrants into American society and preparing them to be productive citizens who could work manufacturing jobs. As a result, the theory of teaching at the time concentrated on maintaining discipline and control, organizing classrooms and covering material efficiently, teaching job skills, and conveying American values and the proper way to behave. As I suggested earlier, this emphasis stemmed from the necessity of teaching large numbers of students as much as from any philosophical theory of teaching. Dewey rejected the teacher's drill sergeant-like role and the student's corresponding conformist role in the prevailing model of education. Rather than approaching schooling by thinking about what students were to become, he began by trying to understand the psychological nature of children and the consequences of that nature for their learning.[178]

Oates: However, while for Dewey, "education is life,"[179] some Progressives saw the purpose of education as preparation for life. For them, this still meant providing students with the skills needed by the economy and society.[180] They focused on changing the emphasis in secondary schools from "literary education" to vocational and commercial education.[181]

Taylor: This is all mildly interesting, but I don't see how it is going to help us formulate a purpose of education going forward.

Moderator: I'm not sure that it will.

Ziegler: The lack of lasting influence the Deweyan Progressives had on educational practices does suggest that purposes that do not align with the needs of society are unlikely to garner much support.[182] [183]

Walter: "Education should indeed be responsive to the needs of society. But this is not the same as regarding yourself as a service station for neocapitalism. In fact, you would tackle society's needs a great deal more effectively were you to challenge this whole alienated model of learning"[184] that we have now.

Anderson: What do you mean by "alienated model of learning"?

Walter: Few students display a genuine interest in school learning, resulting in a situation where they must be bribed with rewards or threatened with punishment in order to play the game.

Ziegler: I'd like to hear about the last half of the 20th century up until the present to help us understand how we came to what we have now.

Harris: After the Soviet Union's launch of Sputnik in 1957, the U.S. became concerned about falling behind technologically.[185] The National Defense Education Act, passed in 1958, aimed to produce more scientists and mathematicians to ensure the U.S. could maintain technological dominance. This was the first time the federal government had tried to impact education.[186]

Foster: The goal of the revamped K–12 math curriculum, which was referred to as the "New Math," was to prepare students to study mathematics in college.[187]

Druley: In the 1960s, the Great Society programs, including the War on Poverty, looked to education to provide equal opportunity and promote equality.[188] Education was seen as the key to improving society.[189]

Walter: I wonder if "there is something amiss in our age-old white, middle-class attempt to bring education and enlightenment to the masses, to provide 'them' with the cultural capital that will allow 'them' to compete a little more equally on a disastrously unequal playing field."[190]

Yann: "Our social progress is checkered. Residential segregation and unequal opportunities still blight our society, economy and schools. Unfortunately, rather than addressing politically unpopular root causes, it was far more convenient to demand schools solve these problems. . . . No serious effort was made to assure equal opportunities, for example. Thus, the achievement gap [between black students and white students] was finessed by blaming the victim."[191]

Karch: In the post-World War II era, there was an increasing emphasis on recognizing and developing the individuality of each student. Educators assured parents that school would help children realize their individual potential and develop their unique talents. However, this remained an empty promise as it ignored what schools had been, were, and continued to be. The structure of schools, which continued to be unexamined, meant that individuality was ignored in the effort to train students for citizenship and work. Students' role was that of passive recipients of information who succeeded or failed based on their ability to memorize facts and regurgitate them on tests. Pursuing student-generated questions, promoting divergent thinking, and attending to individual differences was simply not part of the classroom picture.[192]

Ziegler: I can see how the rhetoric of individualization could divert attention from the achievement gap and lead to blaming the victim. The "you've got to pull yourself up by your own bootstraps" view.

Inglehart: To move into more recent history, the 1983 report, *A Nation at Risk*, which the moderator mentioned at the outset, decried "a rising tide of mediocrity" in schools and warned that the U.S. was losing ground to other countries. The report linked the quality of education to the nation's economic success.[193]

Harris: To provide some background to that, "between 1870 and 1950, the average American's level of education rose by 0.8 years per decade. In 1890, the average adult had completed about 8 years of schooling. By 1900, the average American had 8.8 years. By 1910, it was 9.6 years, and by 1960, it was nearly 14 years. As Claudia Goldin and Lawrence Katz describe in their book, *The Race Between Education and Technology*, America's educational progress was amazingly steady over those decades, and the U.S. opened up a gigantic global lead. Educational levels were rising across the industrialized world, but the U.S. had at least a 35-year advantage on most of Europe. In 1950, no European country enrolled 30 percent of its older teens in full-time secondary school. In the U.S., 70 percent of older teens were in school. America's edge boosted productivity and growth. But the happy era ended around 1970 when America's educational progress slowed to a crawl. Between 1975 and 1990, educational attainments stagnated completely. Since then, progress has been modest. America's lead over its economic rivals has been entirely forfeited, with many nations surging ahead in school attainment. This threatens the country's long-term prospects. It also widens the gap between rich and poor. Goldin and Katz describe a race between technology and education. The pace of technological change has been surprisingly steady. In periods when educational progress outpaces this change, inequality narrows. The market is flooded with skilled workers, so their wages rise modestly. In periods, like the current one, when educational progress lags behind technological change, inequality widens. The relatively few skilled workers command higher prices, while the many unskilled ones have little bargaining power. The meticulous research of Goldin and Katz is complemented by a report from James Heckman of the University of Chicago. Using his own research, Heckman also concludes that high school graduation rates peaked in the U.S. in the late 1960s, at about 80 percent. Since then they have declined. In 'Schools, Skills and Synapses,' Heckman probes the sources of that decline. It's not falling school quality, he argues. Nor is it primarily a shortage of funding or rising college tuition costs. Instead, Heckman directs attention at family environments, which have deteriorated over the past 40 years."[194]

Van Houten: If the main problem with schools is family environments, I don't know how you're going to fix that.

Peterson: Early intervention programs.

Foster: Which cost society (taxpayers) a lot of money.

Peterson: They may cost society less money in the long run than incarceration or rehabilitation and adult job training programs.[195]

Blanchard: I've already heard enough to convince me that, in spite of the challenges family environments pose for schools, there are things that schools should be doing differently.

Ross: In the late 1980s the standards movement began with the publication of math standards. Originally, standards arose within the field of education partly as a reaction against the "back-to-basics" movement of the 1970s. While back-to-basics emphasized rote memorization of facts and procedures, the standards published by the National Council of Teachers of Mathematics in 1989 emphasized problem solving, reasoning, and the ability to communicate mathematically.[196] However, once politicians and policymakers got on the standards bandwagon, they came to be used as a political tool, a way to force improvement in the educational system that would result in more students prepared for college, more students prepared for jobs in technology, more scientists and engineers—all with the goal of helping the U.S. maintain its global economic and technological competitiveness.[197]

Karch: Perhaps partly out of concern over the federal government exercising too much control over education, the No Child Left Behind Act of 2001 required states to develop their own standards and accountability systems but did not establish national standards. However, that approach was subsequently criticized for resulting in inconsistent standards between the states.[198]

Taylor: Reports such as *Goals 2000*, federal education laws such as No Child Left Behind and Race to the Top, and the latest incarnation of standards—the Common Core State Standards—all suggest the purpose of education is to prepare students to compete for jobs in the global economy and, through these jobs, to keep the U.S. ahead of its foreign competitors.[199]

Blanchard: What are the "Common Core State Standards"?

Lawrence: "The Common Core is a set of high-quality academic standards in mathematics and English language arts/literacy (ELA). These learning goals outline what a student should know and be able to do at the end of each grade [K–12]. The standards were created to ensure that all students graduate from high school with the skills and knowledge necessary to succeed in college, career, and life, regardless of where they live. . . . The standards are: research- and evidence-based; clear, understandable, and consistent; aligned with college and career expectations, based on rigorous content and application of knowledge through higher-order thinking skills; built upon the strengths and lessons of current state standards; informed by other top performing countries in order to prepare all students for success in our global economy and society."[200]

Carpenter: No Child Left Behind also aimed to solve social problems such as crime, poverty, and unemployment, primarily through increased student achievement, which it was thought would lead to an improved economy, thereby ameliorating other problems.[201]

Johnson: In our state, the governor and the superintendent of public instruction, together with leaders of the state's business community, formed a group in 1999 whose purpose was to help set education policy.[202] The inclusion of business leaders in this group indicates the importance of education to the economy.

Inglehart: It is not clear how much progress has been made in this area since *A Nation at Risk*. In 2006, The Commission on the Skills of the American Workforce, a group of education and business leaders, claimed that "current teaching is failing to prepare young Americans for the global economy."[203]

Harris: In the early 2000s, the number of graduates in science and engineering in the U.S. had been declining for several years. As a result, there has been a push to increase K–12 science education efforts in order to encourage more students to enroll in science and technology-oriented majors.[204] Furthermore, "research—especially in the science and technology fields—is perceived now as the key to economic development."[205] There are now Faculty Commercialization Awards given to university researchers whose work results in technological developments that have commercial applications that benefit society.[206]

Ziegler: So, to sum up, since the late 1950s the primary purposes of education have been preparing students for college and jobs and improving society—at least improving society economically and technologically.

Harris: And maintaining the United States' standing in the world.

Ziegler: Yes. Education for citizenship and education for life have not been emphasized as much.[207]

Druley: I am concerned that the emphasis on science education overlooks one of the nation's greatest sources of intellectual strength, namely the humanities and social sciences. Many of the most successful people in our country have degrees in one of these fields. Now it seems these areas of study are being denigrated.[208]

Yann: Public colleges and universities have felt this emphasis as well. More and more it seems they are being viewed as vocational schools whose only purpose is job training.

Walter: "An educated student [has been] redefined as an employable one."[209]

Xander: It seems as though educational knowledge is becoming commodified. The president of one of our state universities has suggested that alumni invest in students by funding all or part of their education in return for a small portion of their income once they graduate and are employed. What majors do you think are going to be funded? Business, engineering, science, technology, health care professions. Certainly not philosophy, psychology, sociology, anthropology, foreign languages and literature. The majors that provide the highest short-term return on investment and that serve the needs of powerful private interest groups are those that will be funded. Education is increasingly viewed as a personal investment rather than something that benefits society as a whole.[210]

Walter: "It would not have come easily to the mind of such a man [as Thomas Jefferson], as it does to political leaders today, that the young should be taught to read exclusively for the purpose of increasing their economic productivity."[211]

Carpenter: I find this current emphasis dangerous. "There has been a recognition, running from Aristotle and Adam Smith to the seminal economists of the mid-20th century, that a society cannot long flourish unless economic activity and thought are grounded in the liberal arts. The humanities were seen as a necessary component of a wealthy and stable society. . . . From the Renaissance to the mid-20th century, the humanities were tightly tied to economic success. Figures like Leon Battista Alberti, a 15th-century engineer, architect, and philosopher, insisted that a well-educated citizenry could best maintain stable states, which, in turn, produced wealth. It was a virtuous circle. Every citizen should be able to 'manage a household' (through accounting), but also be well versed in rhetoric, ethics, and history, so as to be an effective and prosperous member of the polity. . . . 20th-century economists continued to be influenced by the liberal arts. Both Carl Menger—founder of the Austrian School of economics, with its animating idea that individuals are fully rational actors who create rational markets—and John Maynard Keynes—who believed in state intervention to regulate economies—studied classics and history. . . . Keynes believed that numbers had to be analyzed through the lens of philosophy, psychology, and history. In so doing, he was walking in the path of the sociologist Thorstein Veblen, who saw economic activity as socially and culturally determined.

   One does not have to ascribe to Keynes's economic theory to agree with his approach. Milton Friedman was trained as an accountant, but he nonetheless wrote, with Anna Schwartz, the deeply researched *A Monetary History of the United States, 1867–1960*. History, Friedman believed, was essential to understanding economics. Seen in this light, the greatest revolution in economics in the past 50 years involves not only the transformation of the discipline into a more quantitative science but also the separation of the business curriculum from the humanities. Training in economics at the college level no longer forces students to think of people as moral agents shaped by religion, culture, and society, but rather as one-dimensional rational actors blindly pursuing material self-interest. . . . With these reductive and often purely quantitative approaches, we are moving further away from the complex, interdisciplinary understandings that first characterized economic analysis."[212]

Johnson: Why must we emphasize one over the other? Why not have balance?

Carpenter: I'm not sure those in power want citizens to be informed or to be able to think for themselves. Just keep your head down and do the job you were trained to do.[213] But I do believe that "knowledge of the structure and function of our government is something that should be—and in some places still is— taught in high school. Education in how our society works and how to function in it is a right of all our minor children. If young Americans figure out how they have been cheated by the use of K–12 as an incarceration system rather than an educational system, the reparations bill will be very large."[214]

Foster: I find it offensive that you refer to our educational system as an incarceration system. Job training is not the same as prison. It benefits individuals and society. To me, it makes sense that as the world has gotten smaller over the last 50 years and a new world order has emerged, we are now part of a global community, so our focus has turned toward remaining a step ahead of other countries. We are a competitive lot, after all.

Grable: Do you have any more clichés?

Walter: How could anyone do that to kids?

Ziegler: What do you mean?

Walter: Saying that the purpose of education is to maintain the United States' standing in the world is essentially placing the burden of the success or failure of the nation's economy on the backs of students.

Taylor: Or their teachers.

Easton: Or administrators.

Xander: Or the college professors who taught their teachers and administrators.

COMPATIBILITY OF PURPOSES

Anderson (to Moderator): I've been thinking about your question concerning the compatibility of the different purposes. May we consider that now?

Moderator: By all means . . .

Anderson: Well, the individual goals of preparing students for college and/ or jobs feed into the social goals of maintaining the United States' economic and technological standing in the world and strengthening national security. So, in this way they also foster the social goal of improving society. Similarly, the individual goals of preparing students for citizenship and promoting moral development support the social goal of creating social harmony.

Ulrich: Hold on! I agree with your first statement. But I'm not sure that greater national security and maintaining global economic competitiveness result in an improved society. We still have college graduates who cannot find employment in their chosen fields . . .

Grable: They should have chosen a different field.

Ulrich: . . . and government funding for higher education has not kept up with inflation, thus making higher education more and more difficult to afford and creating a looming student-debt crisis. Also, there is the potential trade-off between greater national security and loss of individual freedoms. Is that an improved society?

Van Houten: I'm not sure I agree with Anderson's last statement—that citizenship education and moral development will lead to social harmony. It sounds great in theory but given the contentious political climate we live in I think there will be a great deal of disagreement about what constitutes appropriate education in citizenship and morals. I was thinking that there is a potential conflict between the individual goals of preparation for citizenship and the development of critical thinking and freedom of thought. Again, one would think, in theory, that these goals should be compatible. But it all depends on what kind of citizens you want.

Xander: Yes, do we want citizens who will question, challenge, and protest or docile citizens who will "go with the flow" and "walk the company line"?

Grable: Probably no one would choose the latter, but it's also true that we only want the former when they agree with us. An athlete kneeling during the national anthem as a form of protest is perceived as patriotic by half the country and treasonous by the other half.

Yann: By extension, one could foresee a possible conflict between the individual goals of promoting freedom of thought and critical thinking and preparation for jobs. What kind of employees do you want?

Ziegler: Do you think the individual goals of intellectual development and critical thinking support the social goal of improving society?

Anderson: Yes, in spite of our political differences, it will take great thinkers to improve society.

Grable: Hmmm . . . that seems elitist.

Blanchard: I wonder if there is a tension between the social goals of transmitting or preserving culture and changing or improving society.[215]

Easton: We ought to be able to preserve the best parts of our culture and change those aspects that need changing.

Carpenter: We ought to, but I think the social processes that preserve culture are not always compatible with those that change culture. Think civil rights movement or the more recent controversy about gay marriage.

Xander (to Easton): What are the "best parts of our culture"? What is best to you may not seem so to someone else.

Johnson: Things that "ought to be" may seem as if they "ought not to be" when the processes of cultural transmission dominate.

Druley: Maybe this is why "critical thinking" and, ironically, "freedom of thought" are sometimes viewed as "radical" educational purposes. They seem consistent with the social goal of improving society, but not necessarily preserving society.

Lawrence: The social goals of promoting equality and preserving privilege are definitely at odds with each other.[216] Horace Mann's concept of the common school extended the hope of social mobility and equality through education to all,[217] but, as I noted before, the practice of tracking functioned to preserve privilege for the upper middle class.[218] [219]

Karch: Social mobility has come to depend on possessing educational credentials. Tracking provided more valued credentials to those in the higher tracks. Further, the number of credentials required for highly valued jobs continues to increase. This makes it harder for lower class students to obtain such jobs because they cannot afford to pay for (buy) the needed credentials. Still, lower class students have to "play the game" if they want to have any chance of advancing socially and economically.[220]

Grable: Even if the chance is quite small.

Lawrence: Yes, "the Jack Kent Cooke Foundation released a report on diversity at the nation's 91 most competitive colleges as defined by Barron's, which compiles information on higher education. The Cooke report found that fewer than one in 25 students at these schools came from families in the country's lowest socioeconomic quartile, while nearly three in four came from families in the top quartile."[221]

Xander: "What [that] says to me is that the working class is history at these schools, the middle class is on its way out the door and the upper class is dominating. And that's not what the American dream is about."[222]

Ross: This suggests to me that the goal or consequence, however you want to look at it, of social sorting may not be compatible with the goal of social harmony. At some point the lower class may stop believing that our society is a meritocracy and revolt against what they see as the unfairness in the social sorting mechanism.

Peterson: I see one more contradiction in the purposes we stated. Oates hinted at it before. We mentioned "preparation for life" as an individual purpose. But Dewey said, "Education is life." He thought that goals emerge in the course of one's activity—they are not given or imposed from the outside prior to the activity.[223] I think anytime one says, "The purpose of education is to *prepare students for . . . ,*" a quite different curriculum, set of teaching methods, and approach to assessment will arise than if one takes the view that "education is life."

PURPOSES, CURRICULA, AND METHODS OF TEACHING

Moderator: Ah. Great! You have anticipated my next question. How are the different purposes we have discussed related to curriculum and teaching methods?

Harris: What do you mean by "curriculum"?

Moderator: Good question. There may be multiple curricula at any given school. I used the term to refer to the explicit or intended curriculum, that is, the subject matter, the learning objectives, learning materials (textbooks, books, worksheets, manipulatives), and learning activities (lectures, class discussions, seatwork, experiments, field trips) that students engage with.

Anderson: So, are teaching methods part of curriculum?

Moderator: I have allowed them to creep in with my inclusion of learning activities, haven't I? And they certainly are part of the enacted curriculum, the curriculum students actually experience.

Snepp: Karch has already pointed out how the content of the McGuffey readers changed from a focus on religious beliefs and values to a more secular focus on "civics."

Johnson: It makes sense that such a change would accompany a change in purpose from religious indoctrination in the early years of the nation to assimilation of immigrants in the late 1800s.[224]

Blanchard: I recall reading that Thomas Jefferson proposed that schools teach reading, writing, arithmetic, geography, and history. Except for science, that's pretty much what we teach in elementary schools today.

Anderson: I can see that those subjects would have been sufficient for citizenship preparation back then. And reading, writing, and arithmetic would have prepared one to manage one's affairs and to handle any business transactions they might have engaged in.

Easton: The secondary school curriculum today is not much different, except for a few more subjects such as economics, sociology, and psychology.

Yann: We also have to consider how the subjects are dealt with. In 1892, the Committee of Ten proposed that the high school curriculum should focus on preparation for college.[225] However, in 1918, the *Cardinal Principles* recommended that high schools should teach all that was necessary in adult life.[226] A few years later, Franklin Bobbitt suggested analyzing adult roles and occupations in order to determine what content schools should teach.[227] As high school enrollments grew in the first half of the 20th century, these different foci were reflected in the different tracks created for students. The highest-level track focused on preparing students for college. For example, in mathematics this meant Algebra I, Geometry, Algebra II, Trigonometry, and perhaps Calculus. However, for the lower track, mathematics was General Mathematics, which meant arithmetic with whole numbers, fractions, decimals, and percents, ratio and proportion, and perhaps some rudimentary algebra.

Ziegler: So, by employing different curricula for different groups of students, schools were able to address the goals of preparation for college and preparation for life and work.

Yann: There were also vocational schools for students who were not going on to college. In 1917, the Smith-Hughes Act authorized federal funding for vocational education in schools. "The early vocational education was driven by a philosophy of fitting people to their probable destinies. Kids from poor families were tracked off into becoming the worker bees. Others were tracked off to go to universities and be the intelligentsia."[228] The Smith-Hughes Act was an attempt to address economic and social changes in American society. As industrialization expanded, factory owners faced a shortage of skilled labor. And public schools needed to do something with the influx of immigrants from largely poor families.[229]

Johnson: Although the practice of "tracking" was criticized for reproducing existing racial and socioeconomic divisions in society and efforts were made to do away with the practice, it seems to have reappeared in our state with a new name—pathways. We now have different pathways leading to a high school diploma.

Anderson: What about teaching methods?

Karch: There hasn't been much change in teaching methods for more than 100 years. Regardless of grade level or subject matter, the dominant form of instruction has been teacher centered. That means, among other things, teacher talk exceeding student talk, the teacher working with the class as a whole rather than with small groups or individuals, the teacher determining the use of class time, and the classroom arranged in rows of desks facing the teacher.[230] For example, the typical pattern in math classes involves the teacher going over the previous day's homework, then explaining new material, and finally having students work at their seats on the assignment over the new material.

Blanchard: So regardless of which purpose prevailed at any given time, teaching methods did not vary much. What about assessment?

Lawrence: Tests, quizzes, homework, essays, lab reports, the occasional project. Like teaching methods, not much change.

Van Houten: Not much change in classroom assessment. Assessment of teachers and schools is a different issue.

Druley: When you meet with 150 students every day it is hard to think outside the box about assessment. There was a push for the use of portfolios in assessment, but I just couldn't grade 150 portfolios in an intellectually honest way in a limited amount of time at the end of a semester.

Peterson: I would point out that the curricula and methods of teaching and assessment we have discussed correspond to school settings where the purpose of education is considered to be preparing students for one thing or another.

Ross: Schools that employ a model of project-based learning often employ performance assessments. Students work individually or collaboratively on extended projects that may involve research, analysis, and problem solving and then present their findings both orally and in writing. Teachers establish rubrics for scoring the presentations. So there have been some attempts to develop new approaches to assessment, but they tend to be used in "innovation" schools, that is, schools that don't conform to the traditional model of schooling most of us experienced and that most current students still experience.

NOTES

1. Edward B. Fiske, "A Nation at a Loss," *New York Times*, April 25, 2008, https://www.nytimes.com/2008/04/25/opinion/25fiske.html.

2. Ibid.

3. Paraphrased and quoted from Fiske, "A Nation at a Loss."

4. Mathis makes a similar point about the "Chicken Little jeremiad" that followed *A Nation at Risk*. See William Mathis, "Losing Our Purpose, Measuring the Wrong Things," web log comment, September 1, 2017, https://dianeravitch.net/2017/09/01/william-mathis-what-is-the-purpose-of-school-and-what-do-we-measure/.

5. Fiske, "A Nation at a Loss."

6. This statement by E and most of those that follow it to the end of the introduction section are based on an open forum e-mail exchange at a public university. The citation at the end of each statement will identify the individual who made that statement. E's statement here was made by Vytenis Damusis.

7. Dennis Barbour.

8. Vytenis Damusis.

9. Ruth Turpin.

10. Vytenis Damusis.

11. Martin Carnoy and Richard Rothstein, *What Do International Tests Really Show about U.S. Student Performance* (Washington, D.C.: Economic Policy Institute, 2013), https://steinhardt.nyu.edu/scmsAdmin/media/users/sl1716/IGEMS/PISA-TIMSS_paper.pdf.

12. Ibid.

13. Elsa Weber.

14. Michael Witham.

15. Mark Mabrito.

16. Phyllis Bergiel.

17. Michael Witham.

18. Alan Spector.

19. Ruth Turpin.

20. Shawn Slavin.

21. Alan Spector.

22. Edward Perosky.

23. Michael Witham.

24. Michael Roller.

25. Ursula Saqui.

26. Michael Roller.

27. Alan Spector.

28. Frank Stanzione.

29. Jin Lu.

30. Attributed to G. K. Chesterton. Retrieved from http://www.quotegarden.com/education.html.

31. Attributed to Ariel and Will Durant in Gelbrich. See Judy Gelbrich, "Section II–American Education," online course material, 1999a, http://oregonstate.edu/instruct/ed416/ae1.html.

32. E. D. Hirsch's notion of cultural literacy, proposed in 1987, is discussed in Wraga. See William G. Wraga, "The Progressive Vision of General Education and the American Common School Ideal: Implications for Curriculum Policy, Practice, and Theory," *Journal of Curriculum Studies* 31, no. 5 (1999): 523–544.

33. A primary purpose of the McGuffey reader, one of the most commonly used texts in U.S. schools in the 19th century, was to foster good citizens. See Judy Gelbrich, "Section II–American Education," online course material, 1999c, http://oregonstate.edu/instruct/ed416/ae3.html.

34. Mortimer Adler's *Paideia Proposal*, written in 1982, lists the development of citizenship as one of the three primary objectives of schooling. See Purpose of School–Philosophical [Wesleyan University blog], retrieved from http://www.purposeofschool.com/philosophical/.

35. Thomas Jefferson advocated education for citizenship, among other purposes. See Sharon H. Iorio and M. E. Yeager, "School Reform: Past, Present, and Future," paper presented at the School Reform Strategies symposium held at Harris Manchester College, Oxford University, Oxford, England, July 2011, http://webs.wichita.edu/depttools/depttoolsmemberfiles/COEdDEAN/School%20Reform%20Past%20Present%20and%20Future.pdf.

36. Throughout the history of the United States, schools have been expected to produce good workers and good citizens. See Randall V. Bass, "The Purpose of Education," *Educational Forum* 61, no. 2 (1997): 128–132, https://doi.org/10.1080/00131729709335242.

37. Eleanor Roosevelt believed that every citizen should take an interest in government and that one of the purposes of education was to produce citizens. See Eleanor Roosevelt, "Good Citizenship: The Purpose of Education," in *Yearbook of the*

National Society for the Study of Education 107, no. 2 (2008): 312–320, https://doi. org./10.1111/j.1744-7984.2008.00228.x.

38. In the 1960s, the School Mathematics Study Group, concerned that schools were not meeting societal needs, stated that understanding the role of mathematics in society was necessary for intelligent citizenship. See George M. A. Stanic and Jeremy Kilpatrick, "Mathematics Curriculum Reform in the United States: A Historical Perspective," *International Journal of Educational Research* 17, no. 5 (1992): 407–417, https://doi.org/10.1016/S0883-0355(05)80002-3.

39. Horace Mann, an early 19th century advocate of public education, wrote that "education must prepare our citizens to become municipal officers, intelligent jurors, honest witnesses, legislators, or competent judges of legislation—in fine, to fill all the manifold relations of life" Quoted in John A. Nietz, "Horace Mann's Ideas on General Methods in Education," *The Elementary School Journal* 37, no. 10 (1937): 743.

40. Writing in support of the school mathematics reforms proposed by the National Council of Teachers of Mathematics in 1989, Thomas Romberg said, "For a culture to be mathematically powerful, its citizens must have the mathematical understanding and experience to jointly undertake the routine tasks of everyday life, to operate as a society, and to progress as a civilization" Quoted from Thomas A. Romberg, "The Scholarly Basis of the School Mathematics Reform Movement in the United States," *International Journal of Educational Research* 17, no. 5 (1992): 432–433, https://doi. org/10.1016/S0883-0355(05)80003-5.

41. Bass, "The Purpose of Education" also discusses the cultural transmission function of education. Through education, one generation passes along to the next generation knowledge, beliefs, lore, customs, values, and rites.

42. See also Nancy Flanagan, "In Your Opinion, What Should the Purpose of Education Be?" Message 8, November 30, 2011, https://www.ted.com/conversations/7491/in_your_opinion_what_should_t.html; Arthur Camins, "What's the Purpose of Education in the 21st Century?" *Washington Post*, February 12, 2015, https:// www.washingtonpost.com/news/answer-sheet/wp/2015/02/12/whats-the-purpose-of-education-in-the-21st-century/?utm_term=.e532a78f8698; and Public Agenda, *The Purposes of Education: A Public Agenda Citizen Choicework Guide* (New York: Public Agenda, 2005).

43. John Dewey thought that schools should help students learn to participate in a democratic society. See Gene Carter, "What's the Purpose of School in the 21st Century?" *Good*, March 19, 2012, https://www.good.is/articles/what-s-the-purpose-of-school-in-the-21st-century.

44. In addition, see W. F. Warde, "John Dewey's Theories of Education," *International Socialist Review* 21, no. 1 (Winter 1960), https://www.marxists.org/archive/novack/works/1960/x03.htm.

45. Romberg argues that a contemporary purpose of education should be to prepare students to participate as informed citizens of a democratic nation in the 21st century. See Walter G. Secada, "Introduction," *International Journal of Educational Research* 17, no. 5 (1992): 403–406, https://doi.org/10.1016/S0883-0355(05)80001-1.

46. Throughout much of United States' history, one goal of education has been to promote democratic equality by equipping students with the knowledge and skills

necessary to be competent citizens. See David F. Labaree, "The Chronic Failure of Curriculum Reform," *Education Week* 18, no. 36 (1999): 42–44.

47. At the college level, the concept of general education in the 1930s was intended to prepare students for life in a democracy. See Wraga, "The Progressive Vision of General Education."

48. Albert Einstein. Retrieved from http://www.azquotes.com/quote/596853.

49. During the Cold War, James Conant, the president of Harvard University, argued that education was necessary to maintain a democratic society. From colonial times until the mid-19th century in the U.S., public education's primary purpose was to create an educated citizenry that would sustain democracy. Since the mid-19th century, other goals have arisen, for example, workforce preparation, career development, life-long learning, and development of critical thinking skills. Today, the goals of preparation for college and career, development of critical thinking skills, and preparation for citizenship continue to be in competition with each other in discussions about the purpose of education. See Iorio and Yeager, "School Reform: Past, Present, and Future."

50. See Nietz, "Horace Mann's Ideas on General Methods in Education" and Wraga, "The Progressive Vision of General Education."

51. Bass, "The Purpose of Education."

52. View attributed to George Counts, a leader of the social reconstructionism movement in education during the 1930s. See Purpose of School – Philosophical [Wesleyan University blog], retrieved from http://www.purposeofschool.com/philosophical/.

53. John Dewey, 1897, quoted in W. F. Warde, "The Fate of Dewey's Theories," *International Socialist Review* 21, no. 2 (Spring 1960): 54–57, 61, https://www.marxists.org/archive/novack/works/1960/x04.htm.

54. The 1983 National Commission on Excellence in Education report *A Nation at Risk* described a "rising tide of mediocrity" in the nation's schools. American students were performing poorly compared to students in other countries, achievement test scores were declining, there was a high level of functional illiteracy, and the current generation's educational skills were below that of the previous generation. During this time period, poverty, drug abuse, unwanted pregnancies, and violence were all on the rise and confidence in public institutions was decreasing. The calls for education reform that followed *A Nation at Risk* argued that improved education could address these social ills. See Jacob E. Adams Jr., "Education Reform - Overview," retrieved July 11, 2018, from http://education.stateuniversity.com/pages/1944/Education-Reform.html.

55. "Education, then, beyond all other devices of human origin, is the great equalizer of the conditions of men—the balance-wheel of the social machinery." Horace Mann, quoted in Gelbrich, "Section II - American Education," (1999c).

56. Labaree says, "we are chronic social reformers, who are on a mission to solve a series of seemingly intractable social problems and who routinely turn to school as the most accessible if not most effective way to accomplish that mission. From this angle, we see schools as the primary way to accomplish our highest social ideals, or at least to represent these ideals in institutional form." David F. Labaree, "School

Syndrome: Understanding the USA's Magical Belief that Schooling Can Somehow Improve Society, Promote Access, and Preserve Advantage," *Journal of Curriculum Studies* 44, no. 2 (2012): 143–163, https://doi.org/10.1080/00220272.2012.675358.

57. In the middle of the 20th century progressive educators formulated a vision of general education that would result in knowledge that students could apply toward resolving personal and social problems. See Wraga, "The Progressive Vision of General Education."

58. Proponents of the *No Child Left Behind Act of 2001* thought that the educational reforms it mandated would result in reductions in poverty, crime, and unemployment. See Justin Lonsbury and Michael W. Apple, "Understanding the Limits and Possibilities of School Reform," *Educational Policy* 26, no.5 (2012): 759–773.

59. In the 1960s political leaders believed education could reduce poverty, promote equality, and provide equal opportunity. The *Elementary and Secondary Education Act of 1965* was a key part of President Johnson's War on Poverty and the Great Society he envisioned. See Iorio and Yeager, "School Reform: Past, Present, and Future."

60. The curriculum theorist, Joseph Schwab, believed that the purpose of the school curriculum is to shape society in the direction of goodness. See J. Wesley Null, "Curriculum Development in Historical Perspective," in *The SAGE Handbook of Curriculum and Instruction*, ed. F. Michael Connelly (Thousand Oaks, CA: Sage Publications, Inc., 2008), 478–490.

61. "Our progress as a nation can be no swifter than our progress in education." John F. Kennedy, quoted in Judy Gelbrich, "Section II - American Education," online course material, 1999d, http://oregonstate.edu/instruct/ed416/ae4.html.

62. Mackenzie and Evans, 1946, quoted in Wraga, "The Progressive Vision of General Education."

63. See Kathy Castle, "In Your Opinion, What Should the Purpose of Education Be?" Message 59, December 22, 2011, https://www.ted.com/conversations/7491/in_your_opinion_what_should_t.html; Oscar García, "In Your Opinion, What Should the Purpose of Education Be?" Message 45, December 28, 2011, https://www.ted.com/conversations/7491/in_your_opinion_what_should_t.html; and Jan Bartscht, "In Your Opinion, What Should the Purpose of Education Be?" Message 29, December 12, 2011, https://www.ted.com/conversations/7491/in_your_opinion_what_should_t.html.

64. "[A] shared and unifying [educational] experience can be one that creates citizens able to investigate and change their communities' political, cultural, and economic assumptions." Lonsbury and Apple, "Understanding the Limits and Possibilities of School Reform," 770.

65. John Dewey thought that by applying the principles and practices of democracy in schools, students would emerge as "creative, well-adjusted equalitarians [who] would make over American society in their own image." See Warde, "John Dewey's Theories of Education."

66. Horace Mann wrote that the public-school system would "feed and sustain the academies and colleges." Quoted in Karen Cheek, "Education in the Southern Colonies," last modified 1996, http://www3.nd.edu/~rbarger/www7/soucolon.html.

67. In the early 1900s, advances in technology, increasing industrialization, and child labor laws meant that there were fewer unskilled jobs for lower-class children. In order to keep these children off the streets and out of trouble, lawmakers turned to schools to provide job training. See Gelbrich, "Section II - American Education," (1999d).

68. The goal of the United States' education system is to produce employable citizens. Modifications to the system over the last 100 years have primarily attempted to update the system to ensure that graduates are prepared for the workforce. See Adam Burk, "In Your Opinion, What Should the Purpose of Education Be?" Message 1, November 2011, https://www.ted.com/conversations/7491/in_your_opinion_what_should_t.html.

69. One of the justifications of the Common Core Standards was that, by meeting them, schools would ensure their graduates were ready for college or jobs. The Obama administration furthered the Common Core initiative by creating Race to the Top, a $4.3 billion contest among states for education grants. In order to qualify for the grants, states were required to have "college and career ready" standards. See Lyndsey Layton, "How Bill Gates Pulled Off the Swift Common Core Revolution," *Washington Post*, June7, 2014, https://www.washingtonpost.com/politics/how-bill-gates-pulled-off-the-swift-common-core-revolution/2014/06/07/a830e32e-ec34-11e3-9f5c-9075d5508f0a_story.html?utm_term=.509ce44b971d.

70. "American companies are concerned with the readiness of our high school graduates for college programs that will prepare workers for an increasingly competitive global work environment." Greg Fritzberg, "A Brief History of Education Reform," *Response* (Spring 2012), http://spu.edu/depts/uc/response/new/2012-spring/features/history-of-reform.asp.

71. In the 1970s, Roman Pucinski, the chairman of the General Subcommittee on Education in the U.S. House of Representatives, wrote, "the schools have one final chance to prove their worth to the nation, in perhaps the most challenging undertaking of their history, by dedicating themselves to preparation of students for the world of work." Thomas C. Hunt, "Education Reforms: Lessons from History," *Phi Delta Kappan* 87, no. 1 (2005): 86.

72. The purpose of schools in the 1800s was to prepare students for citizenship and provide them with skills necessary to make a living. See Iorio and Yeager, "School Reform: Past, Present, and Future."

73. John Franklin Bobbitt's book, *The Curriculum*, published in 1918, was viewed as providing a scientific approach to studying curriculum. It spawned many efforts to analyze adult roles and occupations in order to determine what schools should teach. See Ellen C. Lagemann, "Contested Terrain: A History of Education Research in the United States, 1890–1990," *Educational Researcher* 26, no. 9 (1997): 5–17.

74. The RAND Corporation's report on standards-based reform illustrates the taken-for-granted nature of the view that the purpose of education is to prepare students for college and jobs. See Laura S. Hamilton, Brian M. Stecher, and Kun Yuan, "Standards-Based Reform in the United States: History, Research, and Future Directions" (Washington, D.C.: Center on Education Policy, 2008), http://www.rand.org/content/dam/rand/pubs/reprints/2009/RAND_RP1384.pdf.

75. In an education policy "white paper," the National Academy of Education also assumes that the purpose of secondary education is to prepare students for college or the workplace. See National Academy of Education, *Standards, Assessment, and Accountability* (Washington, D.C.: National Academy of Education, 2009).

76. The purpose of the Common Core Standards is to indicate what students should know and be able to do in order to be prepared for college. The 2012 Democratic Party National Platform encouraged states "to raise their standards so students graduate ready for college or career and can succeed in a dynamic global economy." Allie Bidwell, "The History of Common Core State Standards," *U. S. News & World Report*, February 27, 2014, https://www.usnews.com/news/special-reports/articles/2014/02/27/the-history-of-common-core-state-standards.

77. A Harvard University report, *General Education in a Free Society*, published in 1945, maintained that "the aim of education should be to prepare an individual to become an expert both in some particular vocation or art and in the general art of the free man and the citizen." Wraga, "The Progressive Vision of General Education."

78. The *Goals 2000: Educate America Act* of 1994 emphasized education for employment more than education for citizenship or for the general task of living. Ibid.

79. Horace Mann thought education could prepare students for work in the field, shop, or office. See Warde, "John Dewey's Theories of Education."

80. "From the mid-19th century to the present a bifurcation of the basic intent of education led in one direction to workforce preparation, then vocational training, and, currently, career development. The other direction mapped education as the process of 'learning how to learn' through development of critical thinking skills, opportunity for experiential learning, emphasis on life-long learning, study of mathematics and sciences, and application of the scientific method to prepare students for post-secondary education and transferable skills for currently unforeseen, future careers." Quoted from Iorio and Yeager, "School Reform: Past, Present, and Future," 33.

81. See also Joy Faber, "In Your Opinion, What Should the Purpose of Education Be?" Message 62, December 21, 2011, https://www.ted.com/conversations/7491/in_your_opinion_what_should_t.html; Camins, "What's the Purpose of Education in the 21st Century?"; and deMarrais & LeCompte (1995) cited in Purpose of School – Philosophical [Wesleyan University blog], retrieved from http://www.purposeofschool.com/philosophical/.

82. "One of the fundamental assumptions of education reform in the mid-1980s was that the quality of K–12 education would determine the nation's economic success." Adams Jr., "Education Reform – Overview."

83. Proponents of the Common Core Standards believed they would help produce a more highly skilled workforce and that this would ensure a strong economic future both for individuals and for the nation. See Layton, "How Bill Gates Pulled Off the Swift Common Core Revolution."

84. This quote was the title of a brief article in a "legislative update" flyer mailed to constituents by Indiana state senator Sue Landske in 2008.

85. Paraphrased from Ted Dintersmith, *What School Could Be: Insights and Inspiration from Teachers across America* (Princeton, NJ: Princeton University Press, 2018), 57.

86. The education reforms associated with the *No Child Left Behind Act* aimed to bring levels of student achievement in line with the needs of business and industry in order to maintain the United States' competitiveness in a global economy. See Lonsbury and Apple, "Understanding the Limits and Possibilities of School Reform."

87. Romberg argues that in order for business and industry to be economically competitive, the school mathematics curriculum must be changed so that it helps produce graduates who will be productive employees in today's workplace. See Romberg, "The Scholarly Basis of the School Mathematics Reform Movement in the United States."

88. "Steelman's (1947) presidential report, *Manpower for Research*, articulated the need for successful secondary school mathematics programs that would eventually increase the number of engineers and other highly technically prepared workers needed for a more scientifically-oriented society. This report was indicative of the kind of high-profile policy documents that would appear over the next 50 years; ones exhorting education to produce more technically literate workers for an evolving economy." John Woodward, "Mathematics Education in the United States: Past to Present," *Journal of Learning Disabilities* 37, no. 1 (2004): 17.

89. While chair of the National Governors Association in 2006–2007, Janet Napolitano developed an initiative that became the impetus for the Common Core Standards. She believed that math and science education must be improved in order to improve the United States' workforce and that this improvement was necessary for the U.S. to lead the world in innovation and remain competitive. See Bidwell, "The History of Common Core State Standards."

90. Personal communication from Diana Underwood regarding an e-mail she received from the Indiana State Teachers Association, dated May 10, 2019.

91. Horace Mann, quoted in Warde, "John Dewey's Theories of Education."

92. Quoted from John Kaag and David O'Hara, "Big Brains, Small Minds," *The Chronicle of Higher Education*, May 13, 2016, https://www.chronicle.com/article/Big-Brains-Small-Minds/236480.

93. Labaree writes, "From the perspective of the social-mobility goal, the point of education is not to learn the curriculum but to accumulate the grades, credits, and degrees that provide an edge in competing for jobs. So when this goal begins to play an increasingly dominant role in shaping education—which has been the case during the 20th century in the United States—curriculum reforms come to focus more on sorting and selecting students and less on enhancing learning, more on form than substance. This turns curriculum into a set of labels for differentiating students rather than a body of knowledge that all children should be expected to master, and it erects a significant barrier to any curriculum reforms that take learning seriously." Labaree, "The Chronic Failure of Curriculum Reform."

94. Ibid.

95. In the early 20th century, the purpose of education in the United States shifted from preserving the republic to sorting people into their appropriate positions in the social order. See Lonsbury and Apple, "Understanding the Limits and Possibilities of School Reform."

96. As the education system expanded to include all children, upper-middle-class parents sought to maintain prestige in the credentials their children were attaining. Tracking was one practice that differentiated the value of credentials. See *The History of Education in America* [online course material for Education 101 at Chesapeake College], retrieved from http://www.chesapeake.edu/Library/EDU_101/eduhist_19thC.asp.

97. Paraphrased from Dintersmith, *What School Could Be*, 126.

98. Burk, "In Your Opinion."

99. View attributed to John Franklin Bobbitt and David Snedden in the 1920s. See Lagemann, "Contested Terrain."

100. C. Medansky, "In Your Opinion, What Should the Purpose of Education Be?" Message 2, December 27, 2011a, https://www.ted.com/conversations/7491/in_your_opinion_what_should_t.html.

101. View attributed to John Dewey. Quoted from Peggy Malone, "Purpose, Processes, and Change," in *Real School Issues: Case Studies for Educators*, ed. Laura Trujillo-Jenks and Rebecca Ratliff Frederickson (Lanham, MD: Rowman and Littlefield, 2017), 149.

102. Dewey, quoted in Warde, "John Dewey's Theories of Education."

103. Hilda Taba and John Dewey, paraphrased by Mark Isham in his 1984 doctoral dissertation at the University of Texas, *Hilda Taba: Pioneer in Curriculum Development*. See Null, "Curriculum Development in Historical Perspective."

104. "Education is, not a preparation for life; education is life itself." John Dewey, quoted in Judy Gelbrich, "Section II - American Education," online course material, 1999e, http://oregonstate.edu/instruct/ed416/ae7.html.

105. Labaree, "The Chronic Failure of Curriculum Reform."

106. Nicholas Negroponte, 2006, computer scientist and founder of MIT's Media Lab, quoted in Kim Jones, "What is the Purpose of Education?" *Forbes*, August 15, 2012, https://www.forbes.com/sites/sap/2012/08/15/what-is-the-purpose-of-education/#466dcc207795.

107. "The object of education is to prepare the young to educate themselves throughout their lives." Quote attributed to Robert Maynard Hutchins, an American educational philosopher. Retrieved from http://www.quotegarden.com/education.html.

108. Attributed to Mandell Creighton, a British historian and bishop of the Church of England. Retrieved from http://www.quotegarden.com/education.html.

109. See Mary T., "In Your Opinion, What Should the Purpose of Education Be?" Message 21, December 26, 2011, https://www.ted.com/conversations/7491/in_your_opinion_what_should_t.html.; and Public Agenda, *The Purposes of Education*.

110. "Education would be much more effective if its purpose was to ensure that by the time they leave school every boy and girl should know how much they do not know and be imbued with a lifelong desire to know it." Quote attributed to British newspaper editor William Haley. Retrieved from http://www.quotegarden.com/education.html.

111. Paraphrased from Seymour B. Sarason, *School Change: The Personal Development of a Point of View* (New York: Teachers College Press, 1995), 144–145.

112. Constance Kamii, *Young Children Reinvent Arithmetic: Implications of Piaget's Theory* (New York: Teachers College Press, 1985).

113. Schools "were created to transmit aspects of the culture to the young and to direct students toward and provide them with an opportunity for self-fulfillment." Quoted from Romberg, "The Scholarly Basis of the School Mathematics Reform Movement in the United States," 423.

114. Augustus Yuan, "In Your Opinion, What Should the Purpose of Education Be?" Message 43, December 28, 2011, https://www.ted.com/conversations/7491/in_your_opinion_what_should_t.html.

115. C. Medansky, "In Your Opinion, What Should the Purpose of Education Be?" Reply to message 2, December 28, 2011b, https://www.ted.com/conversations/7491/in_your_opinion_what_should_t.html.

116. See Darleen Saunders, "In Your Opinion, What Should the Purpose of Education Be?" Message 6, December 2, 2011, https://www.ted.com/conversations/7491/in_your_opinion_what_should_t.html.; Rebecca Zuniga, "In Your Opinion, What Should the Purpose of Education Be?" Reply to message 31, December 10, 2011, https://www.ted.com/conversations/7491/in_your_opinion_what_should_t.html.; and Castle, "In Your Opinion, What Should the Purpose of Education Be?"

117. In 2009, President Obama called on schools "develop standards and assessments that don't simply measure whether students can fill in a bubble on a test, but whether they possess 21st-century skills like problem solving and critical thinking and entrepreneurship and creativity." See National Academy of Education, *Standards, Assessment, and Accountability.*

118. In 1942, the General Education Committee of the Commission on Curricula of Secondary Schools and Institutions of Higher Education of the North Central Association of Colleges and Secondary Schools wrote that secondary schools should emphasize "critical-mindedness, tolerance, social sensitivity, and cooperativeness." See Wraga, "The Progressive Vision of General Education."

119. Romberg argues that the shift from an industrial to an information society means that "instead of training all but a few children to function smoothly in the mechanical systems of factories, all children must be taught critical thinking skills." Quoted from Romberg, "The Scholarly Basis of the School Mathematics Reform Movement in the United States," 429.

120. Attributed to Bill Beattie. Retrieved from http://www.quotegarden.com/education.html.

121. Attributed to American businessman and publisher Malcolm S. Forbes. Retrieved from http://www.quotegarden.com/education.html.

122. Lukas Hostetler, "In Your Opinion, What Should the Purpose of Education Be?" Message 14, December 6, 2011, https://www.ted.com/conversations/7491/in_your_opinion_what_should_t.html.

123. This is a statement given by Michael Scriven and Richard Paul at the 8th Annual International Conference on Critical Thinking and Education Reform in the summer of 1987. Retrieved from https://www.criticalthinking.org/pages/defining-critical-thinking/766.

124. Barry Schwartz, "What 'Learning How to Think' Really Means," *The Chronicle of Higher Education*, June 18, 2015, https://www.chronicle.com/article/What-Learning-How-to-Think/230965.

125. Quotes from David Niose, "Anti-Intellectualism is Killing America," *Psychology Today*, June 23, 2015, https://www.psychologytoday.com/us/blog/our-humanity-naturally/201506/anti-intellectualism-is-killing-america.

126. Quoted from Hunter R. Rawlings III, "Stop Defending the Liberal Arts," *The Chronicle of Higher Education*, December 21, 2017, https://www.chronicle.com/article/Stop-Defending-the-Liberal/242080.

127. "There is only *one* Education, and it has only *one* goal: the freedom of the mind. Anything that needs an adjective, be it civics education, or socialist education, or Christian education, or whatever-you-like education, is *not* education, and it has some *different* goal. The very existence of modified 'educations' is testimony to the fact that their proponents cannot bring about *what they want* in a mind that is free. An 'education' that cannot do its work in a free mind, and so must 'teach' by homily and precept in the service of *these* feelings and attitudes and beliefs rather than *those*, is pure and unmistakable tyranny." Quoted from Richard Mitchell, "The Gingham Dog and the Calico Cat," *The Underground Grammarian* 6, no. 6 (September 1982), http://www.sourcetext.com/grammarian/.

128. Mihai Popeti, "In Your Opinion, What Should the Purpose of Education Be?" Message 18, December 28, 2011, https://www.ted.com/conversations/7491/in_your_opinion_what_should_t.html.

129. Anne Hall, quoted in Frank Bruni, "College, Poetry and Purpose," *New York Times*, February 18, 2015, https://www.nytimes.com/2015/02/18/opinion/frank-bruni-college-poetry-and-purpose.html.

130. View attributed to John Dewey in Laurel N. Tanner, "Curriculum History and Educational Leadership," *Educational Leadership* 41, no. 3 (1983): 38–39, 42.

131. Attributed to the Scottish writer Muriel Spark. Retrieved from http://www.quotegarden.com/education.html.

132. Hannah Martin, "In Your Opinion, What Should the Purpose of Education Be?" Message 57, December 23, 2011, https://www.ted.com/conversations/7491/in_your_opinion_what_should_t.html.

133. See Bartscht, "In Your Opinion, What Should the Purpose of Education Be?"; and Keith Tsui, "In Your Opinion, What Should the Purpose of Education Be?" Message 30, December 10, 2011, https://www.ted.com/conversations/7491/in_your_opinion_what_should_t.html.

134. Sivaprasad Sreenivasan, "In Your Opinion, What Should the Purpose of Education Be?" Message 44, December 28, 2011, https://www.ted.com/conversations/7491/in_your_opinion_what_should_t.html.

135. Quoted from Meghan Florian, "Notes from an Employed Philosopher," *The Chronicle of Higher Education*, April 1, 2013, https://www.chronicle.com/blogs/conversation/2013/04/01/notes-from-an-employed-philosopher/.

136. Quoted from Robert J. Sternberg, "Giving Employers What They Don't Really Want," *The Chronicle of Higher Education*, June 17, 2013, https://www.chronicle.com/article/Giving-Employers-What-They/139877.

137. Quoted from Nicholas Kristof, "Starving for Wisdom," *New York Times*, April 16, 2015, https://www.nytimes.com/2015/04/16/opinion/nicholas-kristof-starving-for-wisdom.html. Kristof attributes the passage quoted here to Lawrence Katz, a labor economist.

138. View attributed to Arthur Bestor in Herbert M. Kliebard, "Why History of Education?" *Journal of Educational Research* 88, no. 4 (1995): 194–199.

139. Matteo Catanzano, "In Your Opinion, What Should the Purpose of Education Be?" Message 41, December 28, 2011, https://www.ted.com/conversations/7491/in_your_opinion_what_should_t.html.

140. Richard Danziger, "In Your Opinion, What Should the Purpose of Education Be?" Message 36, December 2, 2011, https://www.ted.com/conversations/7491/in_your_opinion_what_should_t.html.

141. Quoted from Nel Noddings, *The Challenge to Care in Schools: An Alternative Approach to Education* (New York: Teachers College Press, 1992), 8.

142. Camins, "What's the Purpose of Education in the 21st Century?"

143. Mortimer Adler's *Paideia Proposal*, written in 1982, lists the development of citizenship as one of the three primary objectives of schooling. See Purpose of School–Philosophical [Wesleyan University blog], retrieved from http://www.purposeofschool.com/philosophical/.

144. A Harvard University report, *General Education in a Free Society*, published in 1945, maintained that "the aim of education should be to prepare an individual to become an expert both in some particular vocation or art and in the general art of the free man and the citizen." See Wraga, "The Progressive Vision of General Education."

145. During the 2015–2016 school year, Ted Dintersmith, a retired venture capitalist and father of two, visited 200 schools in 50 states. In his words, "I met with every element of our education ecosystem—governors, legislators, billionaires, school boards, college admissions, textbook and testing executives, bureaucrats, students, parents and teachers. I covered every geography, demographic and school type. I had no ax to grind, no bias to uphold. I just wanted to listen and learn." Quoted from Ted Dintersmith, "Venture Capitalist Visits 200 Schools in 50 States and Says DeVos is Wrong: 'If Choice and Competition Improve Schools, I Found No Sign of It.'" *Washington Post*, March 15, 2018, https://www.washingtonpost.com/news/answer-sheet/wp/2018/03/15/heres-what-our-secretary-of-education-needs-to-hear-by-a-venture-capitalist-who-visited-200-schools-in-all-50-states/?utm_term=.512e659329d8. The statement that Ulrich makes here is paraphrased and quoted from an article written by Dintersmith, based on his visits to schools, that appeared in the Answer Sheet blog of the *Washington Post*. See Ted Dintersmith, "A Venture Capitalist Searches for the Purpose of School. Here's What He Found," *Washington Post*, November 3, 2015, https://www.washingtonpost.com/news/answer-sheet/wp/2015/11/03/a-venture-capitalist-searches-for-the-purpose-of-school-heres-what-he-found/?utm_term=.8c7e18bd30a1.

146. Paraphrased from Dintersmith, "A Venture Capitalist Searches for the Purpose of School."

147. Quoted from Neil Postman, *The End of Education: Redefining the Value of School* (New York: Vintage Books, 1995), x–xi, 7.

148. Quoted from Peter Gray, "A Brief History of Education," *Psychology Today*, August 20, 2008, https://www.psychologytoday.com/blog/freedom-learn/200808/brief-history-education.

149. Ibid.

150. Thomas Jefferson advocated education for citizenship, among other purposes. See Iorio and Yeager, "School Reform: Past, Present, and Future."

151. A primary purpose of the McGuffey reader, one of the most commonly used texts in U.S. schools in the 19th century, was to foster good citizens. See Gelbrich, "Section II - American Education," (1999c).

152. See also Mathis, "Losing Our Purpose."

153. See Labaree, "School Syndrome."

154. "I know no safe depositary of the ultimate powers of the society but the people themselves; and if we think them not enlightened enough to exercise their control with a wholesome discretion, the remedy is not to take it from them, but to inform their discretion by education. This is the true corrective of abuses of constitutional power." Thomas Jefferson, quoted in Judy Gelbrich, "Section II - American Education," online course material, 1999b, http://oregonstate.edu/instruct/ed416/ae2.html.

155. Emphasized by Cotton Mather in a letter to accompany his book, *The Education of Children*. Retrieved from http://www.romans45.org/mather/edkids.htm.

156. Gelbrich, "Section II - American Education," (1999b).

157. Wraga, "The Progressive Vision of General Education."

158. Iorio and Yeager, "School Reform: Past, Present, and Future."

159. Horace Mann, quoted in Mathis, "Losing Our Purpose."

160. National Park Service, U.S. Department of the Interior, "William Holmes McGuffey and His Readers," *The Museum Gazette*, January 1993, https://www.nps.gov/jeff/learn/historyculture/upload/mcguffey.pdf.

161. Gelbrich, "Section II - American Education," (1999d).

162. William Noyes, "Overwork, Idleness or Industrial Education," *The Child Labor Bulletin* 1, no. 4 (1913): 75–87, https://books.google.com/books?id=UclIAAAAYAAJ&pg=PA75&source=gbs_toc_r&cad=3#v=onepage&q&f=false.

163. Wraga, "The Progressive Vision of General Education."

164. Gelbrich, "Section II - American Education," (1999d).

165. Gray, "A Brief History of Education."

166. View attributed to David Labaree. See Michigan State University College of Education, "Professor's Analysis Reveals 'Individualistic Conception' of Public Education," *New Educator* 5, no. 1 (Spring 1999), http://www.educ.msu.edu/neweducator/spring99/analysis.htm.

167. Lonsbury and Apple, "Understanding the Limits and Possibilities of School Reform."

168. Quoted from Gray, "A Brief History of Education."

169. See Gelbrich, "Section II - American Education," (1999d) and Iorio and Yeager, "School Reform: Past, Present, and Future."

170. Paraphrased from Sarason, *School Change*, 131.

171. Quoted from Gray, "A Brief History of Education."

172. "The underlying problem with the current system is that it is based on an industrial metaphor. Schooling is viewed as being analogous to an assembly line; students are the raw material input to the system; teachers are workers passing on a fixed body of mathematical knowledge by telling students what they must remember and do (primarily, they must be proficient at carrying out algorithms); and the output from the system is judged by scores from tests. This metaphor is based on the need to efficiently prepare the majority of students to fit smoothly into a mass-production economy. According to the model devised to meet this need, knowledge is construed as objective, learning as absorption, and teaching as transmission and control." Quoted from Romberg, "The Scholarly Basis of the School Mathematics Reform Movement in the United States," 429.

173. "The idea of the school as an efficient factory assembly line has a long but surprising history. A century ago, the notion of schools delivering finished products to a democratic society was both new and admired. Here is what Professor Ellwood P. Cubberley, of Stanford University said in the early 20th century:

> Our schools are, in a sense, factories, in which the raw products (children) are to be shaped and fashioned into products to meet the various demands of life. The specifications for manufacturing come from the demands of twentieth-century civilization, and it is the business of the school to build its pupils according to the specifications laid down.

In the midst of the progressive-inspired school efficiency movement, sparked by 'scientific management,' Cubberley captured the prevailing beliefs of most school reformers then. Critics of the day, such as John Dewey, did question this efficiency-driven mindset that dominated schools then arguing that the purpose of public schooling in a democracy goes beyond preparation for the workplace. But their voices were drowned out by champions of uniformity, productivity, and more bang for each dollar spent in every aspect of schooling." Quoted from Larry Cuban, "Schools as Factories: Metaphors that Stick," posted May 8, 2014, https://larrycuban.wordpress.com/2014/05/08/schools-as-factories-metaphors-that-stick/.

174. Paraphrased from Sarason, *School Change,* 130.

175. "Following the large-scale expansion of high schools in the early 20th century, Labaree explains, nearly all of the components of the administrative structure of modern schools were in place. This included the use of standardized ability tests to assign students to particular curriculum tracks. No longer was the mission to preserve the republic. That had partly been accomplished by the common schools. Now, the purpose of schools was to efficiently sort the burgeoning masses into their appropriate positions in the social order. Predictably, of course, test outcomes most often reflected students' social class. Regardless, although emerging from different tracks that offered much different rewards, because social mobility was becoming increasingly difficult especially without educational credentials, engaging in even the lowest track made much better sense for the working classes than refusing to participate. One *had* to have access to schools to have any hope to advance socially or economically. Unfortunately, the good sense in schooling reinforced hegemonic economic dynamics and relations, further dividing the masses of people and undermining democratic

equality. It was less a choice that education 'consumers' were making, then, than a necessity. The needs of capital were among the most powerful shapers of the system, not the genuine desires of 'consumers.'" Quoted from Lonsbury and Apple, "Understanding the Limits and Possibilities of School Reform," 763–764.

176. David Tyack claims that, historically, the purpose of schooling has been tied to the nation's social and economic needs. See Purpose of School – Philosophical [Wesleyan University blog], retrieved from http://www.purposeofschool.com/philosophical/.

177. Warde, "John Dewey's Theories of Education."

178. Paraphrased from Sarason, *School Change*, 130–131.

179. "Education is, not a preparation for life; education is life itself." John Dewey, quoted in Gelbrich, "Section II - American Education," (1999e).

180. Labaree, "School Syndrome."

181. Iorio and Yeager, "School Reform: Past, Present, and Future."

182. Carter claims that Dewey's purposes for schools—to transfer knowledge and to prepare students to participate in a democratic society—are inadequate in today's modern world that requires that schools prepare students to compete in the global environment. See Carter, "What's the Purpose of School in the 21st Century?"

183. "Dewey went wrong . . . in his lack of understanding of the forces at work in American society and of the real relations between the educational and the economic systems . . . The modes of life and learning inside the schools were at variance with the realities of the business civilization outside." Quoted from Warde, "The Fate of Dewey's Theories." In short, Dewey overestimated the power of education to overcome social and economic problems.

184. Quoted from Terry Eagleton, "The Slow Death of the University," *The Chronicle of Higher Education*, April 6, 2015, https://www.chronicle.com/article/The-Slow-Death-of-the/228991.

185. Fritzberg, "A Brief History of Education Reform."

186. Iorio and Yeager, "School Reform: Past, Present, and Future."

187. Stanic and Kilpatrick, "Mathematics Curriculum Reform in the United States."

188. Iorio and Yeager, "School Reform: Past, Present, and Future."

189. Adams Jr., "Education Reform – Overview."

190. Quoted from David C. Brotherton, review of *Corridor Cultures: Mapping Student Resistance at an Urban High School*, by Maryann Dickar, *Teachers College Record*, March 3, 2009, http://www.tcrecord.org/library/Abstract.asp?ContentId=15586.

191. Quoted from Mathis, "Losing Our Purpose."

192. Paraphrased from Sarason, *School Change*, 130.

193. See Fritzberg, "A Brief History of Education Reform" and Adams Jr., "Education Reform – Overview."

194. Quoted from David Brooks, "The Biggest Issue," *New York Times*, July 29, 2008, https://www.nytimes.com/2008/07/29/opinion/29brooks.html?mtrref=www.google.com&gwh=9391F281242608C604C227943465E32C&gwt=pay&assetType=opinion.

195. James J. Heckman, "Schools, Skills, and Synapses." *Economic Inquiry* 46, no. 3 (2008): 289–324.

196. Romberg, "The Scholarly Basis of the School Mathematics Reform Movement in the United States."

197. Ibid.

198. David J. Hoff, "National Standards Gain Steam," *Education Week*, March 2, 2009, http://www.edweek.org/ew/articles/2009/03/04/23nga_ep.h28.html?tmp=140352705.

199. See Wraga, "The Progressive Vision of General Education," Iorio and Yeager, "School Reform: Past, Present, and Future," Lonsbury and Apple, "Understanding the Limits and Possibilities of School Reform," Fritzberg, "A Brief History of Education Reform," Woodward, "Mathematics Education in the United States: Past to Present," Bidwell, "The History of Common Core State Standards," Layton, "How Bill Gates Pulled Off the Swift Common Core Revolution," and Carter, "What's the Purpose of School in the 21st Century?"

200. Quoted from *About the Standards* on the Common Core State Standards Initiative website: http://www.corestandards.org/about-the-standards/.

201. Lonsbury and Apple, "Understanding the Limits and Possibilities of School Reform."

202. Steve Walsh, "Next Goal: Full-Day Kindergarten," *Post-Tribune*, March 20, 2006, A1, A5, https://www.chicagotribune.com/suburbs/post-tribune/.

203. Associated Press, "Panel: Upgrade Schools," *Post-Tribune*, December 15, 2006, A9, https://www.chicagotribune.com/suburbs/post-tribune/.

204. Phillip Fiorini, "Discovery Park Appoints Director for K–12 Science Education Efforts," *Research Review* 20, no. 8 (2007): 7, West Lafayette, IN: Purdue University Press.

205. Quoted from an interview with Purdue University president Martin Jischke in the June 2007 edition of *Research Review*. *Research Review* is published by the Office of the Vice President for Research at Purdue University, http://www.purdue.edu/research/vpr/publications/researchreview.html. "Futures are Built on Legacies," *Research Review* 20, no. 6 (2007): 1–3, West Lafayette, IN: Purdue University Press.

206. Amrish L. Shenoy, "Stephen Byrn—Outstanding Commercialization Award Winner," *Research Review* 22, no. 1 (2009): 3, West Lafayette, IN: Purdue University Press.

207. Wraga, "The Progressive Vision of General Education."

208. Jennifer Schuessler, "Humanities Committee Sounds an Alarm," *New York Times*, June 18, 2013, https://www.nytimes.com/2013/06/19/arts/humanities-committee-sounds-an-alarm.html.

209. Quoted from Eagleton, "The Slow Death of the University."

210. Alan Spector, "Re: (OpenForum) From Daniels' Testimony–Students for Sale?" Message posted to OpenForum@lists.purduecal.edu, March 19, 2015.

211. Quoted from Postman, *The End of Education*, 13.

212. Quoted from Jacob Soll, "The Economic Logic of the Humanities," *The Chronicle of Higher Education*, February 24, 2014, https://www.chronicle.com/article/The-Economic-Logic-of-the/144813.

213. Personal communication from Diana Underwood.

214. Quoted from Ruth Turpin, "Re: (OpenForum) What Colleges Will Teach in 2025." Message posted to OpenForum@lists.purduecal.edu, September 29, 2013.

215. Postman writes: "Our citizens believe in two contradictory reasons for schooling. One is that schools must teach the young to accept the world as it is, with all of their culture's rules, requirements, constraints, and even prejudices. The other is that the young should be taught to be critical thinkers, so that they become men and women of independent mind, distanced from the conventional wisdom of their own time and with strength and skill enough to change what is wrong." Postman, *The End of Education*, 60.

216. "We ask schools to promote equality while preserving privilege, so we perpetuate a system that is too busy balancing opposites to promote student learning. We focus on making the system inclusive at one level and exclusive at the next, in order to make sure that it meets demands for both access and advantage." Quoted from Labaree, "School Syndrome," 162.

217. "Education, then, beyond all other devices of human origin, is the great equalizer of the conditions of men—the balance-wheel of the social machinery." Horace Mann, quoted in Gelbrich, "Section II - American Education," (1999c).

218. Tracking works against the unifying ideal of the common school. See Wraga, "The Progressive Vision of General Education."

219. See *The History of Education in America* [online course material for Education 101 at Chesapeake College], retrieved from http://www.chesapeake.edu/Library/EDU_101/eduhist_19thC.asp.

220. Lonsbury and Apple, "Understanding the Limits and Possibilities of School Reform."

221. Quoted from Frank Bruni, "How and Why You Diversify Colleges," *New York Times*, May 14, 2016, https://www.nytimes.com/2016/05/15/opinion/sunday/how-and-why-you-diversify-colleges.html.

222. Harold Levy, executive director of the Jack Kent Cooke Foundation, quoted in Bruni, "How and Why You Diversify Colleges."

223. Kliebard, "Why History of Education?"

224. See Gelbrich, "Section II - American Education," (1999d) and Iorio and Yeager, "School Reform: Past, Present, and Future."

225. Edmund Sass, "American Educational History: A Hypertext Timeline," retrieved July 6, 2018, from http://www.eds-resources.com/educationhistorytimeline.html.

226. All that was necessary in adult life included "health, command of fundamental processes (which meant the three Rs), vocation, worthy use of leisure time, worthy home membership, citizenship, and ethical character." See Lagemann, "Contested Terrain."

227. Ibid.

228. Jim Stone, director of the National Research Center for Career and Technical Education, quoted in Emily Hanford, "The Troubled History of Vocational Education," essay derived from the American Public Media radio documentary, *Ready to*

Work: Reviving Vocational Ed, September 9, 2014, http://www.americanradioworks. org/segments/the-troubled-history-of-vocational-education/.

229. Hanford, "The Troubled History of Vocational Education."

230. David B. Tyack and Larry Cuban discuss the lack of impact of educational reforms on educational practice in their book, *Tinkering Toward Utopia*. See Labaree, "The Chronic Failure of Curriculum Reform."

Chapter Two

Let's Try to Fill It In

REFORM EFFORTS IN THE TWENTIETH CENTURY: PROGRESSIVISM, NEW MATH, BACK TO BASICS, CONSTRUCTIVISM, STANDARDS MOVEMENT

Yann: As Ross's comment about "innovation" schools, suggests, there have been efforts to introduce alternate curricula and methods. In the early 1900s, Progressives reacted against schools' practice of preparing a small number of students for college and preparing the masses for industrialized labor.[1] [2] They also thought the citizenship training schools provided emphasized cultural uniformity and led to passive rather than critical-thinking citizens.[3] [4]

Oates: They also were concerned that adults were using schools to mold students according to the needs and interests of adult society, thereby ignoring the needs of students' maturation. As Rousseau said, "Nature wants children to be children before they are men . . . nothing can be more foolish than to substitute our ways for them."[5]

Quinn: One of the leading progressives, John Dewey, rejected schooling as preparation for a remote and uncertain future.[6] This is why he said education is life itself. He emphasized experiential education; in other words, education based on students' current experiences.[7] He also thought curriculum and methods could promote equal opportunity in society.[8] As Druley noted earlier, Dewey's goal was to integrate school with society by applying democratic practices to learning activities focused on actual problems of life.[9] He emphasized manual training, science, nature study, and art instead of reading, writing, and arithmetic. He believed that problems students encountered in these areas would lead into learning the more traditional branches of knowledge that schools emphasized.[10] For example, building activities in the shop might involve measuring, fractions, geometry, ratios, and proportions.

Oates: Progressives thought the curriculum should emphasize the principles of democracy and promote "critical-mindedness, tolerance, social sensitivity, and cooperativeness."[11] The idea was that public schools would provide students with essential experiences that would enable them to become creative, well-adjusted members of a democratic society who could contribute to social reforms that would alleviate the problems in American society.[12]

Peterson: Dewey "strove to avoid experience that increases specific skills, but confines life to a narrow course. He also sought to avoid experience that is exciting or fun but does not strengthen the disposition for increasingly complex and meaningful experience. The educative experience he sought would foster interest and excitement, strengthen skills and widen horizons, and make knowledge more coherent. . . . It would start with personal concerns and expand these to encompass the wisdom, knowledge, and skills of the child's culture. These should truly become the child's property, that she might enhance its value. Not inert property, but material from which to fashion new experiences—intellectual adventure for the child and for society."[13]

Quinn: Yes. "At its best, schooling can be about how to make a life, which is quite different from how to make a living."[14]

Ross: I like these ideas. I think they are compatible with mine. "The solution which I am urging, is to eradicate the fatal disconnection of subjects which kills the vitality of our modern curriculum. There is only one subject-matter for education, and that is life in all its manifestations. Instead of this single unity, we offer children—algebra, from which nothing follows; geometry, from which nothing follows; science, from which nothing follows; history, from which nothing follows; a couple of languages, never mastered; and lastly, most dreary of all, literature, represented by plays of Shakespeare, with philological notes and short analyses of plot and character to be in substance committed to memory. Can such a list be said to represent life, as it is known in the midst of the living of it? The best that can be said of it is that it is a rapid table of contents, which a deity might run over in his mind while he was thinking of creating a world and has not yet determined how to put it together."[15]

Druley: Apparently your school experience with literature was quite impoverished. I expect my students to write critical analyses of what we read and to look for connections with other things they have read and with their own experience.

Blanchard: So, what happened to Progressivism? I don't see much evidence of these ideas in practice today.

Karch: Dewey's views gained some popularity. Additionally, psychologists highlighted differences in individual children's progression through stages of development and cultural differences received more attention from researchers. However, schools changed very little in response to these changes in focus in educational research and educational discussions. The organization of schools did not change; school practice did not change. In spite of the talk about individuality, schools seemed unable to accommodate the concept.[16]

Druley: I don't think many progressive schools ever fully achieved the goal of student participation in negotiating the purposes that would guide their learning activities. Descriptions of these schools suggest that teachers designed activities and students were given a choice of what to study. But that is not the same thing as involving students in discussions of the nature and point of what they are learning and in negotiating the means and ends of their education.[17]

Newcomer: Are children really capable of doing that?

Inglehart: I do not think young children are and even if they are, as I said before, it is a mistake to allow the taught to assume control of the direction their education takes.

Peterson: Why is that a mistake?

Carpenter: More to the point of why Progressivism failed to have a lasting impact is that the 1950s was a time of cultural conservatism and anxiety about the Cold War.[18] Furthermore, the Progressives overestimated the power of education to solve social and economic problems. The type of education Dewey and the Progressives tried to create did not support the trends of capitalist development.[19]

Inglehart: As Harris mentioned earlier, the Cold War and the Soviet's launch of Sputnik led to another attempt to change the schools' curricula. The goal was to produce more scientists and mathematicians to ensure the U.S. maintained its scientific, technological, and military dominance in the world.

Johnson: The ensuing attempt to reform the math curriculum aimed to prepare students to study mathematics in college. This reform was led by university mathematicians. Their focus was on the content of the mathematics taught in schools, not the methods of teaching it.[20] In general, the goal of the mathematicians and scientists who developed curricula for K–12 education during the 1950s and 60s was to shape students in their own image.[21]

Karch: In mathematics, the name given to the curriculum introduced in the 1960s was the "New Math."

Van Houten: Sets, intersections, unions, associative property, commutative property—I remember it! Well, I remember studying those things; I don't remember much about them.

Karch: Yes, me too. But by the mid-1970s the New Math was widely considered to have failed.[22] As Seymour Papert, himself a mathematician, said in the book *Mindstorms*, the New Math did not grow out of a study children's mathematics, but from a trivialization of mathematicians' mathematics.[23]

Walter: It seems that "it often turns out that all those X's and Y's can inhibit becoming deft with everyday digits."[24]

Inglehart: Wasn't it during the 1960s that Jerome Bruner's ideas about "discovery learning" had some influence on teaching methods?

Blanchard: What's "discovery learning?"

Snepp: The idea was to present students with a problem or an activity that would require them to evaluate, analyze, and perhaps research a topic. Ultimately, this process would lead them to discover some important concept. Here is an example from science: "In this activity, students use a light source, a polystyrene ball, and their bodies to model solar and lunar eclipses, the phases of the moon, and the revolution and rotation of the moon. By observing their models of these phenomena in three dimensions, reality-checking with their notes of their observations of the real moon, drawing simple diagrams and completing complex partial diagrams, students 'discover' the causes of phases and eclipses and the period of the moon's revolution and rotation."[25]

Ross: The problem was that when students did not discover what they were supposed to discover, the teacher had to step in and ask leading questions to guide them to the correct "discovery." The discovery learning process frequently degenerated into a guessing game where students sought hints and teachers supplied them in order to keep the class moving along.

Peterson: Bruner was a psychologist. The New Math curriculum developers were mathematicians. I can imagine that the pairing of New Math with discovery learning might have worked had there been some collaboration between the content specialists and the learning theorists, but without it you've got a recipe for disaster.

Johnson: Perhaps one reason why by the mid-1970s the new educational motto was "back-to-basics."

Harris: Back-to-basics—I always wondered what that meant.

Quinn: Reading, writing, and arithmetic as they had traditionally been taught in schools, ignoring any "progressive" influences. Also, discovery learning faded, replaced by the more familiar teacher-dominated "initiation-reply-evaluation" discourse pattern, the presentation of subject matter as a collection of facts and procedures, and the traditional classroom routine of checking the answers to the previous day's homework problems, introducing new material, and assigning seatwork or homework to be completed individually.

Xander: I think it is worth noting the politics behind the "New Math" and "back-to-basics" movements. "The new math was widely praised at first as a model bipartisan reform effort. It was developed in the 1950s as part of the 'Cold War of the classrooms,' and the resulting textbooks were most widely disseminated in the 1960s, with liberals and academic elites promoting it as a central component of education for the modern world. The United States Chamber of Commerce and political conservatives also praised federal support of curriculum reforms like the new math, in part because these reforms were led by mathematicians, not so-called progressive educators. By the 1970s, however, conservative critics claimed the reforms had replaced rigorous mathematics with useless abstractions, a curriculum of 'frills,' in the words of Congressman John M. Ashbrook, Republican of Ohio. States quickly beat a retreat from new math in the mid-1970s and though the material never totally disappeared from the curriculum, by the end of the decade the label 'new math' had become toxic to many publishers and districts. Though critics of the new math often used reports of declining test scores to justify their stance, studies routinely showed mixed test score trends. What had really changed were attitudes toward elite knowledge, as well as levels of trust in federal initiatives that reached into traditionally local domains. That is, the politics had changed. Whereas many conservatives in 1958 felt that the sensible thing to do was to put elite academic mathematicians in charge of the school curriculum, by 1978 the conservative thing to do was to restore the math curriculum to local control and emphasize tradition—to go 'back to basics.' This was a claim both about who controlled intellectual training and about what forms of mental discipline should be promoted. The idea that the complex problems students would face required training in the flexible, creative mathematics of elite practitioners was replaced by claims that modern students needed grounding in memorization, militaristic discipline and rapid recall of arithmetic facts."[26]

Yann: How could anyone do that to kids?

Foster: What's wrong with teaching the basics?

Yann: It's the way they were taught. Drill-and-practice, rote memorization, the teacher as the sole authority on knowledge, little or no class discussion. That puts students in a passive role, results in boredom with school, and, worst of all, denies the value of their own thinking and understandings.

Karch: Those who advocated a return to the basics believed that an emphasis on factual knowledge—names, dates, places, basic arithmetic facts—provided children with foundational knowledge they must have. They thought returning to the basics would cure the ills wrought by progressivism. How could anyone be against teaching the basics? What these people did not understand was that, although some progressive rhetoric may have crept into discussions about schools, school practice had never abandoned the basics. Focus on the basics continued to preclude time for pursuing students' questions or individual interests. As a result, those who advocated increased emphasis on the basics were contributing to making school an even more mind-numbing place for students.[27]

Ross: As a science educator, I can tell you how the "back-to-basics" philosophy has affected teaching in my field. "As every parent knows, children begin life as uninhibited, unabashed explorers of the unknown. . . . But most of us quickly lose our intrinsic scientific passion. And it's a profound loss. A great many studies have focused on this problem, identifying important opportunities for improving science education. Recommendations have ranged from increasing the level of training for science teachers to curriculum reforms. But most of these studies (and their suggestions) avoid an overarching systemic issue: in teaching our students, we continually fail to activate rich opportunities for revealing the breathtaking vistas opened up by science, and instead focus on the need to gain competency with science's underlying technical details. In fact, many students I've spoken to have little sense of the big questions those technical details collectively try to answer: Where did the universe come from? How did life originate? How does the brain give rise to consciousness? Like a music curriculum that requires its students to practice scales while rarely if ever inspiring them by playing the great masterpieces, this way of teaching science squanders the chance to make students sit up in their chairs and say, 'Wow, that's science?'

In physics, just to give a sense of the raw material that's available to be leveraged, the most revolutionary of advances have happened in the last 100 years—special relativity, general relativity, quantum mechanics—a symphony of discoveries that changed our conception of reality. . . . These are paradigm-shaking developments. But rare is the high school class, and rarer still is the middle school class, in which these breakthroughs are introduced. It's much the same story in classes for biology, chemistry and mathematics.

At the root of this pedagogical approach is a firm belief in the vertical nature of science: you must master A before moving on to B. When A happened a few hundred years ago, it's a long climb to the modern era. Certainly, when it comes to teaching the technicalities—solving this equation, balancing that reaction, grasping the discrete parts of the cell—the verticality of science is unassailable. But science is so much more than its technical details. And with careful attention to presentation, cutting-edge insights and discoveries can be clearly and faithfully communicated to students independent of those details; in fact, those insights and discoveries are precisely the ones that can drive a young student to *want* to learn the details. We rob science education of life when we focus solely on results and seek to train students to solve problems and recite facts without a commensurate emphasis on transporting them out beyond the stars. Science is the greatest of all adventure stories, one that's been unfolding for thousands of years as we have sought to understand ourselves and our surroundings. Science needs to be taught to the young and communicated to the mature in a manner that captures this drama."[28]

Johnson: Apparently "back-to-basics" didn't work very well either because in 1983 *A Nation at Risk*[29] strongly criticized the job schools were doing in educating students. This led to another attempt to move away from the basics.

Lawrence: I think the backlash against back-to-basics was already underway before the publication of *A Nation at Risk*, at least in education circles. At the university level, the learning theory of constructivism[30] influenced the development of alternative math and language curricula. Constructivists reacted against the process-product educational research of the 1970s,[31] which applied behaviorist ideas in an attempt to associate certain teacher actions with observable student outcomes. This research ignored both teachers' and students' thinking. The curricula constructivists developed took children's thinking and understanding as a starting point and emphasized problem solving, discussion, intellectual autonomy, and a focus on meaning as opposed to memorization. In math, the new approach was called "inquiry math," "the new 'New Math,'" or, derisively, "fuzzy math." In language, it was known as the "whole-language" approach.

Newcomer: This is what led to the "math wars."

Lawrence: In part, yes. But first we should note that *A Nation at Risk* served as a precursor to the "Standards" movement in education. The first set of standards was published by the National Council of Teachers of Mathematics in 1989.[32] They described what students should understand and be able to do throughout the K–12 mathematics curriculum and offered a limited number of examples for how to meet the standards. Subsequently, other professional organizations developed standards for language, science, and social studies. All had an inquiry-oriented, critical thinking bent reflecting the influence of constructivist learning theory. As far as the math standards, some mathematicians reacted against both the content of the new standards and the constructivist learning approach. In their view, the mathematics outlined in the standards was not rigorous (it was "fuzzy"), problem sets did not include enough drill-and-practice exercises, technology was used inappropriately, and basic skills needed to be learned prior to learning concepts, not in conjunction with them. Also, some parents were frustrated because the constructivist learning activities were foreign to them, so they were unable to help their children with homework.

Snepp: So, the mathematicians rejected the new curricula because it didn't fit with their view of the structure and processes of formal mathematics. And both parents and mathematicians rejected the approach to teaching the new curricula because it was at odds with the way they learned mathematics.

Grable: If the old way of teaching mathematics enabled them to become mathematicians, it must be okay.

Lawrence: In California, the state legislature rejected the reform curricula based on constructivist learning theory by passing a law requiring the state board of education to adopt instructional materials emphasizing basic computation skills. Through the media, the opponents of "fuzzy math" were able to promote the belief that the reform had failed even before curriculum materials aligned with the reform framework became widely available to teachers.[33]

Xander: How could anyone do that to kids?

Easton: Now what?

Xander: It seems to me that the type of change advocated by the NCTM *Standards* would take many years to develop and many years before it would produce consistent effects, good or bad. The content is different; the approach to teaching is different. I would think it would take five to ten years or more for teachers to become knowledgeable and comfortable with the new curricula and methods. It would take extensive professional development and revamping teacher education programs. I understand that the reformers were starting from children's mathematics while the mathematicians were focused on mathematicians' mathematics. I know the teaching methods were different than those that produced the mathematicians. But wasn't the goal the same: to produce students with a solid understanding of mathematics who would be prepared for further study or employment and who could solve real-life problems? I just don't see why you would deny kids the opportunity to experience a new approach that was supported by many educators even if it was unproven.

Easton: Why should teachers be forced to adopt a new approach?

Anderson: It should be proven to work before it is adopted.

Harris: A poorly taught constructivist lesson might do more harm than a well-taught traditional lesson.

Quinn (to Harris): That statement, while containing a grain of truth, is messed up on several levels. Are you offering that statement as a reason for rejecting a constructivist approach? It is equally true that a poorly taught traditional lesson might do more harm than a well-taught constructivist lesson. What should we conclude from that? If one subscribes to a transmission view of teaching, then any constructivist lesson is a poorly taught lesson. And vice versa. Every teacher occasionally screws up a lesson. One would hope that a reflective teacher would return the next day to address the "harm" done by the previous lesson.

Blanchard: Why couldn't the two sides discuss their differences? Even if the reform approach had ultimately produced lower test scores, I seriously doubt that it would have led to the ruination of the U.S. economy or national defense.

Grable: As with most things that become political these days, the goal is not to discuss, but to show that yours is bigger. Mathematicians and math educators seldom get a chance to do that.

Snepp: Perhaps it was in part a battle over who "owned" mathematics or who knew mathematics better.

Johnson: In any case, the standards movement was not confined to California. Spurred by the support of the National Governors Association, standards became a national political object. Initially, the Governors Association produced the *Goals 2000* report. This was the forerunner of No Child Left Behind, Race to the Top, and, most recently, the Common Core State Standards.[34] None of these have been without controversy. Yet, to date, most states have adopted standards for math and language arts instruction. The primary goal of this line of work has been to raise the level of student academic achievement, ensure students are prepared for college and/or highly skilled jobs in the new technologically-dominated world of work, and thus maintain U.S. competitiveness with businesses in other countries, notably Asia. Perhaps not surprisingly, because the movement has come to be dominated by politicians, it is driven by a business model: develop clear goals, communicate them clearly, develop accurate assessments of meeting the goals, and establish a system of rewards and punishments for those that do and do not accomplish the goals. Unlike what happened in California, for many politicians and policymakers, the content of the standards and the means of achieving them were not important. Their priority was to establish a system that would enable them to hold educators accountable for students' performance. Having no other option, educators learned to work within this standards environment. They agreed with the need to have standards and the need for assessments aligned with the standards. Some thought that making the results of assessments public would provide motivation for schools and school districts to take steps necessary to improve their curricula and instructional strategies. However, many educators who subscribed to this view still held out hope that standards and assessments could promote critical thinking, problem solving, communication, and intellectual autonomy.

Karch: It is also not surprising that the political rhetoric dominates the national discussion of education. So, the original goals of the reform efforts started by educators in the mid- to late 1980s, which Johnson mentioned in his last sentence, have been subordinated to the goal of improving students' performance on standardized tests. In fact, "the implementation of standards has frequently resulted in a much more familiar policy of test-based accountability, whereby test items often become crude proxies for standards. Thus, tests have had a stronger impact on teaching than standards."[35] Teaching-to-the-test is a fairly common practice. Many teachers express disdain for the Common Core State Standards, but it seems the real issue is the emphasis put on the tests associated with the standards.

Van Houten: At my children's school, there were posters in the hallways at least a month before the state standardized test announcing the school's goal of attaining a 93.5 percent passing rate. What message does that convey to kids? And a teacher who several years ago described to me his approach to teaching math, which I thought was sound and thought-provoking, is no longer permitted to teach math because his students' standardized test scores were not considered high enough.

Grable: That school district is all about obtaining high ratings and winning awards. A recent school corporation newsletter devoted an entire page to listing all the awards and four-star and five-star ratings the schools had received. I attended an Elementary National Honor Society banquet where the superintendent congratulated the fourth- and fifth-grade students on their hard work *because they were making the schools look good!* Of course, other school districts aren't fortunate enough to be in that position.

Foster: What's wrong with teaching-to-the-test? Students should be thoroughly prepared for what they will be tested on.

Lawrence: For one, it is difficult to develop standardized assessments that measure higher-order thinking. Most test items focus on relatively low-level skills. Open-ended test items that might encourage higher-order thinking are more susceptible to subjectivity in grading, take longer to grade, and thus increase the costs associated with the test.

Peterson: I would think that teaching-to-the-test also narrows the curriculum. Language arts and math are emphasized at the expense of science and social studies. Not to mention art, music, and physical education.[36]

Carpenter: I think that is especially true in high-poverty districts. These districts are under enormous pressure to score well enough on the standardized tests to avoid being taken over by the state. Schools in low-poverty districts are likely to perform satisfactorily on the tests anyway so their curriculum has a little more variety.

Yann: We might have expected that the ominous warning issued by *A Nation at Risk* would have prompted us to undertake major, perhaps even daring, reforms. But it didn't. Instead, we tried to squeeze small improvements from an outdated system by tightening accountability and imposing a standardized curriculum and standardized tests. It is difficult to see that this approach has resulted in even small improvements. Test scores haven't improved, the achievement gap hasn't narrowed, students still find school boring and are often not well-prepared for higher level coursework or jobs, and teachers are increasingly dispirited.[37]

Walter: "When state and national legislators and others assign teachers and students destinations in the form of national standards and scores on tests constructed by unknown people in remote places, they define the nature of the journey through school. More locally, text and workbook adoption policies constrain the journey further, undermining the participation of teachers and students in the formation of the purposes that guide learning. When students, their parents, and their teachers become preoccupied with narrowly defined destinations, they become collaborators in the narrowing of education, life, and culture."[38]

Oates: Not only have they determined the destinations, but they will soon be specifying the travel schedule![39]

Foster: But if the goal is to produce workers with communication skills, mathematical literacy, and the ability to use technology, then I don't see a problem. Perhaps a little more emphasis on science, but decreased attention to those other subjects may be necessary to meet the goal.

Quinn: The goal is "to prepare drones to keep the U.S. economy going. . . . Our children go to school to learn to be workers. Going to school is largely preparation either to punch a time clock or to own the company with the time clock—depending on how lucky you are in the social-class sorting machine called school. Why else give kids 400 worksheets? Why else give children so little voice in what to learn? Why else teach children a curriculum that avoids controversy and debate and open inquiry? . . . Virtually every newspaper article and editorial, every radio report and discussion, every political speech and government policy that I read or hear says, either implicitly or explicitly, that the aim of our schools is to prepare future workers. . . . The United States is the richest and most powerful country on Earth, and our schools exist to keep it that way, even if our role as citizens should be to question those assumptions and the exercise of that power. . . . These economic purposes of our schools are so entrenched that they have seeped into our children's consciousness. Ask adolescents why they go to school, and you will almost universally hear a response solely concerned with their future employment. . . . If school is not helping children to consciously shape their cultural, political, and moral identities, then we are failing to educate our children to reach their greatest potential."[40]

Taylor: Think of the uproar if schools tried to help children shape their political identities.

Druley: I suggest an experiment: we each ask several kindergarteners or first graders why they have to go to school and then we ask several fourth or fifth graders why they have to go to school. I wonder if the responses of the two groups will differ.

Quinn: Why can't we have curricula that promote a love for learning, empathy, social responsibility, global awareness, creativity and imagination, and media literacy?[41]

Walter: "Students should confront controversy and negotiate the means and ends of their education so that they will become citizens of their school and society—robust, rigorous, and adventurous philosophers and practitioners of educative living."[42]

Grable: Eloquently stated Quinn and Walter, but unlikely to happen.

Lawrence: Yes. For the past century or more, attempts to reform curriculum have had very little influence on what occurs in American classrooms. In the book *Tinkering Toward Utopia,* Tyack and Cuban describe the dominant pattern in education as one of recurring waves of reform rhetoric accompanied by glacial change in educational practice.[43]

Grable: The pendulum swinging back and forth.

Ziegler: That's the analogy we hear frequently applied to education, but from our discussion here it seems that it only applies to policy talk about education. There have been several "progressive" attempts, if you will, to challenge the educational status quo, but these attempts have largely been rebuffed. In any case, they have had minimal impact on classroom practice.

Karch: Reform efforts have introduced educational jargon—"new math," "discovery learning," "critical thinking," "whole language," "back-to-basics," "standards-based practice." Textbooks have changed to keep up with the current reform efforts, although sometimes this amounts to no more than pasting a sheet that demonstrates "alignment" inside the front cover, while the content and approach of the text remains unchanged. In spite of these cosmetic changes, there is ample evidence (large-scale reviews of classroom data[44], historical analyses[45], literature reviews[46]) to suggest that what occurs inside classrooms between students and teachers has changed very little over the past one hundred years or so. The recent standards movement has led most states to adopt standards or frameworks for instruction and develop methods to ensure alignment between the standards, curriculum materials, teaching practices, and statewide achievement tests. Although there is evidence that changes in math and science curricula have led to more students taking advanced courses in math and science, a causal relationship between the curricular changes and student achievement in math and science has not been established.[47] A large-scale assessment of the National Science Foundation's Systemic Initiatives program in mathematics and science reported that "the relationships between student achievement and teachers' reported use of reform practices tend to be positive but small, particularly in comparison to relationships between achievement and student background characteristics such as socioeconomic status and ethnicity."[48] Further, although most states have adopted content standards, the extent to which implementation of the standards is supported or enforced varies considerably.[49] It is quite possible for teachers to modify, replace, or omit sections of "reform" texts to justify their traditional practices.

Blanchard: If educational practices haven't changed much in one hundred years, do you think the emphasis on worksheets, memorization, and low-level tasks and the lack of discussion and debate is really tied to an overriding purpose of preparing workers? Maybe it is just easier for teachers to teach this way.

Walter: Maybe it is the only way to survive if you are a teacher.

EXPLANATIONS FOR THE
FAILURE OF EDUCATION REFORM

Moderator: Hmm. A question I had not thought about, Blanchard. Let's look more closely at the failure of reform efforts to affect practice. If the history of reform is one of failure, we should be keen to identify reasons for such failure if we are to have any hope of improving education.

Easton: Why do you believe those who say education needs to be improved?

Oates: As a parent, seeing some of the things my kids have had to endure in school, I think education can be improved.

Peterson: The suggestion to think about the history of reform and the reasons reform efforts have failed seems important to me. "Policymakers in education have long embraced reform. Unfortunately, education reforms have consistently been plagued by the reformers' lack of knowledge and appreciation of the history of education. Accordingly, the latest reform, touted as a panacea, meets with failure, and the search for the magic elixir begins anew."[50]

Anderson: I agree that schooling, as it exists today, only makes sense if we view it from a historical perspective.[51]

Druley: I think many progressive schools have been unwilling to tackle controversial issues. Progressive educators want to remain neutral or impartial, but somehow produce progressive-minded students.[52]

Lawrence: I think students' role as education consumers whose goal is to acquire credentials (rather than learn anything) together with teachers' need to maintain complex classroom ecologies make classroom practices resistant to reform.[53]

Grable: So, nothing changes because it's all a charade?

Taylor: We noted before that the standards reform movement has not produced the reforms of assessments needed to measure higher-order thinking and this results in tests having a stronger influence on teaching than the standards.[54] Teaching to the test involves a lot of drill and practice. This could be another reason for reform failure.

Blanchard: If policymakers rely primarily on tests to convey the changes in teaching that reform calls for instead of investing in professional development to help teachers learn to teach rigorous subject matter in engaging ways,[55] it's no wonder classroom practice doesn't change. "Districts and states should be held accountable for the professional development and support they provide teachers and schools to enable students to reach high standards."[56]

Van Houten: That is something I worry about in my district. The district is trying to promote a reform approach, an inquiry approach, to teaching math and science. But many teachers don't have the deep understanding needed to make it work. They don't know where they're going with it; they don't know what questions to ask. So, then we are back to "let's direct instruct the inquiry worksheets." I'm afraid that when students' test scores do not rise, administrators and teachers will unfairly blame the inquiry approach to teaching when they were not even really using it.[57]

Snepp: Your comment reminds me of how naïve the reformers who pushed the New Math (and other new approaches) in the 1960s and 70s were about what was needed to actually change classroom practice. They seemed to believe that all teachers needed to implement the new curricula effectively was a few days of training. That was just stupid. Did they think teachers were robots that just needed a new program? They either ignored or were ignorant of the power of taken-for-granted social norms, role relationships, and patterns of belief and action in structuring school practices.[58]

Grable: One can see that happening more recently with the introduction of technology in education. "More technology in the classroom has long been a policy-making panacea. But mounting evidence shows that showering students, especially those from struggling families, with networked devices will not shrink the class divide in education. If anything, it will widen it. In the early 2000s, the Duke University economists Jacob Vigdor and Helen Ladd tracked the academic progress of nearly one million disadvantaged middle-school students against the dates they were given networked computers. The researchers assessed the students' math and reading skills annually for five years and recorded how they spent their time. The news was not good. 'Students who gain access to a home computer between the 5th and 8th grades tend to witness a persistent decline in reading and math scores,' the economists wrote, adding that license to surf the Internet was also linked to lower grades in younger children. . . . The problem is the differential impact on children from poor families. Babies born to low-income parents spend at least 40 percent of their waking hours in front of a screen—more than twice the time spent by middle-class babies. They also get far less cuddling and bantering over family meals than do more privileged children. The give and take of these interactions is what predicts robust vocabularies and school success. Apps and videos don't. If children who spend more time with electronic devices are also more likely to be out of sync with their peers' behavior and learning by the fourth grade, why would adding more viewing and clicking to their school days be considered a good idea?

An unquestioned belief in the power of gadgetry has already led to educational snafus. Beginning in 2006, the nonprofit One Laptop Per Child project envisioned a digital utopia in which all students over 6 years old, worldwide, would own their own laptops. Impoverished children would thus have the power to go online and educate themselves—no school or teacher required. With laptops for poor children initially priced at $400, donations poured in. But the program didn't live up to the ballyhoo. . . . The impoverished students who received free laptops spent more time on games and chat rooms and less time on their homework than before, according to the education researchers Mark Warschauer and Morgan Ames. It's drive-by education—adults distribute the laptops and then walk away."[59]

Carpenter: We also noted before that the math curriculum reform of the 1950s and 60s was led by mathematicians whose focus was on the content of school mathematics, not the methods of teaching it. In general, it seems that "there has been little attention in the United States to incorporating the most up-to-date thinking about cognition and learning progressions into curriculum materials and assessments."[60]

Foster: It is important to distinguish "between the political processes needed to achieve consensus and guide policy decisions versus the scientific expertise needed to develop and rigorously evaluate curricular materials, instructional strategies, and assessments."[61] Success (that is, consensus) in the first case does not necessarily mean success (that is, effective materials and strategies used effectively by teachers and students) in the second case.

Grable: While I agree with Foster's statement, I think that "viewing curriculum reform as a technical rather than a moral and ethical process has led reformers to neglect the basic issues of curriculum discourse."[62] Reform is not simply a matter of producing "research-based" materials and teaching strategies and then testing them for effectiveness. "Reformers are doomed to failure if they neglect value dilemmas or assume that empirical evidence is sufficient to justify reform."[63]

Inglehart: What do you mean by "value dilemmas?"

Grable: For example, earlier, Anderson said that new approaches to teaching and learning should be proven to work before being adopted. But what does it mean for an approach to work? You can find research showing that inquiry approaches promote students' problem-solving abilities. You can find research showing that drill-and-practice promotes rapid recall of facts. What outcome do you value? That's a value dilemma. You can find empirical evidence to justify both approaches. So empirical evidence alone is an insufficient basis for making a decision.

Ulrich: We have already noted that reformers' tendency to ignore the history of education may be another reason for their lack of impact. In the past few decades, politicians, businesspeople, and the general public have expressed concern that schools are not adequately preparing students, especially in math and science. These concerns lead to dire predictions about the country's economic future and national security. As we have stated, in this country, we look to schools to solve our social problems, even when this is not realistic. When the problems persist, we blame schools. What reformers and the public fail to recognize is that the proposals to improve STEM education that we hear today are essentially the same as the remedies proposed after the Soviet Union launched Sputnik in the late 1950s. If those proposals didn't work then, why would they work now? I am afraid that our lack of awareness of history may be even more dangerous than our lack of knowledge of science and mathematics.[64]

Inglehart: I agree with what Ulrich said. It is important to understand where past reform efforts went wrong. But I don't agree with Grable. The development of materials and methods in education should be scientific, just as it is in the field of medicine.

Grable: I didn't say they shouldn't be scientific. I said that science alone is insufficient for determining a curriculum.

Easton: I have another reason for reform failure. I think educational researchers and college of education faculty sometimes come off as arrogant toward practitioners. They tend to ignore the daily problems of teachers and other school personnel. This contributes to the practitioners' view that education research is just theory that has little relevance to their work.[65]

Xander: "I think a lot of us education reformers . . . have been too arrogant. It's not even what you do sometimes, it's the way you treat people in the process of doing it. If your approach is to get a lot of smart people in the room and figure out what 'these people' need and then we implement it, the first issue is who decided that you were smart? And why do you think you can just get in a room and make decisions for a community of people?"[66]

Lawrence: I agree with what Easton and Xander said and, possibly because Inglehart mentioned the field of medicine, I thought of a contrast between the field of education and the field of medicine that relates to the role of educational researchers. Medical researchers have not presented themselves as all-knowing saviors. They do not pretend that they will be able to cure all types of cancers, heart disease, and other diseases within a few short years. And as a public, we understand the difficulties they face, and we realize that our unhealthy lifestyles and environmental practices are a big contributor to the problem. In contrast, educational researchers have promised more than they could deliver. And when they couldn't deliver, they blamed teachers for failing to implement their reforms correctly. Medical researchers don't blame doctors when new treatments or techniques fail. No one holds the field of medicine accountable for problems that have their roots in factors and conditions outside the field. Similarly, the field of education needs to throw off the cloak of arrogance Easton and Xander mentioned and stress that they are no more accountable for societal problems than other social and cultural institutions such as governments, businesses, community groups, and families. Perhaps educational researchers could undertake joint efforts with members from these various groups to address educational and societal problems.[67]

Inglehart: I also have another reason for reform failure. The practice of convening commissions to study education problems and then produce reform reports occurred throughout the twentieth century. But these reports tend to suggest changes in a very general manner and they rarely attend to the significant issues in the implementation of reforms. Thus, their recommendations have little impact on schools.[68]

Johnson: It may be that "reformers often feel they need to speak with more confidence, certainty, and simplicity than they actually feel (in quiet moments of critical reflection). Or they may be compelled to sell themselves first on a reform idea that seems to offer high promise of solving a big problem—letting both the promise and the problem deflect them from looking at the idea too critically—and then start marketing it with vigor to the larger public. Or maybe they harbor no doubts at all. As the history of school reform shows, often simple ideas jump to the fore in a reform movement, based on ideological clarity of vision, leaving complex ideas in their dust."[69] So the reformers can sell the idea of reform, but they cannot make it work.

Oates: I believe there are "fundamental value conflicts in [many] education reform proposals. Because values conflict, reform goals and resources shift as often as their supporting political coalitions shift, or as issues gain and lose salience in legislative deliberations."[70]

Newcomer: The design of many education reform policies is incomplete. Consequently, "reform initiatives do not cause all of the changes in the educational system that are necessary to achieve the results they seek, leaving school improvements, in part, to chance." Also, there is often a lack of motivation or capacity at the local level to undertake reform.[71]

Karch: I think "the organization of schooling shields teaching from education policymaking, protecting classrooms from the turmoil of shifting reform agendas but also fostering a teaching culture of isolated and idiosyncratic practice, rendering uniform changes problematic. This loose coupling of education policy and practice helps explain how constancy and change coexist in public schools."[72]

Anderson: Also, "the prevailing bureaucratic organization of public schooling, with its regulatory and compliance mentality and reliance on collective bargaining, precludes serious change."[73]

Harris: Yes. Earlier, Foster distinguished between achieving political consensus and actually implementing a reform agenda. But achieving political consensus is also a roadblock to reform. "Redirecting large district bureaucracies . . . in the service of children in classrooms is a treacherous process, activating well-organized public workers, political organizations, and unions invested in the status quo."[74]

Xander: "Students' home environments, peer culture, and part-time work explain more differences in student achievement than teacher quality or other school factors. [Therefore, I think] education reforms must extend beyond the boundaries of schools."[75]

Snepp: Reform initiatives imposed from the top down are often hindered by inattention to local cultures—communities' beliefs and practices, home environments—that affect educational practice. Thus, not only do top-down approaches have trouble establishing trust and rapport at the school and district levels, but they ignore critical factors that could make or break their success. Top-down reformers often look at individual districts as 'proof points,' that is, potential exemplars of the merits of their approach to reform.[76] "Education reform comes across as colonial to people who've been here for decades. It's very missionary, imposed, done *to* people rather than in cooperation with people."[77] Much like what Xander said earlier about trying to figure out what 'these people' need.

Carpenter: I would like to follow up on what Xander just said. "It's neither this nation's teachers nor its curriculum that impede the achievement of our children. The roots of America's educational problems are in the number of

Americans who live in poverty. . . . Educational problems also have roots in the number of kids living in dysfunctional families where opioid and other drug addictions, or mental illness, is not treated. . . . Our children are tracked into different neighborhoods on the basis of their family's income, ethnicity, and race. This is where our school problems begin. We seem blind to the fact that *housing policies that promote that kind of segregation are educational policies as well.* . . . Neighborhood schools, affectionately supported in American folk belief as a great equalizer in the melting pot we think of as America, now perform on assessments almost exactly as that neighborhood's income predicts they will. . . . I can predict quite accurately the percentage of kids that score at certain levels on standardized tests by knowing characteristics of the families who send their kids to their neighborhood school. I don't need to know anything at all about the teachers or curriculum at that school. . . . Research demonstrates that if you know the average income, the average level of parental education, and the percentage of single-parent households in a community—just these three variables—you can predict with great accuracy the performance on the standardized test scores used by that community to judge its schools. We don't really have to give the tests because we already can accurately predict the aggregate scores of schools and townships. It's not the quality of our teachers or curriculum that allows such remarkably accurate predictions: demographics allow for that. Although demographics may not be destiny for an individual, it is the best predictor of a school's outcomes—*independent of that school's teachers, administrators, and curriculum!* . . . These differences in school achievement occur as a function of differences in family income and the housing choices associated with family income, as well as the employment policies, health policies, and policies about law enforcement and the sentencing of those found guilty of crimes. It is this profusion of policies, *rarely thought about simultaneously*, that determines the huge differences in achievement scores between schools. . . . Despite the irrefutable relationship of poverty to school achievement, some states . . . go on to promote an insulting and highly misleading educational policy. We . . . grade our schools A–F (based on their test scores). When we do this, of course, all we have done is judge, from A–F, the kinds of lives that are lived by the majority of kids at that school. In reality, it's not the quality of the schools that is assessed. Instead, what is assessed are the lives of the families who attend those schools. The grading of schools serves the real estate community quite well. But those grades tell the public nothing about the quality of teaching and caring in a particular school."[78]

Quinn: "Before education can become what it should be, we must reform society."[79]

Grable: I thought you wanted to use education to reform society.

Foster: How do you reform society?

Carpenter: Politically. But education can contribute to that.

Anderson: It's a circular argument.

Druley: It's not circular. The two are inextricably linked. They influence each other.

Ross: I agree with Druley and I believe she has touched upon another reason for the failure of reform. Many reformers have taken a piecemeal approach to education reform. For example, "if only we could improve teachers' subject-matter knowledge" or "if only we could get teachers to use these new activities" or "if only we could demand accountability to higher standards," etc. When these efforts meet with limited success, we try systemic reform, where the assumption seems to be that if we address all of the parts of the educational system, reform will take hold. However, even the systemic initiatives ignore the relationship between the educational system and other social, political, and economic systems.

Yann: The piecemeal approach is characteristic of our "kludgeocracy."

Foster: Our what?

Yann: "A kludge is a poorly designed software patch intended to fix an immediate problem. Such solutions make sense, in a limited way, and keep things running in the short term. But as one kludge piles on another over time, without any consideration of larger design principles, the resulting system is both overly complex and maddeningly inefficient. This . . . is a fair description of modern American public policy: a kludgeocracy. The federal, nonparliamentary American political system distributes power to states and has an inordinate number of veto points, which have been strengthened in recent years with the radical expansion of the filibuster in the Senate. It's almost impossible to pass bold, common-sensical reform. But the desire for reform is still there. So, politicians do what they can by creating a series of small programs—policy kludges—that eventually add up to an awful mess."[80]

Snepp: Education debates such as the California math wars are fostered by our country's tradition of local control of education, which allows school boards to be controlled by the political belief system of those in power.[81] Competing groups mobilizing against proposals that they see as counter to their interests is simply an example of "a fundamental principle of U.S. politics—that political decisions and actions are the result of competing groups with different resources and capacities vying for influence in a constitutional system that encourages conflict as an antidote to the concentration of power."[82]

Easton: So, reform will never work as long as we have a democracy?

Snepp: I wasn't saying that.

Harris: What I get from Snepp's statement is that as long as there is a lack of agreement on the purpose of education in this country, reform will be difficult to accomplish.

Van Houten: I think market forces sustain traditional practices because they inhibit textbook publishers from making significant changes in their books.[83] Drastic changes are likely to be rejected by teachers and textbook adoption committees because of their unfamiliarity and because of the amount of work they would require of teachers to learn a new approach, especially if the school district is not offering professional development support to learn a new approach.

Taylor: "The education industry thrives on small changes and fads. . . . The massive, entrenched nature of the educational establishment works against real change in our educational system. . . . A radical change in our system of education would upset all of this. Such a change might abolish our need for teachers, as presently defined. It might also abolish our need for schools of education and most if not all of our need for textbooks. Many people in our culture have an economic interest in not just retaining but expanding conventional education. The more hours and years we require young people to go to school, the more teachers, school administrators, education professors, and textbook authors and publishers we can employ. The education business is just like every business; it is constantly trying to expand for the benefit of those who profit from it."[84]

Walter: Here is another possible reason for the failure of reform efforts. The current organizational structure of schools arose in the early twentieth century in an era where large numbers of immigrants needed to be taught American values and learn the skills and habits that would enable them to participate in society as good citizens and productive workers. As Karch suggested before, this governance structure is ill-suited for an era in which the focus is much more on individuality and helping each child realize his or her potential.[85]

Xander: I think that the organization and structure of schools *and* the culture of teaching foster and perpetuate traditional teaching practices.[86]

Foster: What do you mean by the "culture of teaching"?

Xander: For example, the collected wisdom of teachers and folk beliefs about teaching that are passed on as new teachers are acculturated into the profession.[87] My experience is that teachers do think about reform ideals, but these ideals "are barely visible in the complex landscape of competing intentions and the multiple areas of concern that are important to teachers. The circumstances inherent in the practice of teaching itself combine to make rigorous, intellectual teaching difficult even for highly knowledgeable and committed teachers." Many of the distractions with which teachers must cope and which inhibit the implementation of reform ideals stem from school and district policies and organizational norms.[88]

Yann: I think that reform efforts need to pay more attention to teachers' beliefs about teaching and the subject matter they are teaching,[89] their understanding of how to teach that subject matter,[90] and their level of comfort with reform ideas.[91] Without considering these teacher characteristics, reform efforts will not affect classroom practice.

Ziegler: When administrators cope with the pressure of high stakes testing by trying to control teachers' practices, reform curricula and ideas tend to be interpreted and used in a way that sacrifices their intent to the need to teach to the test.[92]

Foster: Good lord!

Harris: What?

Foster: How many reasons for the failure of school reform are there?

Moderator: I believe each one of you has suggested at least one reason. Some of them may overlap to a degree or be closely related. As you were listing them, I was trying to categorize them. I may have missed some, but here is what I have: 1) individual teacher characteristics (for example, lack of knowledge, traditional beliefs about how children learn), 2) the complexity of classroom life and the myriad of students, activities, interruptions, and often conflicting goals with which teachers must cope, 3) the lack of support administrators provide teachers attempting to reform their practices, 4) the structural and organizational features of schools that are designed to inculcate a body of knowledge in a large group of students while maintaining order and efficiency, 5) state and national policies that emphasize high stakes testing at the expense of substantive learning, 6) broad societal beliefs and values about the nature of schooling and the purpose of education that may contribute to political resistance, and 7) inattention to the connection between schools and other social, political, and economic institutions.

Druley: With so many reasons for failure, reform will never succeed.

Blanchard: We may as well give up and watch schools follow the drift of society.

Carpenter: That seems like an anarchic view.

Blanchard: Do you have a solution?

Carpenter: I must confess that I do not.

Anderson: Well, all these explanations suggest to me that "there is no reason even debating the abysmal, atrocious failure of the public-school monopoly anymore."[93] Public schools are doomed. Privatization and the introduction of competition is the only way to improve educational outcomes and lower costs.[94]

Harris: It certainly seems like an outside force is needed.[95]

Blanchard: I don't see how privatization and competition are going to overcome all the obstacles to reform we have just mentioned.

Moderator: Neither do I, but I sense that you are not ready to conclude our discussion on such a pessimistic note.

Druley: Please continue.

RELATIONSHIP BETWEEN
EDUCATION STAKEHOLDERS AND REFORM EFFORTS

Moderator: This may not relieve the pessimism, but I suggest we consider how the different stakeholders in education affect and are affected by reform efforts.

Anderson: By "stakeholders," do you mean parents, teachers, politicians, etc.?

Moderator: Yes, anyone with an interest in our education system.

Inglehart: Wouldn't that be just about everyone?

Moderator: Good point, but let's think about it in terms of the types of groups Anderson mentioned.

Newcomer: Well, students stand to gain from the benefits brought by reform.

Easton: Or bear the brunt of it.

Moderator: In what way will they benefit?

Anderson: They should have more knowledge, increased understanding, and therefore higher test scores.

Lawrence: It's not clear to me how the current goal of preparing students to compete in a global economy will translate into classroom practices that result in more knowledge and increased understanding. We've been trying that since the mid-1980s, and the improvement is marginal at best.[96] [97] [98] [99] [100] It may only lead to students accumulating more credentials.

Carpenter: And if everyone attains more credentials, then no one moves on the social mobility ladder.

Snepp: We may have to create a level of schooling beyond graduate school so that a select few can still have the greatest number of credentials.

Grable: We are starting to rehash the purpose of education. I prefer to focus on how students might affect reform efforts. I think they may also contribute to the difficulty of accomplishing change if they reject new activities or new teaching methods. If students have been in traditional schools, by the time they reach fourth or fifth grade they are used to being told what to do. They are not used to being expected to think for themselves, to engage in open-ended discussions, to explain and justify their reasoning. They expect the teacher to tell them or show them, usually in minute steps, what they are to do. In other words, students may resist attempts at classroom reform through their expectations for the teacher's role.

Inglehart: We have already mentioned how parents may also contribute to resistance when new activities and new methods don't fit with their perception of what school is and when they feel that these activities and methods are hindering their efforts to help their children with homework.

Ulrich: Some parents feel uncomfortable when they can't control their children's success in school.

Druley: Teachers may also resist reform, either intentionally or unintentionally. They may be uncomfortable with reform ideas because the ideas differ greatly from what they experienced in schools. I think many teachers don't understand the philosophy underlying new teaching approaches or the rationale behind new classroom activities. Or they may not agree with the reform philosophy. So, in many cases, teachers transform the reform ideas into something very much like their traditional practice.

Taylor: Teachers may not have the subject matter knowledge or the repertoire of questions that would enable them to teach content more rigorously and for a deeper level of understanding.

Inglehart: "We don't have the infrastructure for reliably supplying teachers who know what they're doing. Not through higher education or through alternative routes. We spend a lot of time arguing about who should be providing teachers, but we have no infrastructure for actually building a cadre of people who would be skillful wherever they teach and who understand that that's their job. Their role is to make sure that every one of their students learns. We are as far from a system like that as you can imagine. The question of a national agreement about what's important to learn is related. Imagine wanting to build a system where you supply teachers who actually know what they're doing. That's pretty hard to do when you can't agree on what they're going to teach when they get out there. If we really wanted to build a system that couldn't work, we almost couldn't have done it better than we have.

I [think] that it's about political will. It's about changing the conversation. It would involve cutting through these polarities about whether it's standards or whether it's federal or whether it's Teach for America or whether it's the ed schools or whether it's preservice or in-service. The problem is located in something much more fundamental. If we can get those things off the table, and actually work on the thing we have in front of us—which is to get ordinary adults who are really committed to having kids become skilled—we could do it. There's no shortage of people who want to try to do that, but we're not equipping them at all. It's like sending people out into a very difficult environment with almost no skills or tools to do it. No wonder they leave the profession. . . . We have to supply large numbers of adults in schools, and we have to build schools to house those kids and teachers that actually enable them to reach those goals. The reason some people are questioning standards is that it really does very little to simply announce that you have high standards. . . . We have hugely escalated standards, but we're going to have big waves of additional failure because we don't have enough in place to help those kids actually reach those standards. . . . We shouldn't think it's okay to put people in classrooms who don't know what they're doing. You don't think it's okay to have a plumber come to your house who might completely wreck your drain when your drain isn't working, or your toilet. . . . We're doing kind of the analog of that. We're having people who don't know what they're doing with our kids, and we somehow think that's okay. We think it's okay to let people who lack the skills to teach try to figure them out at the expense of the students in front of them."[101]

Easton: This sounds like teacher bashing.

Oates: I'm not sure it was teacher bashing, but the idea that we can't supply teachers who know what they're doing because we can't agree on what they're going to teach when they get out there suggests to me a belief that teachers should just follow the orders of their superiors. That view shows no respect for teachers' autonomy. It seems contradictory to develop a group of teachers with a deep understanding of subject matter, students' learning, and pedagogy and then tell them what to do.

Ross: Saying teachers are not adequately prepared to enact reform is not teacher bashing. If anything, it's an indictment of reformers' inadequate implementation efforts and the quality of teacher education programs.

Karch: The adequacy or inadequacy of implementation efforts becomes a matter of time and money. In my experience, it may take two or three years of weekly or sometimes even daily work with a mentor for a teacher to truly transform his or her practice. The results may be great for the teacher and his or her students, but reform will never happen on a large scale if this is what it takes.

Ulrich: Several of us have asked, "How can anyone do that to kids?" but "How can anyone do that to teachers?"

Grable: What? Work with them for two or three years?

Ulrich: No. It seems that the responsibility for the success or failure of schools has been placed squarely on teachers' shoulders. Administrators don't accept the responsibility. Policymakers don't accept the responsibility. Some of teachers' lack of knowledge and lack of familiarity with reform ideas could be addressed by serious professional development. But if such professional development is not provided and those who are so quick to hold teachers accountable for students' test performance fail to consider the impact of cultural and socioeconomic influences on student performance, then teachers are being placed in a position where they are expected to produce results that are simply not in their power to produce.

Druley: The same thing may soon happen in medicine. There are those who want to implement outcome monitoring, that is, essentially scoring doctors' success rates in treating patients. But a doctor in a wealthy suburb has a tremendous advantage over a doctor in an inner city simply because of the difference in the nature of the cases they encounter and the overall general health of the populations they serve.[102]

Foster: I agree with Ulrich's point about lack of professional development, but I'm not sure I agree with her second point. Of course, cultural and socioeconomic factors play a big role in students' success in school, but, given that, shouldn't teachers be able to promote some growth in all students over the course of a year? In other words, it might not be fair to judge teachers against teachers in different schools, or even in the same school, but we should be able to see growth in students within a given class.[103]

Ziegler: So, are you saying that rather than holding teachers accountable by comparing the test scores of their students, we could hold them accountable by the growth they promote?

Grable: What is the appropriate amount of growth? Some growth will occur even without a teacher or school.

Carpenter: And won't you still end up comparing teachers based on which ones had the largest student growth?

Druley: And isn't it possible that growth shown in a given year may be in some way dependent on the previous year's teacher? And how will this "growth" be measured if not by test scores? Would a teacher have to show a certain percentage of growth in a student to pass the test of accountability? If something like this had to be done for each student, this would be a nightmare! I would resign![104]

Easton: Might as well just stick with comparing test scores.

Snepp: I think administrators are also in a tough position with regard to reform. As Ulrich and Foster both alluded to, socioeconomic factors are the strongest predictors of students' test scores. Let's say you are an administrator in a relatively high SES district and your district's test scores have been good. Someone comes up with a reform proposal. Why would you take a chance on it? Most reform ideas aren't tested scientifically before they are implemented. So, there is no guarantee it will work.

Ziegler: What do you mean by "scientific"?

Oates: Why should they be tested scientifically?

Snepp: By "scientific" I meant something similar to medical trials comparing the effects of two drugs. One class is taught with the standard approach, another class is taught with the reform approach. Then we see which class does better.

Xander: How will you determine which class does better?

Snepp: Compare their scores on a common test.

Van Houten: A standardized test?

Snepp: Yes.

Newcomer: How will you control for the teacher variable in your experiment? And how would you allow for different student variables from class to class— meaning the various academic levels and the socio-economic makeup of different classes?[105]

Ross: I'm sure that can be addressed by having multiple classes taught with each method and thus multiple teachers, but I'm more concerned with the assumption that everything worth knowing can be measured by a standardized test. Grable touched on this idea before. Let's say the reform group doesn't do quite as well on the standardized test. But perhaps they would do much better on more conceptual items the test doesn't include and much better applying their knowledge in practical, real-life situations. But we reject the reform approach because they didn't score as well on the standardized test?

Inglehart: So, you don't object to the experiment, but you object to the means of comparing the two groups?

Ross: That would be fair to say.

Oates: I object to the experiment. It is just another example of the attempt to "scientize" education.

Inglehart: "Scientize?"

Oates: Umm, that's probably not a word. But never mind. Teaching is an art, not a science.

Moderator: Ahh! A bold statement that we should pursue when we talk about educational research and reform. But right now, does anyone have more to add regarding school administrators and reform?

Peterson: I was thinking about Snepp's statement that administrators in high-performing districts might be reluctant to engage in reform practices. I think administrators in low-performing districts could be just as reluctant. As Snepp noted, reforms are generally unproven. It would take a great leap of faith to commit to something new and unfamiliar when one's job and reputation is on the line. I think a much more comfortable strategy for administrators is to assume that the problem can be addressed by making improvements in schools' traditional approach. Often this leads administrators to exert greater control over the instructional process. They require teachers to submit lesson plans, to write the day's objectives on the board, to all be at the same place in the textbook at the same time, to give the same practice exams in preparation for standardized tests. In essence, they are trying to teacher-proof their curriculum by exerting control over instruction in the hope of raising test scores.

Druley: An asinine practice! In my experience teaching middle and high school, no two classes are ever the same. If you try to stay at the same place at the same time with all similar classes, some students are being held back and others are being left behind.[106]

Ulrich: Once again I will say "How can anyone do that to teachers?" What I mean is that not only does this deny teachers autonomy, but what really bothers me is that it is the teachers who will still be blamed for low test scores. If the administrators are controlling instruction—"teacher-proofing" it, if you will— then they should accept the responsibility for low test scores.

Quinn: Why stop at administrators? In most states, it is politicians and education bureaucrats who are responsible for policies that encourage administrators to act in controlling ways.

Easton: Why do politicians think education is not working?

Taylor: From reports such as *A Nation at Risk* and *Goals 2000*.

Newcomer: And the typical response has been to set high standards, hold teachers and schools accountable through performance assessments (that is, standardized tests), and get rid of those who don't perform satisfactorily. That's the business approach to improvement.

Foster: "Education should be run like a business. The products we turn out are graduates and we're responsible for making sure they're prepared to go out in the world and do well by their families."[107]

Oates: I have three children in school, and I have to say that I have never thought of them as products, nor do I assume that it is schools' responsibility to ensure that they "do well by their families."

Foster: Don't teachers still have the freedom to decide how they will meet the standards?

Lawrence: I think that is what many legislators believe.[108] What they don't think about is that the approach to accountability they are supporting may inhibit reform as we discussed earlier.

Peterson: I doubt that an externally-imposed system of accountability is capable of promoting real learning.[109]

Quinn: What do businesspeople and politicians know about education? Why should they be making decisions about it?

Easton: They know just as much as anyone else. They went to school like everyone else.

Blanchard: Would you say that they know just as much about medicine as everyone else? They have gone to the doctor like everyone else.

Easton: Of course not. Doctors have a lot more specialized knowledge than the average person.

Harris: The average person has sat in classrooms for ten years or more. So, they have a lot more experience with education than they do with medicine.

Blanchard: Don't teachers and educational researchers have specialized knowledge? They have gone to school to become specialists in their field.

Yann: This is why I object to Oates's statement that teaching is an art, not a science. I think that view contributes to devaluing their specialized knowledge.

Grable: Artists go to art school. Don't they have specialized knowledge that the average person doesn't have?

Yann: Yes, but evaluating art is subjective. Some may think a particular piece is beautiful, others may find it hideous. I think that subjectivity works with the "teaching is an art" view to suggest that there are no (or very few) general principles that apply to teaching. You do your own thing and if it is well received, great. If not, then you don't have what it takes to be a teacher. If teaching is an art and not a science, then what is the point of educational research or teacher education programs?

Foster: I have often wondered that myself.

Taylor: Apparently our governor wonders that, too, as he recently described courses in pedagogy as "mumbo jumbo." Also, our state's professional standards board enacted a policy that reduces the influence of schools of education in teacher licensing and certification.[110]

Karch: I think Yann's comments are relevant to the history of educational research. When schools of education began to form at universities in the early 1900s, they tended to be looked down upon by subject-matter specialists—linguists, historians, mathematicians, biologists, etc. Perhaps partly to prove they belonged and partly because even then science was becoming seen as the way to solve social problems, educational researchers worked to make educational research a science. They embraced the scientific method and the behaviorism of the psychologists Thorndike and Skinner.[111] The process-product research of the 1970s illustrates the use of the scientific method to identify general principles of teaching from empirical data.

Blanchard: Can you clarify what you mean by the "scientific method?"

Karch: Scientific method refers to the process of constructing hypotheses, deriving predictions from those hypotheses, and conducting experiments that produce observable results that will verify or falsify the hypotheses based on the agreement or disagreement of the observations with the predictions.

Blanchard: So why don't teachers, politicians, and the general public accept educational researchers' expertise?

Snepp: Education research has not yielded dramatic improvements in practice of the kind one can point to in medicine.[112]

Lawrence: Evaluation studies in the mid-1960s suggested that education was not as all-powerful as had been believed in terms of solving social problems.

This led policymakers in Washington to fear that education research was "a lot of jive" that did not yield "practical results."[113]

Karch: Additionally, because of its behaviorist roots, the process-product research of the 1970s treated individuals' minds and classrooms as black boxes. In other words, it ignored people's thinking, beliefs, and motivations and it ignored classroom social norms that influenced interactions between students and teachers. It focused only on observable behaviors. As a result, the general principles it developed tended to be viewed by teachers as irrelevant to their particular circumstances. For example, a general recommendation about pacing of content, derived from study of multiple classrooms, may be regarded by a teacher as inappropriate for his or her particular group of students, as Druley alluded to earlier. If I may borrow Oates's word, the "scientizing" of education may have contributed to practitioners' view that educational theories are pie-in-the-sky fantasies.

Anderson: So, in contrast to medical researchers, educational researchers are not viewed with respect by subject matter experts, politicians, or teachers.

Inglehart: We expect medical research to be esoteric, but not educational research.

Karch: It's not so much that it was esoteric, but by ignoring contextual factors, it just wasn't applicable to classrooms. Or it wasn't clear how it could be applicable.

Foster: Some educational research is esoteric, mumbo jumbo. How about *Validity and Self-Reflexivity Meet Poststructuralism: Scientific Ethos and the Transgressive Self?*[114]

Harris: What?!

Grable: A brilliant article, no doubt!

Newcomer: When thinking about educational research "teachers are hindered by visions of abstract and impersonal truth. . . . Thus does the predominant notion of legitimate research separate teachers from their students and their own experience."[115] "Education is not helped by the idea that the important people and the criteria of truth reside far from elementary school classrooms."[116] However, it is important to note that "statements about 'what works' in general, derived from positivist research conducted across many classrooms, can carry considerable weight with audiences of higher-level decision makers. . . . Such statements . . . serve to support belief in the fundamental uniformity of practice in teaching. Such belief is functional for decision makers, since it justifies uniform treatment by general policy mandates that are created by centralized decision making and implemented in 'top down' fashion."[117]

Van Houten: I would add that, unfortunately, "teachers are not overly confident in their ability to make change and see themselves as implementers more than creators of education policy."[118]

Lawrence: Another difficulty with educational research is that different studies sometimes appear to draw completely opposite conclusions. One study will show that skills-based drill-and-practice is best for learning; another study will show that inquiry-based problem solving is best. What people often don't realize is that the two studies applied completely different definitions of "learning." In the first case, learning meant being able to recall basic facts quickly and accurately as measured by timed tests. In the second case, learning meant being able to apply concepts and strategies to solve open-ended problems. But if you don't see that underlying difference, it appears the two studies contradict each other. This leads people to place little value in educational research. It doesn't mean educational research is political. Well, think tank educational research may be political. For the most part, academic educational research is not political. And by that, I mean political with a capital "P," that is, Republican vs. Democrat. But certainly, different educational researchers are influenced by different paradigms that are related to their views of teaching and learning and these differences affect their research questions and the conclusions they draw. And I think in education there is still a degree to which the "my research is better than your research" mentality prevails.

Taylor: And so as one paradigm rises to prominence for a span of time, only to fade away, we have the sense that education reform proposals are like a pendulum swinging back and forth. In contrast, we don't feel this way about the field of medicine—we believe that it progresses.

Lawrence: I'm not sure it's quite accurate to suggest that the pendulum swings from one paradigm to another. A push for reform from the field of educational research certainly followed the rise of the constructivist paradigm. But the swing back in the other direction didn't result from a competing paradigm in the field as much as it did from pushback from parents, politicians, teachers, students . . . really many of the obstacles to reform we noted earlier.

Xander: Another problem I've noticed is that even more recent educational research that focuses on students' thinking and identifies levels of development in their thinking is presented in a way that is difficult for teachers and administrators to understand.

Ziegler: You mean it's full of jargon?

Xander: Partly . . . I just think it's hard to convey the entirety of, let's say, an inquiry approach to teaching mathematics—all of the important aspects of it that a teacher needs to attend to—in print. You have to see it in action, you have to be able to ask questions about it, you have to try it and make mistakes, you have to make adjustments, you need someone to continually talk to about it.

Druley: And that's why, as Karch pointed out before, that it may take two or three years for just a handful of teachers working with a mentor to fully acclimate to a reform approach.

Quinn: "The majority of educators . . . have focused their attention on the engineering of learning, their journals being filled with accounts of research that show this way or that to be better for teaching reading, mathematics, or social studies. The evidence for the superiority of one method over another is usually given in the language of statistics, which, in spite of its abstract nature, is strangely referred to as 'hard evidence.' This gives the profession a sense of making progress, and sometimes delusions of grandeur. I recently read an article in *The American Educator* in which the author claims that teaching methods based on research in cognitive science are 'the educational equivalents of polio vaccine and penicillin.' From what diseases cognitive science will protect our students is not entirely clear. But in fact, it does not matter. The educational landscape is flooded with similar claims of the miracles that will flow from computer science, school choice, teacher accountability, national standards of student assessment, and whole-language learning. Why not cognitive science, as well? There was a time when educators became famous for providing reasons for learning; now they become famous for inventing a method. There are, of course, many things wrong with all of this, not least that it diverts attention from important matters—for example, the fundamental simplicity of teaching and learning when both teacher and student share a reason for the enterprise. As Theodore Roszak has written: 'Too much apparatus, like too much bureaucracy, only inhibits the natural flow [of teaching and learning]. Free human dialogue, wandering wherever the agility of the mind allows, lies at the heart of education. If teachers do not have the time, the incentive, or the wit to provide that; if students are too demoralized, bored or distracted to muster the attention their teachers need of them, then *that* is the educational problem which has to be solved—and solved from inside the experience of the teachers and the students.'"[119]

Snepp: "The only kind of educational research that will ever actually improve education is research done *by teachers*, in their own classrooms, to solve what *they* see as their own problems."[120]

Ross: What I've seen happen is that a group of educational researchers may work with a small group of teachers for five years or so. And amazing things start to happen in some of those teachers' classrooms. But the project is conceived of as a research project. The researchers are there to gather data about children's learning and activities that will promote their learning. Eventually, they leave. The teachers may carry on for a while, but without the researchers' support they become increasingly subjected to standardized test accountability pressures, they retire, they move on, and eventually, after 10 or 15 years, there is no evidence of any reform practices in that school.

Druley: And to add to that and to what Xander said, the researchers may develop a curriculum that they mass market, but you can't expect teachers to take this new curriculum and implement it in a way that maintains fidelity with what the researchers intended.

Oates: I am aware of this research that tries to understand how children learn certain concepts and then develops activities to promote that learning. I've read about learning trajectories or learning progressions. What bothers me is that this type of research and the resulting curriculum is still specifying the journey for students. These reformers talk about student autonomy, but it is an illusion.

Anderson: How can students become acculturated if an adult member of the culture does not lead them to construct the correct knowledge? You are advocating educational anarchy!

Grable: And maybe cultural anarchy.

Easton: Are you saying there are no correct learning progressions?

Taylor: There may be several learning progressions that lead to the same endpoint.

Peterson: If children argue and discuss among themselves long enough, they will construct the correct knowledge.

Snepp: In theory, maybe. In practice, it doesn't always work that way.

Oates (to Easton): I reject the premise of that question.

Oates (to Anderson): You are imprisoned by your traditional conception of education.

Anderson (to Oates): You are imprisoned by your insanity!

Carpenter: I'm not sure I am willing to go as far as Oates in rejecting approaches that try to develop activities to promote students' learning in the direction of so-called learning trajectories. If you look at recent educational reform history, you can see these efforts as an outgrowth of the standards movement and the emergence of the constructivist paradigm. We have already noted that the initial standards often were not accompanied by many suggested learning activities. So, I think it makes sense for educational researchers to do that. But what I have noticed is that educational researchers were drowned by the political tidal wave of reform. The educational researchers were not trying to reform education so that students would be better prepared to compete in a global economy. They were simply trying to improve students' understanding of subject matter by employing an approach they believed in philosophically, because of its view of learning, and perhaps ethically, because of its view of teacher-student relationships. Lacking political savvy, the educational researchers weren't able to convey their rationale effectively and succumbed to the politicians' economic rationale for reform. The NCTM *Standards* has the requisite statement that reform is necessary to maintain the United States' standing in the world economy. Perhaps educational researchers intentionally went along with this rationale because they realized it would resonate with a larger group of people and thus, they may have thought it would help propel reform efforts. What politicians and businesspeople did not appreciate or fully understand is the tremendous difficulty in sustaining any type of reform. Businesspeople are used to snapping their fingers and getting results.[121] When it appeared the educational researchers weren't delivering the results quickly enough (and they really couldn't for the multitude of reasons we mentioned), the business leaders decided they would have to take charge of reform.[122] [123] Hence, the strict accountability policies, the emphasis on high-stakes tests, and the resulting failure of reform as the educational researchers initially conceived it.

Blanchard (to Moderator): You were right. This discussion did not relieve my pessimism.

NOTES

1. "Dewey, following his co-educator, Francis Parker, rejected so commercial-minded an approach to elementary education. They opposed slotting children prematurely into grooves of capitalist manufacture. The business of education is more than education for the sake of business, they declared. They saw in too-early specialization the menace of uniformity and the source of a new division into a master and a subject class." Quoted from W. F. Warde, "John Dewey's Theories of Education," *International Socialist Review* 21, no. 1 (Winter 1960), https://www.marxists.org/archive/novack/works/1960/x03.htm.

2. "A Brief Overview of Progressive Education," College of Education and Social Services, The University of Vermont, retrieved August 6, 2018, from https://www.uvm.edu/~dewey/articles/proged.html.

3. See chapter 7 in John Dewey, *Democracy and Education* (New York: The Macmillan Company, 1916), http://www.gutenberg.org/files/852/852-h/852-h.htm#link2HCH0007.

4. Dewey believed education was more than assimilation. He argued that it should promote habits that would enable people to deal effectively and intelligently with their environment. See Warde, "John Dewey's Theories of Education."

5. Ibid.

6. Herbert M. Kliebard, "Why history of education?" *Journal of Educational Research* 88, no. 4 (1995): 194–199.

7. Sharon H. Iorio and M. E. Yeager, "School Reform: Past, Present, and Future," paper presented at the School Reform Strategies symposium held at Harris Manchester College, Oxford University, Oxford, England, July 2011, http://webs.wichita.edu/depttools/depttoolsmemberfiles/COEdDEAN/School%20Reform%20Past%20Present%20and%20Future.pdf.

8. Laurel N. Tanner, "Curriculum History and Educational Leadership," *Educational Leadership* 41, no. 3 (1983): 38–39, 42.

9. Warde, "John Dewey's Theories of Education."

10. Ibid.

11. From *General Education in the American High School*, published in 1942 by the General Education Committee of the Commission on Curricula of Secondary Schools and Institutions of Higher Education of the North Central Association of Colleges and Secondary Schools and quoted in William G. Wraga, "The Progressive Vision of General Education and the American Common School Ideal: Implications for Curriculum Policy, Practice, and Theory," *Journal of Curriculum Studies* 31, no. 5 (1999): 523–544.

12. Warde, "John Dewey's Theories of Education."

13. Quoted from John G. Nicholls and Susan P. Hazzard, *Education as Adventure: Lessons from the Second Grade* (New York: Teachers College Press, 1993), 84.

14. Quoted from Neil Postman, *The End of Education: Redefining the Value of School* (New York: Vintage Books, 1995), x.

15. Quoted from Alfred North Whitehead, "The Aims of Education," *Daedalus* 88, no. 1 (1959): 198. Whitehead's essay, "The Aims of Education," was reprinted in the journal *Daedalus* from Whitehead's *The Aims of Education and Other Essays,* Macmillan Company, 1929.

16. Paraphrased from Seymour B. Sarason, *School Change: The Personal Development of a Point of View* (New York: Teachers College Press, 1995), 131.

17. Nicholls and Hazzard, *Education as Adventure*, 102.

18. College of Education and Social Services, The University of Vermont, "A Brief Overview of Progressive Education."

19. W. F. Warde, "The Fate of Dewey's Theories," *International Socialist Review* 21, no. 2 (Spring 1960): 54–57, 61, https://www.marxists.org/archive/novack/works/1960/x04.htm.

20. George M. A. Stanic and Jeremy Kilpatrick, "Mathematics Curriculum Reform in the United States: A Historical Perspective," *International Journal of Educational Research* 17, no. 5 (1992): 407–417, https://doi.org/10.1016/S0883-0355(05)80002-3.

21. Tanner, "Curriculum History and Educational Leadership."

22. Terese A. Herrera and Douglas T. Owens, "The 'New New Math'? Two Reform Movements in Mathematics Education," *Theory into Practice* 40, no. 2 (2001): 84–92.

23. John Holt, *How Children Fail* (New York: Da Capo Press, 1982), 211.

24. Quoted from Andrew Hacker, "The Wrong Way to Teach Math," *New York Times*, February 27, 2016, https://www.nytimes.com/2016/02/28/opinion/sunday/the-wrong-way-to-teach-math.html.

25. See Ann Bykerk-Kauffman, "Phases and Eclipses of the Moon," retrieved June 1, 2018, from https://serc.carleton.edu/sp/library/guided_discovery/examples/moon_phases.html.

26. Quoted from Christopher J. Phillips, "The Politics of Math Education," *New York Times*, December 3, 2015, https://www.nytimes.com/2015/12/03/opinion/the-politics-of-math-education.html.

27. Paraphrased from Sarason, *School Change*, 145.

28. Quoted from Brian Greene, "Put a Little Science in Your Life," *New York Times*, June 1, 2008, https://www.nytimes.com/2008/06/01/opinion/01greene.html.

29. National Commission on Excellence in Education, *A Nation at Risk: The Imperative for Educational Reform* (Washington, DC: U.S. Government Printing Office, 1983).

30. Constructivism holds that knowledge cannot be transmitted from one person to another or absorbed from the environment. Individuals must construct knowledge for themselves by making sense of their interpretations of experiences. Piaget's concepts of assimilation and accommodation illustrate the dialectic of sense making: Experiences are interpreted in terms of ones' current knowledge (assimilation), but in the course of interpreting experiences, one's knowledge may be modified (accommodation). While constructivism focuses on individual knowledge construction, socioconstructivism, as elaborated by Paul Cobb, considers the importance of social interaction in stimulating individual knowledge construction and in the construction of knowledge that is "taken-as-shared" by a community. (See Paul Cobb, Erna Yackel, and Terry Wood, "Interaction and Learning in Mathematics Classroom Situations," *Educational Studies in Mathematics* 23, no. 1 (1992): 99–122; Paul Cobb, "Where is the Mind? Constructivist and Sociocultural Perspectives on Mathematical Development," *Educational Researcher* 23, no. 7 (1994): 13–20; and Paul Cobb, Marcela Perlwitz, and Diana Underwood-Gregg, "Individual Construction, Mathematical Acculturation, and the Classroom Community," in *Constructivism and Education*, ed. Marie Larochelle, Nadine Bednarz, and Jim Garrison (New York: Cambridge University Press, 1998), 63–80.) Teaching-by-telling is incompatible with this view of how one comes to know. Instead, (socio)constructivism is viewed as supporting "inquiry" approaches to instruction. An inquiry approach is based on the view that students learn by resolving problematic situations that challenge their current understanding. There is an emphasis on exploration and problem solving and on discussion among students (who often work together in small groups) and between the teacher and students. Teachers help students develop intellectual autonomy so that students do not have to rely on the teacher or a textbook to validate their intellectual activity. Thus, the teacher's role is more that of a guide or a facilitator than a transmitter of information. Also, students demonstrate understanding by explaining and justifying their arguments rather than by following procedural instructions to obtain answers.

31. Process-product research tried to establish correlations between teachers' observable classroom behaviors and students' behaviors (e.g., time-on-task, test performance). The goal was to be able to say that certain teacher behaviors increased student learning or motivation or decreased discipline problems. A classroom observer recorded teachers' behaviors in pre-coded categories so that researchers could count, for example, how many times a teacher praised students' responses or what type of disciplinary method a teacher used most frequently.

32. See National Council of Teachers of Mathematics, *Curriculum and Evaluation Standards for School Mathematics* (Reston, VA: National Council of Teachers of Mathematics, 1989).

33. Jerry P. Becker and Bill Jacob, "The Politics of California School Mathematics: The Anti-Reform of 1997–99," *Phi Delta Kappan* 81, no. 7 (2000): 529–537.

34. Allie Bidwell, "The History of Common Core State Standards," *U. S. News & World Report*, February 27, 2014, https://www.usnews.com/news/special-reports/articles/2014/02/27/the-history-of-common-core-state-standards.

35. Quoted from National Academy of Education, *Standards, Assessment, and Accountability* (Washington, D.C.: National Academy of Education, 2009), 1, 3.

36. The National Academy of Education has the following to say about the practice of "teaching-to-the-test": "Tested subjects receive much more instructional time than non-tested subjects, driving out art, music, and physical education, but also reducing time for science and social studies, especially for disadvantaged and minority students assigned to increased doses of reading and mathematics. Citizens and policy makers are generally aware of the problem that teachers face strong incentives to emphasize content that is tested, which in some cases can become so strong that they actually 'teach the test.' Many educators, parents, and policy makers believe it reflects a necessary trade off—arguing that reading and math are the most essential skills and must be mastered even at the expense of other learning. However, research on teaching the test shows that pressure to raise test scores changes not only *what* is taught but *how* it is taught. If teaching the test means practicing excessively on worksheets that closely resemble the test format, then it is possible for test scores to go up without there being a real increase in student learning. This problem of test score inflation can explain why scores are rising more dramatically on high-stakes state tests than on NAEP, although it is difficult to estimate the exact amount of inflation. More significantly for the students themselves, the emphasis on rote drill and practice often denies students an opportunity to understand context and purpose that would otherwise enhance skill development. It is much more interesting to work on writing skills, for example, after reading a book about Martin Luther King than it is to practice writing to test prompts. Some teachers also report focusing their efforts on 'bubble kids,' those who are closest to the proficiency cut score, so that a small improvement can make a big difference in the school's percent proficient number. These kinds of problems—gaming, distortion, and perverse incentives—are well known in the economics literature on incentives and can be expected to occur when performance indicators are imperfect measures of desired outcomes. How these problems can and should be weighed by educators and policy makers is a thorny question for which the available findings on unintended consequences of test-based accountability provide useful but insufficient information." National Academy of Education, *Standards, Assessment, and Accountability*, 3.

37. Paraphrased from Ted Dintersmith, *What School Could Be: Insights and Inspiration from Teachers across America* (Princeton, NJ: Princeton University Press, 2018), 14–15.

38. Quoted from Nicholls and Hazzard, *Education as Adventure*, 191–192.

39. Paraphrased from Nicholls and Hazzard, *Education as Adventure*, 191.

40. Quoted from Steven Wolk, "Why Go to School?" *Phi Delta Kappan* 88, no. 9 (2007): 648, 650–652.

41. Ibid., 652–656.

42. Quoted from Nicholls and Hazzard, *Education as Adventure*, 182.

43. See David F. Labaree, "The Chronic Failure of Curriculum Reform," *Education Week* 18, no. 36 (1999): 42–44 and Stanic and Kilpatrick, "Mathematics Curriculum Reform in the United States."

44. Kenneth A. Sirotnik, "What You See is What You Get—Consistency, Persistency, and Mediocrity in Classrooms," *Harvard Educational Review* 53, no. 1 (1983): 16–31.

45. See Larry Cuban, *How Teachers Taught: Constancy and Change in American Classrooms, 1890–1980* (New York: Longman, 1984) and Richard A. Gibboney, *The Stone Trumpet: A Story of Practical School Reform, 1960–1990* (Albany, NY: State University of New York Press, 1994).

46. Thomas A. Romberg and Thomas P. Carpenter, "Research on Teaching and Learning Mathematics: Two Disciplines of Scientific Inquiry," in *The Handbook of Research on Teaching*, 3rd ed., ed. Merlin C. Wittrock (New York: MacMillan, 1986), 850–873.

47. Thomas M. Smith, "Curricular Reform in Mathematics and Science Since *A Nation at Risk*," *Peabody Journal of Education* 79, no. 1 (2004): 105–129.

48. Laura S. Hamilton et al., "Studying Large-Scale Reforms of Instructional Practice: An Example from Mathematics and Science," *Educational Evaluation and Policy Analysis* 25, no. 1 (2003): 18.

49. Smith, "Curricular Reform in Mathematics and Science."

50. Quoted from Thomas C. Hunt, "Education Reforms: Lessons from History," *Phi Delta Kappan* 87, no. 1 (2005): 84.

51. Peter Gray, "A Brief History of Education," *Psychology Today*, August 20, 2008, https://www.psychologytoday.com/blog/freedom-learn/200808/brief-history-education.

52. "The liberal thinkers of the Progressive school found themselves in a dilemma whenever they bumped up against these realities of capitalist life. On the one hand, they opposed any indoctrination in the schools. As advocates of 'the open mind,' they said that children should not have any preconceptions imposed upon them by their elders but should be encouraged to inquire freely and arrive at their own conclusions. It was an enigma how neutral and impartial teachers in neutral and impartial schools were to produce progressive-minded students. After all, the 'free intelligence' they hoped to cultivate did not operate in a void or in a society where everyone shared 'a common knowledge, a common worth or a common destiny,' as Dewey put it. Progressive education had to make its way in a society torn by antagonistic class interests. The disciples of Dewey could not in fact adhere to their angelic impartiality if they wished to further the cause of progressive education. The progressive educationists were in a small minority pitted against a majority of teachers with orthodox views not only on education but on most other matters. . . . Professor Harold Rugg of New York University, himself a leading light among the progressive educationists, detected this retrograde tendency some time ago: 'From 1942 to 1945 I spent forty-

odd days in a score of older progressive schools, choosing principally those that had the advantage of many years of uninterrupted experiment under fairly continuous administration,' he wrote in *Foundations of American Education*, pp. 19–21. 'I saw some good teachers in action—occasionally true artist-teachers—who respected their young people as Persons and carried on their groups as societies of equals. I saw them reflecting the American psychology of freedom and action—the young people free to move about and talk, and each one expected to speak of what he sees in his own unique way. . . . Their climate of opinion was marked by a spirit of inquiry rather than of dogmatism; teachers sent young people to sources and put responsibility on them for organizing material and for facing issues. Thus, the old dissectional atomism of the mechanical school had largely disappeared and young people were being offered a program in which total jobs, total enterprises, could be confronted and to which each could bring as much of himself as possible. In psychological terms this was no mean achievement. But . . . something seemed to be missing in these schools. A strange aloofness from society seemed to mark them. . . . They seemed afraid of forthright realistic dealings with the actual conditions of their local communities.'" Quoted from Warde, "The Fate of Dewey's Theories."

53. View attributed to Labaree in Justin Lonsbury and Michael W. Apple, "Understanding the Limits and Possibilities of School Reform," *Educational Policy* 26, no. 5 (2012): 759–773.

54. National Academy of Education, *Standards, Assessment, and Accountability*.

55. Ibid.

56. National Research Council, 1999, quoted on p. 7 of National Academy of Education, *Standards, Assessment, and Accountability*.

57. Interview with Ms. Lawrence, an elementary school teacher in a suburban school district in the Midwest.

58. Paraphrased from Seymour B. Sarason, *The Predictable Failure of Educational Reform* (San Francisco: Jossey-Bass, 1990), 90–91.

59. Quoted from Susan Pinker, "Can Students Have Too Much Tech?" *New York Times*, January 30, 2015, https://www.nytimes.com/2015/01/30/opinion/can-students-have-too-much-tech.html.

60. National Academy of Education, *Standards, Assessment, and Accountability*, 7–8.

61. Ibid., 8.

62. Stanic and Kilpatrick, "Mathematics Curriculum Reform in the United States," 407.

63. Ibid., 415.

64. Paraphrased from Sarason, *School Change*, 192.

65. See Ellen C. Lagemann, "Contested Terrain: A History of Education Research in the United States, 1890–1990," *Educational Researcher* 26, no. 9 (1997): 14.

66. Howard Fuller, former Milwaukee schools superintendent, quoted in Dale Russakoff, *The Prize: Who's in Charge of America's Schools?* (New York: Houghton Mifflin Harcourt, 2015), 210.

67. Paraphrased from Sarason, *The Predictable Failure of Educational Reform*, 38–39.

68. Rick Ginsberg, "Education Reform – Reports of Historical Significance," retrieved July 11, 2018, from http://education.stateuniversity.com/pages/1944/Education-Reform.html.

69. Quoted from David F. Labaree, "School Syndrome: Understanding the USA's Magical Belief that Schooling Can Somehow Improve Society, Promote Access, and Preserve Advantage," *Journal of Curriculum Studies* 44, no. 2 (2012): 160, https://doi.org/10.1080/00220272.2012.675358.

70. Quoted from Jacob E. Adams Jr., "Education Reform – Overview," retrieved July 11, 2018, from http://education.stateuniversity.com/pages/1944/Education-Reform.html.

71. Ibid.

72. Ibid.

73. Ibid.

74. Quoted from Russakoff, *The Prize*, 210.

75. Quoted from Adams Jr., "Education Reform – Overview."

76. See Russakoff, *The Prize*.

77. Shavar Jeffries, former Newark, NJ school board president, quoted in Russakoff, *The Prize*, 207.

78. Quoted from David Berliner, "Education Professor: My Students Asked Who I Would Vote For. Here's What I Told Them," *Washington Post*, October 22, 2018, https://www.washingtonpost.com/education/2018/10/22/education-professor-my-students-asked-who-i-would-vote-heres-what-i-told-them/?tid=ss_mail&utm_term=.d0ad82c5a7c2.

79. View attributed to Horace Greeley in Warde, "The Fate of Dewey's Theories."

80. Quoted from Kevin Carey, "The Kludging of Higher Education," *The Chronicle of Higher Education*, November 25, 2013, https://www.chronicle.com/article/The-Kludging-of-Higher/143215. According to Carey, the term "kludgeocracy" was coined by Steven Teles, a political scientist at Johns Hopkins University.

81. Stephen L. Gessner, "What the Want Ads Can Tell Us about the Educational Wars," *Education Week* 17, no. 42 (1998): 40.

82. Quoted from Richard F. Elmore, "The Politics of Education Reform," *Issues in Science and Technology* 14, no. 1 (Fall 1997): 42.

83. Robert E. Reys, "Curricular Controversy in the Math Wars: A Battle Without Winners," *Phi Delta Kappan* 83, no. 3 (2001): 255–258.

84. Quoted from Peter Gray, "Forces Against Fundamental Educational Change," *Psychology Today*, August 27, 2008, https://www.psychologytoday.com/blog/freedom-learn/200808/forces-against-fundamental-educational-change.

85. See pp. 130–131 of Sarason, *School Change*.

86. Cuban, *How Teachers Taught*.

87. Ibid.

88. Quoted material from Mary Kennedy, *Inside Teaching: How Classroom Life Undermines Reform* (Cambridge, MA: Harvard University Press, 2005), 17, 61.

89. Alba G. Thompson, "Teachers' Beliefs and Conceptions: A Synthesis of the Research," in *Handbook of Research on Mathematics Teaching and Learning*, ed. Douglas Grouws (New York: MacMillan, 1992), 127–146.

90. Deborah L. Ball and Hyman Bass, "Interweaving Content and Pedagogy in Teaching and Learning to Teach: Knowing and Using Mathematics," in *Multiple Perspectives on Mathematics Teaching and Learning*, ed. Jo Boaler (Westport, CT: Ablex Publishing, 2000), 83–104.

91. Jeffrey Frykholm, "Teachers' Tolerance for Discomfort: Implications for Curricular Reform in Mathematics," *Journal of Curriculum and Supervision* 19, no. 2 (2004): 125–149.

92. Paul Cobb and Kay McClain, "The Collective Mediation of a High Stakes Accountability Program: Communities and Networks of Practice," *Mind, Culture, and Activity* 13, no. 2 (2006): 80–100.

93. Mitch Daniels, quoted in Carol Burris, "A Telling Story of School 'Reform' in Mike Pence's Home State, Indiana," *Washington Post*, December 21, 2017, https://www.washingtonpost.com/news/answer-sheet/wp/2017/12/21/a-telling-story-of-school-reform-in-mike-pences-home-state-indiana/?utm_term=.8cb9b39614d3.

94. Views attributed to a group of businesspeople discussing school reform in Burris, "A Telling Story of School 'Reform'."

95. Ibid.

96. With the adoption of state standards came efforts to ensure alignment between the standards, curriculum materials, teaching practices, and statewide achievement tests. Smith indicates that changes in mathematics and science curricula since the publication of *A Nation at Risk* have led to more students taking advanced mathematics and science courses, but that a causal relationship between the curricular changes and student achievement in mathematics and science has not been established. In addition, although most states have adopted content standards in math and science, the extent to which the implementation of the standards is supported or enforced varies considerably. See Smith, "Curricular Reform in Mathematics and Science."

97. In a large-scale assessment of the National Science Foundation's Systemic Initiatives program in mathematics and science, which supported standards-based reform, Hamilton et al. report that "the relationships between student achievement and teachers' reported use of reform practices tend to be positive but small, particularly in comparison to relationships between achievement and student background characteristics such as socioeconomic status and ethnicity." Quoted from Hamilton et al., "Studying Large-Scale Reforms of Instructional Practice," 18.

98. Ross, McDougall, and Hogaboam-Gray used a survey to classify teachers in a district using a standards-based textbook series into "high reform" teachers and "low reform" teachers. They found that the high reform teachers used the text to support their efforts to implement standards-based teaching and supplemented the text with activities consistent with the standards. In contrast, the low reform teachers were able to use the text to justify traditional practices. They modified, replaced, or omitted sections of the text to deemphasize the standards. See John A. Ross, Douglas McDougall, and Anne Hogaboam-Gray, "A Survey Measuring Elementary Teachers' Implementation of Standards-Based Mathematics Teaching," *Journal for Research in Mathematics Education* 34, no. 4 (2003): 344–363.

99. Tarr et al. report that of 24 middle school teachers using NSF-supported, *Standards*-based curricula only one-third had classrooms characterized by a strong

"standards-based learning environment." See James E. Tarr et al., "The Impact of Middle Grades Mathematics Curricula and the Classroom Learning Environment on Student Achievement," *Journal for Research in Mathematics Education* 39, no. 3 (2008): 247–280.

100. Reviewing standards-based mathematics education reform across three states, Haug reports that "state policies combined with local capacity of school districts was sufficient for successful reform in certain cases with select teachers, but these circumstances did not exist in most schools and districts in this study. As a result, standards-based mathematics reform was unevenly implemented." Quoted from page 27 of Carolyn A. Haug, "Local Capacity and State Policies in Colorado: Obstacles to Standards-Based Mathematics Education Reform," paper presented at the annual meeting of the American Educational Research Association, New Orleans, April 2000.

101. Deborah Ball, quoted from an interview with Ball and Bob Moses that was conducted by *Phi Delta Kappan*. See Joan Richardson, "Equity and Mathematics: An Interview with Deborah Ball and Bob Moses," *Phi Delta Kappan* 91, no. 2 (2009): 54–59.

102. Interview with Dr. Eggleston, family practitioner.

103. Interview with Ms. Palmer, chair of state senate's education committee in a Midwestern state.

104. Jane Bentz, high school English teacher, personal communication.

105. Ibid.

106. Ibid.

107. Quote from a school board member in a Midwestern state. See Mark Lazerus, "Board Member Blames Buzea," *Post-Tribune*, June 15, 2007, B1, https://www.chicagotribune.com/suburbs/post-tribune/.

108. Interview with Ms. Palmer.

109. Carl B. Frederick, review of *The Nature and Limits of Standards-Based Reform and Assessments: Defending Public Schools*, by Sandra Mathison and E. Wayne Ross, editors, *Teachers College Record*, April 22, 2009, http://www.tcrecord.org/Content.asp?ContentID=15622.

110. Brian A. Howey, "A 'Revolution' Begins . . . Next Week," *Howey Politics Indiana* 14, no. 44 (2009): 1, 4–5, http://www.in.gov/library/files/HPR14z44.pdf.

111. Lagemann, "Contested Terrain."

112. Ibid.

113. Quotes from Sproul, Weiner, and Wolf, 1978, in Lagemann, "Contested Terrain," 12.

114. Kate Lenzo, "Validity and Self-Reflexivity Meet Poststructuralism: Scientific Ethos and the Transgressive Self," *Educational Researcher* 24, no. 4 (1995): 17–23, 45.

115. Quoted from Nicholls and Hazzard, *Education as Adventure*, 187.

116. Ibid., 188.

117. Frederick Erickson, 1990, quoted in Nicholls and Hazzard, *Education as Adventure*, 190–191.

118. Quoted from Brandi Hinnant-Crawford, "Education Policy Influence Efficacy: Teachers Beliefs in Their Ability to Change Education Policy," *International Journal of Teacher Leadership* 7, no. 2 (2016): 1–27, https://files.eric.ed.gov/fulltext/EJ1137496.pdf.

119. Quoted from Postman, *The End of Education*, 26–27.

120. Quoted from Holt, *How Children Fail*, 212.

121. Interview with Dr. Schultz, director of a statewide science, technology, engineering, and mathematics (STEM) project in a Midwestern state and professor of science education at the "managing partner" university for the project.

122. Interview with Dr. Quisenberry, a mathematics educator and administrator at one of the STEM network's regional partner institutions.

123. Interview with Ms. Roth, the vice president of a venture capital economic development initiative. With a state university as a partner to manage day-to-day operations, her firm launched the STEM project in an effort to improve K–12 math and science education in the state.

Chapter Three

Another Brick in the Wall

VISIONS FOR EDUCATION: A STATEWIDE REFORM EFFORT

Moderator (to group): Let's consider your ideas for education. What vision do you have for our schools? How would you like to see education improved? [1]

Snepp: Here's an idea—why not ask teachers first? If you wanted to improve hospital care, wouldn't you start by asking nurses? If you want to improve anything, you should start by asking those who do the work. [2]

Grable: Not if you don't value their opinions or if you believe they're incompetent or if you think you know better than anyone else what is needed to fix the problems.

Walter: Earlier Druley mentioned how hard it is for teachers to think outside the box about assessment. I wonder if that is true regarding educational reform in general. Perhaps teachers are so caught up in the daily grind of schooling that all they can think about are minor tweaks. We should ask teachers, yes, but I think the perspective of those outside the system could be valuable.

Taylor: Those outside the system tend to suggest reforms that are impractical and do not work because their proponents do not understand the system.

Easton: Hold on. I have a question. Why do you think education needs to be improved?

Harris: Well, I can tell you that over the past five years as my venture capital firm has worked with companies and universities and individuals who all have some interest in life sciences, I would say 99.9 percent of them have a huge interest in K through 12 science education and math education, and they kept saying to us, "So when are you guys going to do something in the K through 12 area?" [3]

Lawrence: What did they mean by that?

Harris: They were concerned because they were seeing a workforce that wasn't adequately prepared. Graduates were coming to them without necessary skills so the businesses had to train them before they could do their jobs properly.[4]

Druley: So, what did your firm do?

Harris: We launched a four-pronged effort to improve math and science education across the state. It consisted of 1) teacher professional development aimed at improving the preparation of middle school teachers, 2) a science, technology, engineering, and mathematics (STEM) network comprised of universities throughout the state that serve as regional points of contact for local school systems and a website that inventories resources for teaching K–12 math and science and chronicles workshops, conferences, and programs for teacher professional development in these areas, 3) the promotion of inquiry-based curriculum materials endorsed by the National Science Foundation, and 4) a marketing campaign to change the "dinner-table" conversation across the state into a conversation about the benefits and value of a college education.[5]

Foster: That makes a lot of sense to me. As a state senator, my view has been to ask, "What do we want the state's economy to look like in ten years and what do we have to do to get there? How do we know what kind of jobs we need to have and how do we prepare these kids so they'll have good jobs, how do we make sure that our state residents' per capita income is not the top of the bottom third, but that we're moving the per capita income up? What part does education play in all that?" And so, the relationship between economic development and education has never been more important and I think we're looking at those two things as being inextricably linked as we move forward.[6]

Anderson: Education is not a priority in many families in certain parts of the state.[7]

Druley: And how is anyone ever going to change that? Kids are a product of their families, and if the family is not engaged in the education of their children, the children themselves will not feel compelled to be engaged. Teachers will always have to fight family values (or lack thereof) about education. It is a constant battle, and one that is frequently impossible to win. When teachers are faced with these battles, it can detract from what they are able to accomplish in their classrooms. And what does this do to accountability? Will the family be held at fault?[8]

Harris: That's why we want to change the dinner-table conversation. It is difficult to attract new businesses to certain parts of the state when they are concerned about the pool of qualified workers.[9]

Carpenter: You know, a lot of poorer families don't have many dinner-table conversations because the parents are working two or three jobs. Maybe your money would be better spent trying to address policies and practices that sustain poverty.

Inglehart: There is another economic reason for improving student achievement and the quality of schools in addition to workforce preparation. I have been involved with the STEM initiative Harris described and one of the biggest challenges communities throughout the state face in attracting new business and industry is getting the companies' "high-octane" people to live in their community. In other words, the companies' CEOs and middle managers want to know, "Where will my kids go to school?" Too often I have heard local folks say, "We got the company, but, darn it, all the middle managers and the CEOs live in a different community because they want their kids to go to [school in a well-to-do suburb]."[10]

Ziegler: So, workforce issues are driving the STEM initiative.[11] And the linking of education and the country's economic stability appears to be taken-for-granted by business leaders and some academic leaders as well.

Blanchard: The "economic benefit to society" rationale linking education and economic development does not fit particularly well with American culture. Aren't we all about individuality, creativity, and entrepreneurship?[12]

Lawrence: That's why the social benefit rationale tends to be interpreted in terms of, or accompanied with, an individual benefit rationale: Doing well in school is important because it will help one get into college, obtain a well-paying job, and secure a respectable position in life. This rationale has been driven home to kids.

Druley (to Harris): Is your firm's STEM initiative entirely a private effort? Is the state involved in it in any way?

Harris: Well, the state Department of Education does not view itself as any kind of networking info-structure provider. We are working with universities across the state. I think we're going to try to work with the universities pretty closely the first two years just because we've gone out and raised all the money. So, we want to be sure that it gets off on the right foot and doesn't become an academic research project.[13]

Xander: What do you have against academic research?

Harris: Nothing per se, but if the primary focus becomes research, the initiative will not create and sustain the momentum and scale of support necessary to be successful. Also, individual universities don't have enough critical mass to really sway the public sector into a certain type of behavior.[14]

Johnson: Businesspeople are tired of waiting for educators to do something to fix education, so they are going to take the bull by the horns and do it themselves.[15]

Inglehart: One problem with that sort of attitude is that, as Carpenter said, lots of business and industry folks, especially the leadership, are used to snapping their fingers and getting things done. The "attention span" of the governor's office, the legislature, and even local folks, too, could be a major roadblock to the success of this STEM initiative because they will establish an unreasonable timeline for seeing results. The governor would probably like for everything to be better in time for the next election.[16]

Harris: I think the business community is frustrated that their previous invest-ments in STEM education have not had much of an impact. We need a systemic overview of the K–12 education system in the state and we need to develop an enterprise-wide strategy for creating a more efficiently working, cost-effective educational system.[17]

Inglehart: We're wary that the educational bureaucracy will inhibit the STEM network's efforts to work directly with teachers. The thing I'm most concerned about in terms of making this network work is identifying the right products and services that we need to provide and getting them out on the street and going. If we get hung up in too much bureaucracy in the Department of Education, or in school corporations, that will hinder us. It's not that we're trying to avoid them; they are key players . . . [18]

Newcomer: I'm not sure why you are concerned about the DOE hindering your efforts. I'm the associate director for mathematics curriculum there. Our role is to implement laws passed by the legislature and to oversee "administrative code"—rules set by the state board of education. We don't try to promote a certain type of reform. We have our Standards, which reflect a compromise between various approaches to subject matter. In the end it is political, and compromise is what you do, that's part of government, but once the Standards are set, I think our role for things like that is to get out of the way. Our goal is to leave decisions about textbooks, curriculum, and teaching approaches to the local level where they can decide best what works for their students.[19]

Anderson: As the governor's policy director for education, I would echo that. We tend to think of curriculum and teaching approaches as local issues. People would get pretty mad at us if we tried to get involved in things that were that specific. I mean, I'll say that without a lot of research, the governor has been kind of skeptical of [recent reform textbooks in math and science and the whole-language approach to teaching reading], but that's just kind of a gut feeling, not a big policy statement. I like to be aware of all the research and all the hap-penings, but just because we know about them and have opinions about them doesn't mean that we're out there making policy about them.[20]

Druley (to Harris): Are you skeptical of inquiry approaches to math and sci-ence?

Harris: Oh, no. I think many of us who work in business and the sciences can see that inquiry, problem solving, critical thinking, and cooperative work could be useful in preparing students for their jobs.[21] Generally speaking, I think you will find that employers are more concerned that prospective employees possess "creative, critical, practical, and wisdom-based decision-making and problem-solving skills, along with a mindset of lifelong learning and a strong work ethic" than they are with grades, test scores, and the specific knowledge and skills that correspond to a certain major.[22]

Foster: I agree with what Newcomer and Anderson just said about the state not dictating curriculum and teaching approaches. As chair of the state senate's education committee, I'm concerned about the educational performance of the state's children. Improving test scores is tied very directly to instruction and it's tied to expectations for what kids can and should be doing, but overall we're not teachers, so when you look at what we do and what we have the ability to do, whether it's right or wrong, we're going to look at how the state's kids are doing on their scores on the state standardized test and we're going to attach some significance to that, you know, are we making improvements or are we losing ground? How are our kids doing in the eighth grade in math? And we don't know really, we rely on people who teach math teachers how to do instruction. So, even if we wanted to improve math instruction, how could we really do that? Part of it is because, as legislators, we don't really micromanage too much how people teach and that's really not our responsibility directly. It is indirectly our responsibility in that if it's not working we're going to care, but the idea that legislators could micromanage a certain kind of curriculum . . . the closest that we have ever come to that in my fourteen years there has been in the area of reading where we have said that phonics needs to be included as a part of the toolbox for teaching reading. What I would like to do is be able to treat, from a legislative standpoint, teachers as professionals and assume that in the same way that I wouldn't tell an accountant how to figure taxes or I wouldn't tell a lawyer how to try a case, it's a bit presumptive of me to say, "but I would like to tell you how to teach math." All I can really do is look at and measure the effectiveness of what you're doing.[23]

Snepp: Wait a minute! You are not going to tell me how to teach, but you are going to judge my teaching by my students' scores? You need a lesson in basic statistics—in particular about validity. A test is valid if it measures what it was designed to measure. A math assessment given to an 8th grader has validity if it measures 8th grade math ability. Such an assessment is not designed to measure teaching ability. Thus, using that math assessment to measure teaching is not valid.[24]

Anderson: But 8th graders' math ability should reflect their teacher's teaching ability.

Snepp: A teacher in a wealthy suburban district is more likely to have higher scores than a teacher in a rural district or a teacher in a high-poverty, inner-city district. Similarly, the students in the suburban district are more likely to show larger gains in achievement from one year to the next. Does that mean the teacher in the suburban district is a better teacher?

Karch: "Research shows that the outcomes of standardized tests don't reflect the quality of instruction, as they're intended to. . . . The results show that it's possible to predict the percentages of students who will score proficient or above on some standardized tests. We can do this just by looking at some of the important characteristics of the community, rather than factors related to the schools themselves, like student-teacher ratios or teacher quality. . . . Though some proponents of standardized assessment claim that scores can be used to measure improvement, we've found that there's simply too much noise. . . . According to the technical manuals published by the creators of standardized assessments, none of the tests currently in use to judge teacher or school administrator effectiveness or student achievement have been validated for those uses. . . . The tests are simply not designed to diagnose learning. They are simply monitoring devices, as evidenced by their technical reports. The bottom line is this: Whether you're trying to measure proficiency or growth, standardized tests are not the answer. . . . Although some might not want to accept it, over time, assessments made by teachers are better indicators of student achievement than standardized tests. For example, high school GPA, which is based on classroom assessments, is a better predictor of student success in the first year of college than the SAT."[25]

STANDARDS AND TESTING

Karch: Thinking about Newcomer's and Fosters's comments, it seems that the Standards, albeit a result of compromise, are viewed as a set of objective goals and the standardized test is regarded as an objective measure of student performance. Isn't it possible that the nature of the Standards might make them more amenable to certain curricula or certain approaches to instruction? And the content and format of the state standardized test could affect curriculum choices and teaching practices.

Foster: Again, I don't believe it's the state's job to become involved in that. Another problem is that, due to political biases, you don't have anybody who anybody really considers to be an honest broker on education policy. Depending on where you stand on the issue, you tend to believe or disbelieve research.[26]

Ziegler: What do you mean by "an honest broker on education policy"?

Foster: I mean that both sides, Democrats and Republicans, have their sources for educational information and often the sources do not agree.[27]

Blanchard: I can see that education policy is political, but education research?

Easton: Science is not political.

Oates (to Foster): How ironic. You treat the Standards as objective and educational research as subjective!

Grable: The notion of objective research is a fallacy.

Snepp: It is also ironic that there is a state law requiring school improvement plans to incorporate research-based practices,[28] yet there are supposedly no "honest brokers on education policy." That puts teachers in the position of being expected to meet external standards without guidance from the legislature while at the same time being open to the charge that they have drawn on biased, unsound research to do so.

Van Houten: I think many business leaders and politicians have a dim view of academic educational research.

Newcomer: There seems to be, from where I'm sitting at the DOE, more influence from think-tank research because they understand their audience better. Maybe they mean something slightly different by research or a little different than an educational researcher . . . but a think tank report will have a very nice executive summary, it will have lots of charts and graphs, and it will talk directly about the implications of what they've found for policy. Part of it is the way it's presented. There's less, how would I say . . . there's more confidence in what their findings are in a sense. They present the information in a way with fewer notations of possible exceptions or problems. It's not about the findings from one particular incident; it's about what you should do tomorrow and in the next two weeks and in the next two years as a policymaker to improve education. That's a much different kind of information for somebody who has a very limited time to think about this particular issue. They are thinking about math right now, but they may need to move on to science in two hours. It is something that I think education researchers need to think about if they want to be influential in these kinds of things. How do we present our information to other audiences?[29]

Easton: I would like to make a comment about our state's academic Standards. We have excellent Standards. The state General Assembly directed the Department of Education to develop Standards that are "world-class, clear, concise, [and] jargon-free." Teachers, community members, and university-level content experts contributed to their development. Achieve, Inc., stated that our state's Standards are "among the clearest, most understandable, and most rigorous Standards in the nation." Additionally, the Thomas B. Fordham Foundation gave the Standards an "A."[30]

Ulrich: The Standards may be great, but how are they being implemented in classrooms? What kind of support is the state providing to teachers to implement the Standards?

Ziegler: Isn't that what Harris's firm's STEM initiative is trying to do—provide teachers with needed support?

Ulrich: Yes, although that's primarily a private venture.

Ross: What I'm hearing is that legislators' want higher test scores and it's up to teachers and school administrators to decide how best to produce higher scores. And this is considered to be respecting teachers' professional judgment?

Anderson: School districts can choose textbooks and teachers can choose how to teach in order to best meet the Standards.

Xander: But as Karch pointed out, the Standards and especially the standardized test may dictate certain practices. If the test emphasizes remembering facts and using low-level skills, then a drill-and-practice approach might produce higher test scores. If it emphasizes problem solving and deep understanding of concepts, then an inquiry approach might produce higher test scores. So, based on the importance of the test, how much freedom to choose do school districts and teachers really have?

Easton: We need randomized comparative experiments in order to establish the effectiveness of instructional approaches and curricula. For example, have three groups: in the first group, teachers use a drill-and-practice approach; in the second, they use an inquiry approach; and in the third they use a hybrid of the first two methods. Whichever group has the higher test scores will indicate the best way to teach.

Blanchard: What will the test measure?

Easton: Problem solving, explanation of concepts, and recall of facts.

Peterson: On what grounds do you believe that application of the scientific method is as appropriate for comparing different approaches to instruction as it is for comparing different treatments of a disease?

Grable: The scientific method can be applied to solve any problem, can't it?

Easton: Teaching is a science, isn't it?

Quinn: Or is it an art?

Johnson: Didn't we already discuss this?

Blanchard: I have a question for Foster. Are teachers evaluated based on their students' performance on the state standardized test?

Foster: Yes, we have passed a law that states that components of the evaluation include both classroom observations and "objective measures of student achievement and growth," such as scores on statewide standardized tests.[31]

Newcomer: Secretary of Education Duncan "made it very clear to states that, to be eligible for a share of [Race to the Top funds], they must adopt policies that promote teacher merit pay and charter schools. In particular, state policies must allow the use of student test scores as part of teacher evaluation and compensation, and states must remove caps on charter school growth and increase funding for those schools. . . . Little or no research actually supports policies linking teacher compensation to student test scores. What the research does show is that the technical hurdles to developing a fair, workable system have yet to be cleared. And research is also clear that tests developed and validated for one purpose (student evaluation) are not necessarily applicable to another (teacher evaluation)."[32]

Ziegler: I read that New York City has begun serial testing of kindergarteners. The mayor of New York, with Secretary Duncan at his side, "announced that teachers should be retained or fired based on their students' test scores. These types of scenarios are being played out in every state and school district nationwide."[33]

Yann: How has this affected school administrators and teachers?

Peterson: "Even the most unbiased, carefully constructed, 'authentic' measure of what students know is likely to be worrisome, psychologically speaking, if too big a deal is made about how students did, thus leading them (and their teachers) to think less about learning and more about test outcomes."[34]

Karch: As Xander suggested earlier, different kinds of tests emphasize different kinds of knowledge. Certain curricula and teaching methods might promote the type of knowledge a test tests; different curricula and teaching methods might promote knowledge a test does not address. If a small set of standardized tests are considered the gold standard, then there is little room for variety in curricula and teaching methods. Under the pressure induced by such high-stakes tests, it is little wonder that schools embrace rigid accountability measures. But it is far from clear that such measures improve student learning or even improve student test scores.[35]

Taylor: As an elementary school principal, I can tell you that we want everybody to pass the state standardized test. That's the biggest . . . we're test driven in this state, so . . . it affects instruction highly. It's not that you ever want to teach to the test, but you become more restricted in what you teach and that limits you. Teachers who have for years done their favorite unit on such and such, and they love doing it, if it's not in the Standards, you better stop doing it because there isn't enough time. So, it limits creativity. It is about the test regardless of how we want to dress it up. Bottom line is the test scores go in the paper and that's what people want to see, that's what they know. We don't want the humiliation of not measuring up so there is pressure because we want to make sure that the kids have what they need to be successful on the test.[36]

Snepp: As a middle school teacher, I can tell you that the message I have heard is that the Standards are supposed to drive everything I do from the time I walk into the building until the time I leave.[37]

Peterson: It seems that the goal of helping students make sense out of subject matter has taken a back seat to the goal of having "world-class" Standards that will produce students who will secure their own, the state's, and the nation's economic future.

Easton: You make it sound as if those are mutually exclusive. Having world-class Standards should result in students who have a thorough understanding of subject matter.

Johnson: I'm the director of curriculum and instruction for my school system. The battle I'm fighting is if you just look at, say, here's the test, here's the Standards, there's this thought that we're just going to teach the test. That's constraining because if you just teach to the test, then all you're concerned about is getting students to reach that level to pass so that it shows up as a [pass rate] percentage and you really don't go for deep understanding of the concepts. You're not really working towards having students reach their fullest potential. You're going to lose the students at the high end because you just want to make sure that everybody has the knowledge and the skills to pass the test. So, I worked at a meeting with our principals, who work with the teachers, and I tried to emphasize that we don't want to get caught up in this teaching to the test. We are more than that. We are about students learning and reaching their fullest potential.[38]

Snepp: You may not want to say that we teach to the state standardized test, but we do.[39]

Taylor: I think that as a state we've lowered our expectations in order to have more students pass the standardized test. We're not shooting for that higher-level thinking. That test is mainly skills based. They did add an applied skills portion of the test and it was supposed to become a larger and larger part of the test, but due to the cost of scoring it, that part has actually been curtailed.[40]

Johnson: Standardized tests are easy to construct, administer, and score. But what do they measure? Bits and pieces of knowledge that are easy to assess in that type of format. They don't test for connections students have made between ideas or their ability to use what they have learned to analyze new situations and problems. Standardized tests do not provide an authentic assessment of students.[41]

Van Houten: "Teachers are forced to choose between teaching with integrity and ensuring each child has a chance to succeed on high-stakes tests."[42]

Snepp: Not only that but what sense does it make to rank school corporations based on state standardized test results when those corporations are not testing students from the same socio-economic environment? A fairer approach would be to measure student academic growth over time.[43]

Ulrich: In my recent travels across the United States, I visited all 50 states and 200 schools. I found that our emphasis on measurement through standardized testing is destroying the teaching profession and discouraging students. Due to the myriad of factors beyond their control, many teachers know there is no way for them to win the test-score game they are forced to play. As a result, they are leaving the profession in large numbers. Furthermore, many young people, based on what they have heard and what they have experienced first-hand, have no interest in becoming teachers. As others have noted, standardized tests emphasize recall of facts and procedures, just the type of thing computers do easily. Rather than teach analytical, creative, and interpretive skills, we are teaching skills that will have no use. And students certainly have no use for standardized tests or the hours upon hours of test prep they are subjected to. But parents do. Especially wealthy parents. No wonder there is still an achievement gap in standardized test score results between students from rich and poor backgrounds. Wealthy parents have bought their children's higher scores by paying for tutors and test-prep materials and by offering their children monetary incentives for their performance.[44]

Karch: "A major new report [by the Rand Corporation] concludes that a $575 million project partly underwritten by the Gates Foundation that used student test scores to evaluate teachers failed to achieve its goals of improving student achievement." This was particularly true for low-income minority students. I think "the findings revive questions about whether the country is well-served when America's wealthiest citizens choose pet projects and fund them so generously that public institutions, policy and money follow—even if those projects are not grounded in sound research."[45]

Yann: "The [American Statistical Association] (ASA) just slammed the high-stakes 'value-added method' (VAM) of evaluating teachers that has been increasingly embraced in states as part of school-reform efforts. VAM purports to be able to take student standardized test scores and measure the 'value' a teacher adds to student learning through complicated formulas that can supposedly factor out all of the other influences and emerge with a valid assessment of how effective a particular teacher has been. These formulas can't actually do this with sufficient reliability and validity." Further, the ASA noted that VAMs based solely on standardized test scores do not measure other teacher contributions such as encouraging students' creativity or helping colleagues improve their teaching. Additionally, VAMs measure correlation, not causation, so that effects attributed to a teacher may actually be due to factors that were not considered in the statistical model.[46]

Peterson: "Simply focusing on teachers as being the only potential cause of growth in students is pretty obviously myopic. A lot of high-stakes accountability has become self-defeating—focusing solely on the identification of bad schools, the bad teachers, as opposed to creating a signal and involving teachers in processes that lead to investigations and changes."[47]

Ziegler: It sounds like the biggest problem is that no one has come up with a cost-effective, logistically-feasible, research-based alternative to standardized tests. As long as it is the primary means of judging the effectiveness of students, teachers, and administrators, it will continue to confront those groups with the pressures we have been discussing.

Oates: It's the biggest problem for those who subscribe to the approach to education reform we have been discussing.

Lawrence: I don't think there is anything wrong with standards per se. But the way we are implementing them—assuming that high-stakes standardized tests will force teachers to remain faithful to the standards and implement them correctly—works against the improvement in learning the standards were created to address. Our focus on technical aspects of accountability is strangling the last bit of life from teaching and learning.[48]

Xander: I would not say that finding an alternative to current standardized tests is the biggest problem facing reformers. I believe there is a much more deep-rooted problem. "The degrading of public education has involved impugning its effectiveness, cutting its budget, and busting its unions. Educational measurement has been the perfect tool for accomplishing all three: cheap and scientific looking. International tests have purported to prove that America's schools are inefficient or run by lazy incompetents. Paper-and-pencil tests seemingly show that kids in private schools—funded by parents—are smarter than kids in public schools. We'll get to the top, so the story goes, if we test a teacher's students in September and June and fire that teacher if the gains aren't great enough. There has been resistance, of course. Teachers and many parents understand that children's development is far too complex to capture with an hour or two taking a standardized test. So, resistance has been met with legislated mandates. The test company lobbyists convince politicians that grading teachers and schools is as easy as grading cuts of meat. A huge publishing company from the United Kingdom has spent $8 million in the past decade lobbying Congress. Politicians believe that testing must be the cornerstone of any education policy. The results of this cronyism between corporations and politicians have been chaotic. Parents see the stress placed on their children and report them sick on test day. Educators, under pressure they see as illegitimate, break the rules imposed on them by governments. Many teachers put their best judgment and best lessons aside and drill children on how to score high on multiple-choice tests. And too many of the best teachers exit the profession. When measurement became the instrument of accountability, testing companies prospered, and schools suffered. I have watched this happen for several years now."[49]

Van Houten: "Notice how unfair No Child Left Behind and Race to the Top have been in treating so-called 'failing schools' by assuming all schools that do not meet the bar are full of pitiful teachers. Oh, never mind why the kids failed the test; they did! Never mind that the school might be low on resources, full of kids with behavior problems, full of kids from bad families and communities, full of poor kids, in the middle of a community that does not support the school—none of that is relevant! Yet when [we] confront these radicals with this wrong-headed crap about NCLB and Race to the Top, all we ever get are replies that assume we do not want teachers to be held accountable. . . . Our government supports the fact that the biggest laws and regulations running our public schools are written by those who are clueless about teaching. . . . [President] Obama himself has said that the greatest influences in children's lives are their teachers. . . . [So] only teachers have any major impact on kids? Parents' income has little impact? If a kid comes from a family in which the parents have no respect for learning and education, neglect their kids and let them run wild, and so on, then it is my fault that they do badly in school? If the community does not want to support my school, if the school leaders do not want to provide us with any decent resources, if school leaders and politicians want to restrict my freedom in teaching so that it becomes virtually impossible for me to do anything that helps kids learn because it isn't teaching to the test, because it doesn't focus on getting kids to memorize only trivial stuff that appears on the exams, and so on, then it is my fault that the kids did not learn anything?"[50]

Quinn: "At some moment no one announced, public education in [our state] became less about childhood advancement than punishing schools and teachers who can't get students to master bad tests. [The state] misplaced the point of public education. It's about children. When schools are transformed into partisan political war zones, predictable devolution always damages the higher good. The [state legislature] has decided its function is to punish bad schools and bad teachers by taking money and resources away from the spendthrift offenders. Of course, holding resources hostage hardly ever makes a school better. . . . [Instead,] the effect is a statewide battery of badly designed tests mandated by amateurs whose only knowledge of public education is the instinct to impose 'accountability.' Political hostility does not seem the best management tool to decide educational policy. The [problem] has little to do with professional educators and almost everything to do with . . . state leaders who bridle when their orders are questioned."[51]

Ziegler: To go back to what Xander said, why do people want to degrade public education?

Lawrence: For money. A small number of companies control the $20–$30 billion textbook and standardized test market. These companies create the standardized tests. By suggesting what scores should count as passing and failing, they have tremendous influence on the success or failure of public schools. Schools that are deemed to be failing because their test scores are too low can then be taken over by the state and replaced by a charter school. There has been a huge growth in the number of charter schools in the last 10 years. Charter schools receive the same per-student funding from the state that public schools get. But charter schools typically cut money for instruction, particularly teacher salaries, and raise administrative costs. In Michigan, administrative costs increased $774 per student while instruction costs decreased $1140 per student, resulting in a profit for the charters of $366 per student. Applying that per student profit to the approximately 55.4 million K–12 students in the U.S.

could give a yearly profit of $20 billion. In Ohio, charter school teachers make 59 percent of what public school teachers make. If all teachers in the country were paid at the Ohio charter school rate, the potential profit arising from this reduction in salary would approach $118 billion.[52]

Quinn: "[Our state's governor was] a keynote speaker for The American Legislative Exchange Council's (ALEC) policy summit [recently]. [He] was surely awarded the coveted speaking spot . . . for his commitment to ALEC's legislative goals to fabricate failure in public schools in order to create a sales opportunity for their corporate membership. ALEC is a Washington, DC, based group that is funded by corporations and the super-rich who pay $7,000 to $25,000 to be members. Its members are in turn granted access to state legislators to propose model legislation which benefits their corporate interests. ALEC is responsible for writing model legislation in [our state] that promotes private company takeovers of public schools, school vouchers, constriction of collective bargaining and due process for teachers, teacher evaluations based on high stakes test scores and other anti-public school bills."[53] Since 2005, ALEC has offered a template law called 'The Virtual Public Schools Act' to introduce online education.[54]

Anderson: That makes it sound like ALEC is out to get public education for no reason. They are just pursuing their mission of promoting "the principles of free markets, limited government, federalism and individual liberty."[55]

Druley: To the detriment of students' learning.

Carpenter: But public education—like police and firefighters—is not a "free market" entity. If you believe that all children are entitled to a free education, then you cannot tie that to profits.[56]

Yann: I also would like to go back to something Xander said. We have discussed how the Standards and the emphasis on the standardized test may affect teachers, but Xander's comment suggests something mostly absent from our discussion, namely, how they affect students. In particular, how do they affect student motivation?

Foster: Well, they should be motivated to do well in school so that they can go to college and then get a good job. In addition, I think if we can get them interested in things other than just the academics of school—drama, singing, band, whatever—if they're involved in that, they're probably going to be okay.[57]

Peterson: So, you're not concerned that some type of external motivation is necessary to get students to "buy in" to their education. Don't you want students to be intrinsically motivated to learn?

Foster: It's not that I don't want them to be intrinsically motivated. That would be great. But, as I said before, I'm focused on results. I'm less concerned about how schools and teachers produce those results.[58]

Ziegler: That makes me think about two students, Tim and Peter, in my second-grade classroom. "Tim is always working his imagination on something. He is far slower than Peter at the aspects of schoolwork that are captured on standardized tests, but he constantly brings things into the class to work with. . . . You know, it's common to hear the claim that motivation is important because it increases achievement. If that is why motivation is important, then curiosity, aesthetic appreciation, and pleasure in challenge are but means to the end of high test scores. If achievement as the tests define it is, in the end, the important thing, Tim is a failure and Peter the ideal student. If schools and parents communicate this to Tim, how will his vigorous and sensitive commitment to constructing a humane, artful, and interesting world survive? It is a triumph of second-grade spirit—a too rarely celebrated secular miracle—that students like Tim, much less able than Peter on the tests, remain imaginative creators, wily inquirers, and thirsty savorers of nature."[59]

Grable: By the time he's in fourth grade Tim's enthusiasm for learning will be extinguished.

Anderson: If teaching is driven by the standardized tests, then maybe we just need to develop more intelligent tests. "If we get the right tests, we will produce independent, creative thinkers."[60]

Oates: "That smacks of a torturer threatening prisoners: 'We have ways of making you think.'"[61]

Peterson: I am a little uncomfortable with this bashing of standardized tests though I have participated in it myself. I think we should recognize that "monitoring our students' progress in schooling is a valid concern, especially considering the continuing disparities along gender, race-ethnic, class, and other lines. In this sense and for their future success, student performance *is* a big deal."[62]

Karch: I agree that it is important to monitor student performance. However, as Ulrich alluded to, "standardized testing puts children of color and those living in poverty, who generally score lower on such tests, at a cumulative disadvantage. The extensive use of tests for high-stakes decisions tends to act as a vehicle of social reproduction rather than working to ameliorate disadvantages due to social background."[63]

Xander: At the beginning of our discussion, Druley mentioned students exhibiting a "consumerist mentality" toward education. Because it stems from a business view of accountability, "standards-based education reform and the rhetoric surrounding it map quite nicely onto the consumerist values of privileged parents. . . . [As a result] parent involvement and parental expectations can harm public schools, because they silence the voice of parents whose involvement does not conform to consumerist values. Thus, parents and their children, whose 'cultural values and social expectations conflict with the values of the institutions within which they are trying to find footing,' are put at a further disadvantage."[64]

Blanchard: So, as Ziegler said, the challenge is to find an alternate way to measure student performance.

Newcomer: I understand what Karch and Xander are saying about the disadvantageous effects of standardized tests, but I wonder if we aren't setting up standardized tests as a "straw villain." Suppose there were no standardized tests. Or suppose we found alternative ways of monitoring student performance that we thought were fairer. Do you think what goes on in classrooms would change that much? Teachers would have more time for science and social studies and might be able to include their favorite "fun" units on certain topics, but in terms of teaching methods and teacher-student role relationships, would there be any change?

Oates: Good point. As long as education is conceived of as information transfer—"I know something, and I have to get you to know it"—classroom practice will not change significantly.

Ulrich: There may be another reason why not much would change. Minnesota's commissioner of education offered grants to encourage schools to develop and adopt novel approaches that would not be subject to standardized test accountability requirements, but very few districts applied. She hypothesized that the test prep, standardized testing mindset had become so much a part of educators' worldview that they found it extremely difficult to imagine alternatives. Even though they didn't like it, the routine of a known commodity outweighed the risk and uncertainty of a novel approach. She is trying to encourage them to feel safe in taking risks.[65]

Carpenter: I fear that many so-called "inquiry" approaches, which might appear to be "novel," are still characterized by the "I know something, and I have to get you to know it" conception of education.

Anderson: That's why they're no more effective than traditional "teacher-centered" approaches.

Blanchard: I'm feeling pessimistic again.

Lawrence: "My present point of view is suffused with pessimism if only because for the past thirty years I have seen no signs that reformers (and, therefore, the public) have started with a reexamination of the purposes for schooling. More correctly, they start with the present structure and seek to make it do what it patently cannot do and never has done. There are a few people who know the game and the score, but they, like me, are politely listened to, patted on the back, given brownie points for the afterlife, and then business goes on as usual. I do not say this out of pique or frustration, but rather with sadness."[66]

Snepp: As the old aphorism says, "A man said to his friend, 'This is the best of all possible worlds.' To which his friend replied, 'I am afraid you are right.'"[67]

Walter: When the purpose of school is conceived as preparing students for jobs that will help the United States' economic standing in the world, it is not surprising that the language of business dominates national discussions about education. Accountability, efficiency, standardization, output measurement, and cost-effective procedures are key components of such discussions. Of course, this has implications for curricula, teaching practices, and what qualities and skills we value in students. Not only has this purpose and its attendant practices come to exclude the other worthy purposes we mentioned, but perhaps even worse is that it ignores how students feel and what they think about their educational experiences. Students really are treated as if they are parts being shuttled along an assembly line.[68]

Inglehart: K–12 schools are not going to change as long as colleges rely on SAT and ACT scores in admissions. These tests don't assess high-level thinking, analytic ability, problem solving, or creativity. They are in the same vein as the standardized tests used at the K–12 level. If this is what colleges base admissions on and the primary purpose of K–12 education is to prepare students for college, what do we expect?[69]

Peterson: I think school personnel assume that it is up to them to make sure that students are ready for the next grade level, ready for college, ready for jobs. This is a controlling view because underlying it is the belief that students are incapable of motivating themselves to seek experiences that fit their interests and that would enable them to prepare themselves for future learning. If students aren't capable of this, then it is up to schools to do it for them. In a strange way, this ensures that schools remain relevant.[70]

Van Houten: I think there is another reason for schools' recalcitrance to change. "It pains me to say this, but professionals in our field often seem content to work within the constraints of traditional policies and accepted assumptions—even when they don't make sense. Conversely, too many educators seem to have lost their capacity to be outraged by outrageous things. Handed foolish and destructive mandates, they respond only by requesting guidance on how to implement them. The Cowardly Lion was able to admit that he lacked what made the muskrat guard his musk. Cowardly humans are more likely just to change the subject. Propose something that makes a meaningful difference, and you'll hear, 'But we've always . . . ,' 'But the parents will never . . . ,' 'But we can't be the only school in the area to . . .' . . . We have to be willing to fight for what's right even in the face of concerted opposition. Maureen Downey, a reporter for The Atlanta Journal-Constitution, wrote several years ago about how tough that can be in a culture where those 'who speak up when they believe their students' welfare is at stake, and who question the system, earn the label of troublemaker.' . . . It takes guts, not just talent, for a teacher to lead students beyond a predictable search for right answers—and to let them play an active role in the quest for meaning that replaces it. That entails not only accepting some unpredictability and messiness but also giving up some control. . . . These days, the greatest barrier to meaningful learning is the standards-and-testing juggernaut—top-down, corporate-style mandates that are squeezing the life out of classrooms. This, therefore, is where courage may be needed most desperately. . . . I understand how real fear keeps more of us from doing what we know should be done. I don't want to blame the victims or minimize the culpability of those who pass bad laws. But if every educator who understood the damage done by those policies decided to speak out, to organize, to resist, then the policies would soon collapse of their own weight. Many teachers and administrators debate whether to do so, or struggle with whether to respond to students' interests rather than conform to prescriptive state (or national) standards. They know the risks, but they also realize that Jonathan Kozol was right: 'Abject capitulation to unconscionable dictates from incompetent or insecure superiors can be contagious.'"[71]

Harris: This is related to Ulrich's description of Minnesota's difficulty in getting schools to apply for change grants. When you have been stuck in a rut that looks a mile deep, it can seem impossible to get out. I think change is possible, even within the constraints of accountability policies. Students who are interested in what they are learning will score well on standardized tests; they don't need hours and hours of test prep. They will still get into the colleges of their choice. But school leaders need a "shift in mind-set" in order to bring about change in school and classroom practices.[72]

Grable: If all it takes is a shift in mind-set, why aren't a lot more people doing it?

Ross: I think Van Houten's comment is related to something I have been thinking about. Earlier, Yann noted the absence of student motivation from our discussion. I would like to point out something else that is missing. The business-scientific view of schooling that I think underlies the STEM initiative we were discussing does not consider ethical issues related to decisions about curricula and pedagogy. For example, what are the ethical dimensions of role relationships between teachers and students, between teachers and parents, between teachers and administrators, between teachers and politicians and business leaders, etc.? Furthermore, don't we have an obligation to speak out against dehumanizing classroom conditions stemming from bad laws and policies?

Foster: Classrooms are dehumanizing?

Ross: When students' understandings, interests, and ways of thinking are ignored, they are intellectually dehumanizing.

WHO SHOULD DECIDE THE PURPOSE OF EDUCATION?

Druley: I think Ross's question is related to one I've been wondering about since the moderator first asked, "What is the purpose of education?" And my question is, "*Who* should decide the purpose of education?"[73] [74]

Snepp: Teachers.

Ulrich: Parents.

Johnson: Local school boards.

Anderson: State school boards.

Inglehart: State politicians.

Grable: National politicians.

Harris: Business and industry leaders.

Yann: University educators and educational researchers.

Oates: Students.

Foster: Good lord!

Easton: Yes!

Foster: We've just named every group that has an interest in education.

Ziegler: Even people who don't belong to one of those groups should have an interest in education.

Druley: Does that mean everyone should be involved in deciding the purpose of education?

Ross: Shouldn't it be that way? The purpose of education is a cultural production; it is determined by the input and interactions of all those groups.

Xander: But that doesn't really say anything. It is that way in any culture. Druley's question was "Who *should* decide the purpose of education?" not "Who *does* decide the purpose of education?" Which group should have the greatest influence?

Newcomer: Local communities should have the greatest influence. Community members should elect local school board members who will represent their interests. The school board will hire a superintendent, who will hire curriculum directors and principals, who will hire teachers, who will pursue the communities' purpose of education in their classrooms.

Van Houten: Teachers who will work together with students to negotiate the purpose of education in classrooms.

Karch: I like Newcomer's suggestion. One thing that bothers me about the STEM initiative that Harris described earlier is that not every area of the state has the same workforce development needs. I've been working with business leaders and schools in a ten-county area whose bread and butter is advanced manufacturing, not science and engineering. What they want and what they're actually pushing is what the leader of the group calls, "There are other ways to win." That is, you don't have to go to college to have a career in this region.

What you need to do is have a good solid high school education that provides twenty-first century skills as well as a good foundation in math and literacy and then you go to work for Honda, or you go to work for Cummins. Workforce development is not just sending everybody to college; it's also making people aware that there are entry-level jobs that turn into careers.[75]

Carpenter: Harris's firm's initiative is primarily a top-down initiative. It did not use local concerns and goals as a starting point in its design.[76]

Johnson: Well, remember, they wanted to maintain control so that the initiative got started in the right direction.

Walter: The right direction being their vision for reform.

Van Houten: I wonder how Harris would like it if I started telling her how to do her job. I have some experience in making investments.

Grable: She would just ignore you.

Snepp: The problem with Newcomer's suggestion is that in some areas lobbying groups are now spending thousands, maybe millions, of dollars to influence the outcomes of school board elections. So, it's not clear that local communities really have the greatest influence in these elections.

TEACHER AND STUDENT ROLES

Grable: I would like to return to Ross's comment about the ethical dimensions of role relationships between teachers and students. I think that is part of the appeal of an inquiry approach to teaching. I was glad to hear Harris say that her initiative supports inquiry-oriented curricula. I endured the transmission approach to teaching all through school. I can't remember elementary school, but I remember many courses in high school and college where the time spent in class was largely wasted. All we did was take notes. After about five minutes, I would be behind in my note taking. The teacher would be talking about something he or she had written on one part of the board, but I would still be copying down something on another part of the board. So, I wasn't even listening to what was being said. No learning occurred in class. Learning took place later when I reviewed my notes and thought about them or when I worked through homework problems. Learning does not occur just from a teacher talking. Learning could occur if I got stuck on a problem and went to the teacher's office to ask about it, but those were two-way conversations where the teacher would explain an idea and I could say, "Wait, what about this?" or "I don't see how that works?" Those are the types of situations where learning occurs. So, the constructivist view that knowledge cannot be transmitted from one person to another but must be constructed by each individual through their experiences, which may include conversations with others, makes a lot of sense to me.

Oates: "It is just as true of intelligence as it has always been true of school subjects that teaching—'I know something you should know and I'm going to make you learn it'—is above all else what *prevents* learning."[77]

Anderson (to Grable): What does that have to do with ethics?

Grable: As I understand an inquiry approach, the role relationships between students and teacher are much different than in a transmission approach. In the transmission approach, the teacher is the sole authority for knowledge, the final arbiter of what is right and wrong. In an inquiry approach, students are helped to develop intellectual autonomy so that they can judge correctness of answers and validity of arguments for themselves. The teacher is not the sole authority; the teacher and the students collaborate as a community of thinkers that negotiate agreements about what works, what is valid, what is correct. Even if Easton's randomized comparative experiment shows that a drill-and-practice approach produces higher scores on whatever measure might be used, I still would not support such an approach. Educational decisions cannot, or should not, be reduced solely to criteria of the scientific method.

Peterson: "It is often said that children find security in drill, in repetitive work. In this kind of situation, where the child is in command, master of his materials and sure of what he is doing, the statement is probably correct. But not one percent of school drill is work of this nature. It is mumbo-jumbo, and the notion that if a child repeats a meaningless statement or process enough times it will become meaningful is as absurd as the notion that if a parrot imitates human speech long enough it will know what it is talking about."[78] "Human beings are born intelligent. We are by nature question-asking, answer-making, problem-solving animals, and we are *extremely* good at it, above all when we are little. But under certain conditions, which may exist anywhere and certainly exist almost all of the time in almost all schools, we stop using our greatest intellectual powers, stop wanting to use them, even stop believing that we have them. The remedy is not to think of more and more tricks for 'building intelligence,' but to do away with the conditions that make people act stupidly, and instead make available to them a wide variety of situations in which they are likely once again to start acting intelligently. The mind and spirit, like the body, will heal itself of most wounds if we do not keep tearing them open to make sure they are healing."[79]

Snepp: Many teachers think, for example, "If a child doesn't know how to multiply, you show him how, and give him practice and drill. If he still makes mistakes, you show him how again, and give more practice. If after you have done this about a dozen times he still makes mistakes, you assume that he is either unable or unwilling to learn—as one teacher put it, either stupid, lazy, disorganized, or emotionally disturbed."[80] These teachers do not seem to believe that "it is their business to put themselves into contact with the intelligence of their students, wherever and whatever that may be."[81] "To get in touch with the intelligence of these children, to give them solid ground to move and stand on, it may be necessary to go way, way back, to the very beginning of learning and understanding. Equally important is respect for these children, a conviction that under the right circumstances they can and will do first-class thinking."[82] "Too often teachers' help consists in trying to get students to learn the recipes for the problems that they are supposed to know how to do. They don't try to find out, as for years I never did, just what students do know about numbers, what sort of mental model students have of the world of numbers and how they behave."[83]

Van Houten: "I am convinced that in my classroom it is not clever materials, or puzzles, or teaching ideas that make my class a better place for the children, but the fact that it is a different kind of human situation. And it is not as an inventor of clever materials that I am of most use to these children, but as a human being who has done a few interesting things in her life, who has many interests, who loves books, reading, writing, sports, and above all music, who is generally fairly kind and patient with them but who can now and then get very angry, who does not pretend to be something other than she is, but generally says what she thinks and shows what she feels, and who above all generally likes, enjoys, trusts, and respects them."[84] "What helps my students is the fact that, certainly compared with most school classes, our class is a lively, interesting, cooperative, and generally unthreatening place. . . . One student's mother told me that for six years her daughter had come home from school silent and remained silent all through the evenings. Now, she said, her daughter gets in the car talking, and talks all the way home and right through the evening. About what? About her gifted teacher, Ms. Van Houten? Not at all. She talks about all the interesting things that were said and done *by the other children in the class*. That is where she gets her food for thought."[85]

Taylor: "I doubt very much if it is possible to teach *anyone* to understand *anything*, that is to say, to see how the various parts of it relate to all the other parts, to have a model of the structure in one's mind. We can give other people names, and lists, but we cannot give them our mental structures; they must build their own."[86] "I used to think that a good teacher could use clever demonstrations of concepts to teach math and science and thereby help children learn more quickly and efficiently than they could through self-discovery. But the problem with such reasoning is that every child is different and no teacher, no matter how brilliant, can get into every child's mind and come up with just the trick that will engage that mind at that exact time. That's why self-learning—learning in which the child is in charge—is almost always, in the long run, more efficient and enduring than anything that can be taught by even the most brilliant teacher."[87]

Ziegler: The teacher may be able to see the concepts and their relationships in the demonstration materials, but that is because he or she already has developed that understanding and made the connections. For students who have yet to develop these ideas, clever demonstrations and manipulatives may be just as meaningless as abstract symbols.

Carpenter (to Taylor): What do you mean by "self-learning" or saying that the child is in charge of learning? To me, that suggests an image of a student stumbling around in a fog occasionally bumping into concepts. Furthermore, to say there is a "trick" to learning also makes it seem like happenstance. I agree that demonstrations are of little value to many students and that in order to really understand something you have to make sense of it in your own mind. But "self-learning" doesn't seem very efficient to me. Don't you think teachers can present tasks, problems, activities, or situations that might be helpful in engaging students' minds in thinking about certain concepts?

Taylor: Perhaps, but I have seen too many cases where, when the students don't construct the idea that the teacher thinks they are supposed to learn, the teacher engages the students in a series of leading questions that ultimately produces a "correct answer," thus creating the appearance, to both teacher and students, that the students understand, when, in fact, they have learned nothing from the experience except, possibly, how to play the "leading question-answer" game.

Yann: "What makes school really hard for *thinkers* is not just that teachers say so much that doesn't make sense, but that they say it in exactly the way they say things that are sensible, so that the child comes to feel—as he is intended to—that when he doesn't understand it is his fault. What seems simple, natural, and self-evident to us may not seem so to a child."[88]

Lawrence: I think Grable's point about role relationships between students and teachers is an important one. I have noticed that if you read the various commission reports and other policy proposals calling for educational reform, they all talk about improving student learning, doing a better job preparing students, or perhaps just raising test scores, but they never talk about students' role in the classroom. They appear to assume that improvement can be mandated through imposition of new standards and new curricula without any change in classroom social norms, role relationships, or patterns of interaction—the culture of the classroom. And when the reform efforts fail, as they surely must if no attention is given to the interactional structure of the classroom, this assumption leads to assigning blame in all the wrong places and for all the wrong reasons.[89]

Johnson: I like the idea of enabling a more active role for students, but I think we have to be careful. "There has been much talk outside classrooms to the effect that students should discover or construct scientific knowledge. Inside classrooms, it is more common to find a different ethic. The typical science class requires every student to 'complete the same readings, worksheets, experiments and tests—and to come to essentially the same conclusions.'"[90] "Students almost never pose questions or devise ways to answer them. They are sometimes admonished to discover things, but the meaning of such 'discovery' is revealed when student 'experimenters' ask their teachers, "'Is this what was supposed to happen?' or 'Have I got the right answer?'"[91] "A preoccupation with questions for which scientists are presumed to have right answers is unduly narrow and can make it hard for students to experience anything like scientific exploration. . . . If science education is primarily a matter of acquiring well-structured knowledge, it is unlikely to be an adventure."[92]

Ross: I also like the idea of inquiry-oriented instruction but based on our earlier discussion of the use of Standards and high-stakes tests, I am skeptical of the viability of such approaches.

Quinn: As long as learning is "equated with standards, objectives, tests, and ultimately, mere numbers,"[93] not much learning is going to occur.

Snepp: "One ironical consequence of the drive for so-called higher standards in school is that the children are too busy to think. I have noticed many times that when the workload of the class is light, kids are willing to do some thinking, to take time to figure things out; when the workload is heavy, the 'I-don't-get-it' begins to sound, the thinking stops, they expect us to show them everything."[94] "When kids are in a situation where they are not under pressure to come up with a right answer, far less to do it quickly, they can do amazing things."[95]

Druley: To me, "it looks as if the test-examination-marks business is a gigantic racket, the purpose of which is to enable students, teachers, and schools to take part in a joint pretense that the students know everything they are supposed to know, when in fact they know only a small part of it—if any at all."[96]

Quinn: "No matter what tests show, very little of what is taught in school is learned, very little of what is learned is remembered, and very little of what is remembered is used. The things we learn, remember, and use are the things we seek out or meet in the daily, serious, non-school parts of our lives."[97]

Van Houten: "I feel angry and disgusted with myself for having given these tests. The good students didn't need them; the poor students, during the months of preparation and review, had most of whatever confidence and common sense they had picked up during the year knocked right out of them. . . . Are we trying to turn out intelligent people, or test takers?"[98]

Blanchard: Are schools more interested in having children learn something real or having them get good marks on tests?[99]

Snepp: "What schools want is good test takers. Nothing else is anywhere near as important."[100]

Peterson: I'm not sure it's fair to say that's what schools want, if by "schools" you mean the teachers and administrators who work in schools. The politicians who oversee education policy seem to want good test takers more than anything else.

VISIONS FOR EDUCATION:
BEYOND STANDARDS AND TESTING

Van Houten: "There must be a way to educate young children so that the great human qualities that we know are in them may be developed. But we'll never do it as long as we are obsessed with tests. At faculty meetings we talk about how to reward the *thinkers* in our classes. Who is kidding whom? . . . For all our talk and good intentions, there is much more stick than carrot in school, and while this remains so, children are going to adopt a strategy aimed above all else at staying out of trouble. How can we foster a joyous, alert, wholehearted participation in life if we build all our schooling around the holiness of getting 'right answers'?"[101]

Peterson: The fact that you are trying to come up with ways to reward kids for thinking illustrates part of the problem.[102]

Quinn: "Reward and punishment is the lowest form of education."[103]

Taylor: "For all the labor and psychometric sophistication that goes into [standardized tests], they provide very crude information about student knowledge. Teachers need more specific information to guide the complex, unpredictable business of daily teaching. Do the students have a sense of the point of the topic at hand? Do they have conceptions of what they are about that guide their attempts to make meaning and polish their skills? What intrigues students, what confuses them, what words or symbols are strange to them, what might they best learn next? These tests cannot help teachers discern what a child understands about addition of two-digit numbers, the nature of sentences, the source of rain, how to tell how long it will be until lunchtime, or any of the other myriad topics that will come up in the next few days. Each topic has many aspects that can be understood at many levels and in many ways. Children's knowledge changes rapidly. Even if these behemoth tests could provide information at the level of detail a responsive teacher could use, by the time the results came back from scoring, the information would be dated. . . . This psychometric enterprise has nothing to do with the delicate, idiosyncratic, evolving, forward-looking, creative process of teaching. The common response of legislators and deans of schools of education to teachers' negative attitudes toward tests is that teachers should learn more about existing tests and how to use them, that they should accept these tests as useful."[104] "But these tests do nothing to increase the likelihood that students will play an active role in letting the teacher know what does and does not puzzle them. They do not help students develop the power to evaluate their own knowledge. They undermine the atmosphere of mutual trust and joint commitment to construction of meaning that makes it possible to monitor student knowledge in the very act of fostering the development of that knowledge. Assessment in this more constructive sense is no more separable from teaching than the attempt at mutual understanding is separable from an ongoing conversation among friends."[105]

Snepp: I am thinking about a girl in my class who "started the year scared and then became almost wild. . . . But now she combines flash, verve, and intellectual passion with a resilient, persistent concern for those without her force of character. These talents will never show on the standardized tests," but I am convinced they will serve her better in her future schooling and in her life than anything she learned for the tests.[106]

Xander: "When school is construed as a test or a contest, even students who can safely expect to be near the top of the pack can resist the prospect that education might be a collaborative adventure. Such resistance must long have puzzled and frustrated teachers with the romantic notion that children are 'naturally' disposed to explore. Children can also—when faced with achievement tests, mad minutes, and the next grade—be disposed to measure their worth against their peers' competence. Then the idea of adventure or exploration can have the appeal of a ride over Niagara Falls in a fragile barrel. The security of workbooks, which the teacher can be induced to lead them through, becomes alluring. These cut-and-dried assignments avert immediate worries about abilities and seem to offer a way to accumulate the answers children think they will need to pass the tests that guard the narrow way to status and self-esteem."[107]

Druley: "But what avail is it to win prescribed amounts of information about geography and history, to win ability to read and write, if in the process the individual loses his [or her] own soul: loses his [or her] appreciation of things worthwhile, of the values to which these things are relative; if he [or she] loses desire to apply what he [or she] has learned and, above all, loses the ability to extract meaning from his [or her] future experiences as they occur?"[108]

Van Houten: "A mother said to me not long ago, 'I think you are making a mistake in trying to make schoolwork so interesting for the children. After all, they are going to have to spend most of their lives doing things they don't like, and they might as well get used to it now.' Every so often the curtain of slogans and platitudes behind which most people live opens up for a second, and you get a glimpse of what they really think. This is not the first time a parent has said this to me, but it horrifies me as much as ever. What an extraordinary view of life, from one of the favored citizens of this most favored of all nations! Is life nothing but drudgery, an endless list of dreary duties? Is education nothing but the process of getting children ready to do them? It was as if she had said, 'My boy is going to have to spend his life as a slave, so I want you to get him used to the idea, and see to it that when he gets to be a slave, he will be a dutiful and diligent and well-paid one.' It's easy to see how an adult, in a discouraged moment, hemmed in by seemingly pointless and petty duties and responsibilities, might think of life as a kind of slavery. But one would expect that people feeling this way about their own lives would want something better for their children, would say, in effect 'I have somehow missed the chance to put much joy and meaning into my own life; please educate my children so that they will do better.' This woman . . . shares with many parents and teachers a belief about her child and children in general which is both profoundly disrespectful and untrue. It is that they never do anything and never will do anything 'worthwhile' unless some adult makes them do it. All this woman's stories about herself and her boy have the same plot: at first, he doesn't want to do something; then, she makes him do it; finally, he does it well, and maybe even enjoys it. She never tells me stories about things that her boy does well without being made to, and she seems uninterested and even irritated when I tell her such stories. The only triumphs of his that she savors are those for which she can give herself most of the credit. Children sense this attitude. They resent it, and they are right to resent it. By what right do we assume that there is nothing good in children except what we put there? This view is condescending and presumptuous. More important, it is untrue, and blinds us to the fact that in our clumsy and ignorant efforts to mold the character of children we probably destroy at least as many good qualities as we develop, do at least as much harm as good."[109]

Taylor: "School tends to be a dishonest as well as a nervous place. We adults are not often honest with children, least of all in school. We tell them, not what we think, but what we feel they ought to think; or what other people feel or tell us they ought to think. . . . The fact is that we do not feel an obligation to be truthful to children. . . . We think it our right and our duty, not to tell the truth, but to say whatever will best serve our cause—in this case, the cause of making children grow up into the kind of people we want them to be, thinking whatever we want them to think. . . . We present ourselves to children as if we were gods, all-knowing, all-powerful, always rational, always just, always right."[110]

Oates: "Behind much of what we do in school lie some ideas that could be expressed roughly as follows: (1) Of the vast body of human knowledge, there are certain bits and pieces that can be called essential, that everyone should know; (2) the extent to which a person can be considered educated, quali-fied to live intelligently in today's world and be a useful member of society, depends on the amount of this essential knowledge that he carries about with him; (3) it is the duty of schools, therefore, to get as much of this essential knowledge as possible into the minds of children. Thus, we find ourselves trying to poke certain facts, recipes, and ideas down the gullets of every child in school, whether the morsel interests him or not, and even if there are other things that he is much more interested in learning. These ideas are absurd and harmful nonsense. We will not begin to have true education or real learning in our schools until we sweep this nonsense out of the way. Schools should be a place where children learn what they most want to know, instead of what we think they ought to know."[111]

Peterson: "It is not subject matter that makes some learning more valuable than others, but the spirit in which the work is done. If a child is doing the kind of learning that most children do in school, when they learn at all—swallowing words, to spit back at the teacher on demand—he is wasting his time, or rather, we are wasting it for him. This learning will not be permanent, or relevant, or useful. But a child who is learning naturally, following his curiosity where it leads him, adding to his mental model of reality whatever he needs and can find a place for, and rejecting without fear or guilt what he does not need, is grow-ing—in knowledge, in the love of learning, and in the ability to learn. He is on his way to becoming the kind of person we need in our society, and that our 'best' schools and colleges are *not* turning out."[112]

Quinn: "We cannot have real learning in school if we think it is our duty and our right to tell children what they must learn. We cannot know, at any moment, what particular bit of knowledge or understanding a child needs most, will most strengthen and best fit his model of reality. Only he can do this. He may not do it very well, but he can do it a hundred times better than we can. The most we can try to do is help, by letting him know roughly what is available and where he can look for it. Choosing what he wants to learn and what he does not is something he must do for himself."[113]

Newcomer: So, you believe the teacher's role should be that of a "guide"?

Quinn: Yes.

Carpenter: But "guide" should not simply mean that the teacher points students to books or Internet websites on a certain subject. The "teacher-guide" should be able to introduce activities, assignments, problems, and questions that stu-dents might find interesting, that might engage their thinking, and that might encourage them to want to continue learning. The "teacher-guide" should also have students work together whose interests, ideas, points of view, and ways of thinking will stimulate each other to learn.

Peterson: To follow up on what Quinn said, "If you think it your duty to make children do what you want, whether they will or not, then it follows inexorably that you must make them afraid of what will happen to them if they don't do what you want. . . . The alternative—I can see no other—is to have schools and classrooms in which each child in his own way can satisfy his curiosity, develop his abilities and talents, pursue his interests, and from the adults and older chil-dren around him get a glimpse of the great variety and richness of life. In short, the school should be a great smorgasbord of intellectual, artistic, creative, and athletic activities, from which each child could take whatever he wanted, and as much as he wanted, or as little."[114] "Children who are learning on their own, learning what interests them, *don't* get all upset every time they meet something unusual or strange. To young children, everything is strange. They may think and fantasize a great deal about what they do not understand, but they worry about it very little. It is only when other people, adults, start trying to control their learning and force their understanding that they begin to worry about not understanding, because they know that if they don't understand, sooner or later they are going to be in some kind of trouble with those adults."[115]

Van Houten: Your comments remind me of student who once said, "'You know, kids really like to learn; we just don't like being pushed around.'"[116]

Ziegler: Peterson's and Quinn's comments make me think of a school I have read about—the Sudbury Valley School. "The Sudbury Valley model of education is not a variation of standard education. It is not a progressive version of traditional schooling. It is not a Montessori school or a Dewey school or a Piagetian constructivist school. . . . To understand the school, one has to begin with a completely different mindset from that which dominates current educational thinking. One has to begin with the thought: *Adults do not control children's education; children educate themselves.* . . . The Sudbury Valley School is first and foremost a community in which children and adolescents experience directly the privileges and responsibilities of democratic government. [Staff members] are people who are kind, ethical, and competent, and who contribute significantly and positively to the school's environment. Students are free, all day, every day, to do what they wish at the school, as long as they don't violate any of the school's rules. . . . None of the school's rules have to do with learning. The school gives no tests. It does not evaluate or grade students' progress. There is no curriculum and no attempt to motivate students to learn. Courses occur only when students take the initiative to organize them, and they last only as long as the students want them. Many students at the school never join a course, and the school sees no problem with that. The staff members at the school do not consider themselves to be teachers. They are, instead, adult members of the community who provide a wide variety of services, including some teaching. Most of their 'teaching' is of the same variety as can be found in any human setting; it involves answering sincere questions and presenting ideas in the context of real conversations. Learning at Sudbury Valley is largely incidental. It occurs as a side effect of students' self-directed play and exploration. The most important resource at the school, for most students, is other students, who among them manifest an enormous range of interests and abilities. . . . Much of the students' exploration at the school, especially that of the adolescents, takes place through conversations. Students talk about everything imaginable, with each other and with staff members, and through such talk they are exposed to a huge range of ideas and arguments. Because nobody is an official authority, everything that is said and heard in conversation is understood as something to think about, not as dogma to memorize or feedback on a test. Conversation, unlike memorizing material for a test, stimulates the intellect. Studies have shown that the school works well as an educational institution. . . . To a considerable degree [graduates of the school] maintain, in adulthood, the playful (and that means focused and intense as well as joyful) attitude to careers and life that they developed and refined while at the school."[117]

Johnson: I think a "barrier to the kind of change in schooling that [you just described] is that it cannot be done gradually within a school or school system. The change requires a paradigm shift, from one in which teachers are in charge of the educational process to one in which each student is truly in charge of his or her own education. You can't do that a little at a time. As long as teachers set a curriculum, no matter how many choices they offer within that curriculum, students will see it as teachers' jobs, not theirs, to decide what to learn. As long as teachers evaluate students' progress, no matter how they do so, students will see that their job is to meet teachers' expectations, not to establish and meet their own expectations. In fact, the addition of choices and of less clearly defined means of evaluation within the conventional schooling system can make students' lives even more stressful than before. After such 'liberal' changes, it becomes each student's job to guess what it is that the teachers want them to do and to guess at the real, unspoken criteria for evaluation."[118]

Ziegler: I agree with your first point—it cannot be done gradually. However, at Sudbury Valley, the teachers do not set the curriculum and they do not give tests, so the students are not in a position of guessing what is expected.

Blanchard: I have read about a similar school, Acton Academy. At Acton Academy, students are entirely responsible for their own learning. They determine their own projects and establish a timeline for completing them. Instead of teachers, the school employs a small number of adults who provide guidance and suggest resources, but do not directly answer student questions.[119]

Taylor: "I am truly amazed by what young people—as young as six years old—can do when adults stop micromanaging them and give them space to think and grow."[120] "When you give your kids choice and make them responsible for their learning, test scores go up, engagement goes up, motivation goes up."[121]

PURPOSE AND CONTROL

Ross: Thinking about our earlier discussion of the purpose and history of education, it seems that "everyone involved in the founding and support of schools had a clear view about what lessons children should learn in school. Quite correctly, nobody believed that children left to their own devices, even in a rich setting for learning, would all learn just exactly the lessons that they (the adults) deemed to be so important. All of them saw schooling as inculcation, the implanting of certain truths and ways of thinking into children's minds. The only known method of inculcation, then as well as now, is forced repetition and testing for memory of what was repeated."[122]

Walter: And "with the rise of schooling, people began to think of learning as children's work. The same power-assertive methods that had been used to make children work in fields and factories were quite naturally transferred to the classroom. . . . Everyone assumed that to make children learn in school the children's willfulness would have to be beaten out of them. . . . Play was not considered to be a vehicle of learning. In the classroom, play was the enemy of learning. In recent times, the methods of schooling have become less harsh, but basic assumptions have not changed. Learning continues to be defined as children's work, and power-assertive means are used to make children do that work."[123]

Ulrich: "It is, in fact, nothing short of a miracle that the modern methods of education have not yet entirely strangled the holy curiosity of inquiry; for this delicate plant, aside from stimulation, stands mainly in need of freedom; without this it goes to wrack and ruin without fail. It is a very grave mistake to think that the enjoyment of seeing and searching can be promoted by means of coercion and a sense of duty."[124]

Xander: "Knowledge that is acquired under compulsion obtains no hold on the mind."[125]

Yann: "Men are born ignorant, not stupid; they are made stupid by education. Education is one of the chief obstacles to intelligence and freedom of thought."[126]

Newcomer: "I am beginning to suspect all elaborate and special systems of education. They seem to me to be built up on the supposition that every child is a kind of idiot who must be taught to think."[127]

Druley: "It is among the commonplaces of education that we often first cut off the living root and then try to replace its natural functions by artificial means. Thus, we suppress the child's curiosity and then when he lacks a natural interest in learning he is offered special coaching for his scholastic difficulties."[128]

Snepp: "[A veteran teacher] summed up his life's work [to me] in these words: 'I teach, but they don't learn.' . . . Why *don't* they learn what we teach them? The answer I have come to boils down to this: *Because* we teach them—that is, try to control the contents of their minds."[129]

Ulrich: I agree with Yann. "Nobody starts off stupid. . . . But what happens, as we get older, to this extraordinary capacity for learning and intellectual growth? What happens is that it is destroyed, and more than by any other one thing, by the process that we misname education—a process that goes on in most homes and schools. We adults destroy most of the intellectual and creative capacity of children by the things we do to them or make them do. We destroy this capacity above all by making them afraid, afraid of not doing what other people want, of not pleasing, of making mistakes, of failing, of being *wrong*. . . . We destroy the disinterested (I do *not* mean *un*interested) love of learning in children, which is so strong when they are small, by encouraging and compelling them to work for petty and contemptible rewards—gold stars, or papers marked 100 and tacked to the wall, or A's on report cards, or honor rolls, or dean's lists, or Phi Beta Kappa keys—in short, for the ignoble satisfaction of feeling that they are better than someone else. We encourage them to feel that the end and aim of all they do in school is nothing more than to get a good mark on a test, or to impress someone with what they seem to know. We kill, not only their curiosity, but their feeling that it is a good and admirable thing to be curious, so that by the age of ten most of them will not ask questions and will show a good deal of scorn for the few who do. In many ways, we break down children's conviction that things make sense, or their hope that things may prove to make sense. We do it, first of all, by breaking up life into arbitrary and disconnected hunks of subject matter . . .

Furthermore, we continually confront them with what is senseless, ambiguous, and contradictory; worse, we do it without knowing that we are doing it, so that, hearing nonsense shoved at them as if it were sense, they come to feel that the source of their confusion lies not in the material but in their own stupidity. We encourage children to act stupidly, not only by scaring and confusing them, but by boring them, by filling up their days with dull, repetitive tasks that make little or no claim on their attention or demands on their intelligence. . . . But why must this busywork be so dull? Why not give tasks that are interesting and demanding? Because, in schools where every task must be completed and every answer must be right, if we give children more demanding tasks, they will be fearful and will instantly insist that we show them how to do the job. When you have acres of paper to fill up with pencil marks, you have no time to waste on the luxury of thinking."[130]

Snepp: "The only difference between bad and good students in this respect is that the bad students forget right away, while the good students are careful to wait until after the exam. If for no other reason, we could well afford to throw out most of what we teach in school because the children throw out almost all of it anyway."[131]

Yann: I think the efforts to control students' learning, to pour information into them, constrains their achievement. Let me try to illustrate this by drawing two hypothetical graphs. [Yann uses a flip chart on an easel that has been set up for just such an occasion. See Figures 3.1 and 3.2 on the following page.] The top graph shows the range of achievement of students in a more controlled environment; the bottom graph shows the range of achievement of students in a less controlled environment.

Ross: What does the vertical axis represent in your graphs?

Yann: It is vague isn't it. I said "achievement," but I did not mean "standardized test score." I have to say I was thinking more along the lines of "creativity" or "learning with understanding."

Oates: I understand the point you are trying to make, but I am not comfortable with your representation of each student by a single number, even if it represents creativity or conceptual learning.

Johnson: To me, your bottom graph suggests a situation in which the achievement gap would increase, however you define achievement.

Yann: I was thinking that the graphs represented a single class of students with relatively similar socioeconomic backgrounds, but I see how it could suggest that. Still, I'm not sure that closing the achievement gap in schools as they presently exist is any sort of victory. But your concern is definitely valid if we don't also take steps to level the playing field for students from differing racial, class, and gender backgrounds.

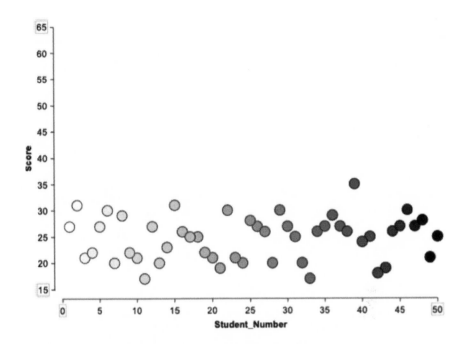

Figure 3.1. Student Achievement in a More-Controlling Environment.
Created by the author using Version 1.1 of the TinkerPlots software published by Key Curriculum Press, 2009.

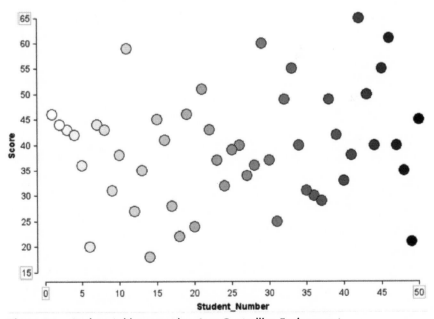

Figure 3.2. Student Achievement in a Less-Controlling Environment.
Created by the author using Version 1.1 of the TinkerPlots software published by Key Curriculum Press, 2009.

Oates: To say "level the playing field" makes it sound as though you view education as a competition between students.

Yann: A poor choice of words. I would like to have said that we need to help children from differing backgrounds be prepared to engage with their peers in discussions centered around common interests and to solve challenging problems related to those interests.

MOTIVATION

Druley: I'd like to return to Ulrich's analysis of how schools destroy the intellectual and creative capacity of students. Compared to their life beyond school—in the world—most students find classroom life to be incredibly uninteresting. They don't see the point of learning all these disparate, irrelevant facts.[132] Following World War II, it seems that students increasingly came to see school as disconnected from the "real world." It may be a cliché, but as the world became smaller, as access to information and the ability to travel increased, students' interest in the world outside of school increased as their tolerance for what was going on inside schools waned. This was especially true in the upper grade levels. In response, governments and other funding agencies spent millions of dollars on projects that claimed they would "make schools interesting."[133] As today's students will attest, such projects had little effect.

Lawrence: Earlier we considered why it is "so difficult to institute fundamental changes within the school system. . . . Conventional schooling has promoted ways of thinking and acting that turn its own premises into self-fulfilling prophecies. . . . Here's an example of such a premise: *Schools need to motivate children to learn.* . . . One reason for the perception that school-aged kids are not motivated to learn on their own comes from our culture's general acceptance of the school system's definition of learning. . . . Another example of a self-fulfilling prophecy is this: *Good performance in school predicts subsequent success.* We have made this prophecy come true by setting up a world for children in which we essentially define 'success' as good performance in school."[134]

Harris: When you say that one reason for the perception that kids are not motivated to learn on their own comes from our culture's acceptance of a certain definition of learning, do you mean learning as measured by standardized tests and learning as work instead of play?

Lawrence: Yes, and this results in a situation where kids think that the only reason to go to school is to prepare for college.[135]

Foster: That should be motivation enough.

Easton: Yes, education that serves a worthwhile purpose does not have to be inspiring. If students are being prepared for college, being prepared for careers, then the education system is functioning properly even if students find some of the content boring. As long as students are acquiring skills that they can cash in, school doesn't need to be inherently satisfying.[136]

Druley: Students learn very little, even of instrumental value, through the academic grind of memorize and regurgitate, of "learn this because, well, you just have to." I would argue that to learn something that truly has lasting instrumental value, one needs to have some intrinsic motivation.

Snepp: I believe that motivation is a huge problem, especially in middle school and high school. "A friend [of mine] gave up teaching high school mathematics because she could not answer, to her own satisfaction, the students who asked, 'Why do we gotta do this stuff?' Do we have to choose between giving up mathematics and selling it with lame appeals to later occupations or the need to balance a checkbook? Why is it so hard to take this question seriously and negotiate new curricula with students?"[137]

Yann: I doubt if motivation is a problem at the Sudbury Valley School.

Foster: At that school I would think a lot of students sit around and never do anything.

Newcomer: Not doing anything gets boring after a while.

Ziegler: Students who wish to graduate from the school must write and defend a thesis that demonstrates they have prepared themselves for responsible adult life.[138]

Harris: I was wondering how that school could have graduates if they do not give tests and do not evaluate students' progress in any way.

Blanchard: There must be a "hidden curriculum" at that school if students have to show they are prepared for adult life.

Quinn: Notice that Ziegler said the students have to show that *they have prepared themselves* for adult life. There are myriad ways to do that.

Van Houten: Don't you think you could sit down and talk to an 18-year-old about what they have been doing in their school, what their ambitions are, and what important things they believe they have learned and be able to discern in 30 minutes or less whether or not they are ready for adult life?

Peterson: Perhaps one of the root causes of the motivation problem in traditional schools is that "practically everything we do in schools tends to make children answer-centered."[139] "When children worry about the next grade and whether they will measure up, their conceptions of complex, controversial topics are irrelevant. Relevant are their conceptions of intelligence, of how one gets to be superior or inferior to others at intellectual tasks. In our society, the question of how competent one is cannot easily be answered by posing questions about matters such as why dinosaurs died out. It is too hard to tell whose answers are right and whose are wrong. Intelligence tests never employ such questions. They are full of questions with unambiguously right or wrong answers. Furthermore, these questions are not chosen by the children. Someone else has always decided what questions one needs to answer to show how intelligent one is. When children worry about how they will measure up in the next grade, they worry about being unable to get enough right answers to questions that have already been posed by someone else. When second graders think of intelligence, they see it as a matter of accumulating bits of information. They have a quiz-show conception of intelligence."[140]

Blanchard: I read about a school in Louisiana that rates itself based on the percentage of its graduates that go to college and the quality of the colleges they go to. In order to receive a diploma from the school, students must be accepted by at least two colleges. What kind of message does that send to kids?[141]

Grable: If you don't go to college, you're a failure.

Oates: When students start to perform poorly and fall behind, the typical response is to get them tutors, keep them after school or in the summer for additional help, inundate them with test prep—basically an intense effort employing the same methods that were not working for them in the first place. And when they still perform poorly on the tests, kids do view them themselves as failures in spite of the many things they can do well. But those aptitudes are not measured by the standardized tests so they must not be important.[142]

Taylor: What sense does it make to rank schools based on a single criterion? Besides, some students are just not good test-takers although they have other outstanding skills and abilities. When the tests cover material that students have no interest in and that they see no point for learning, it's no wonder they don't do well. Instead of spending all our time on test prep, we should be pursuing some of the other important purposes of education we have mentioned.[143]

Quinn: Don't you think it is strange that "adults so rarely confront students with more than the financial consequences of their commitments? We threaten students with poverty and low status when they declare school to be foolish, but we neglect their desire for socially useful knowledge."[144]

Snepp: Adults, parents in particular, also don't ask, "'How will schooling affect my child's ability to inquire about what knowledge is worthwhile?' Early in the year, [I] heard from parents such things as 'I hope Elizabeth will be challenged this year.' Challenge is code for 'move ahead on the pre-assigned path to elite colleges as quickly as possible.' It does not mean, 'I hope Elizabeth will be challenged to examine and justify, to herself, her peers, and us, the value of the activities she engages in.'"[145]

STUDENT INVOLVEMENT IN FORMULATING PURPOSES

Lawrence: "Researchers and educators of many persuasions assert that students are active learners. Active learner generally means someone who is busy, who chooses, or who makes meaning of the tasks the teacher presents. It almost never means someone who is an educational theorist ready and able to negotiate the purposes that govern learning."[146] "If adults spent more energy provoking children to think about what knowledge is worthwhile and less energy trying to hold their noses to the grindstones assigned by test and textbook selection committees, everyone might have more energy."[147]

Druley: "How free and how brave is a people that does not provoke its children to participate in the formation of the purposes that govern their activities—that does not celebrate the vigorous examination of life?"[148]

Van Houten: Yes, I think that "children who want to learn also want to select their own challenges and can do this. What sort of challenge, in any event, is it to meet someone else's goals?"[149]

Peterson: "Students might be more involved if we engaged them in the formation of the purposes that govern their activities. But the reason students should confront controversy and negotiate the means and ends of their education is so that they will become citizens of their school and society—robust, rigorous, and adventurous philosophers and practitioners of educative living. This must mean living through times of discontent as well as times of excitement. Students who continually express themselves and want learning to be fun are missing something. One cannot confront the questions of what knowledge is worthwhile, what sort of person one is to become, or what sort of society one is to construct without confronting controversy and venturing into uncertainty. Respectful disagreement and confrontation of controversial topics involve strains that mere self-expression, ignoring others, or shouting them down does not. . . . The challenge of gaining personal strength while contributing to the polyglot conversational graffiti is the challenge of maintaining liberty and community. Full membership means becoming a theorist who reflects on the nature, direction, and details of the conversation. We might develop more skill at provoking our students to join."[150]

Ulrich: On my travels to schools I repeatedly had teachers describe instances of struggling, unmotivated students who suddenly became thoroughly engaged when they were given the opportunity to pursue projects of interest to them. Is it possible that if school activities were tied to real-life concerns all students' learning would increase? And the gap in learning between rich and poor students would decrease?[151]

Newcomer: We do not expect teachers and their students to be able to engage in the sort of dialogue you describe Peterson. Educational researchers, who seem to consider it their job, and theirs alone, to solve educational problems, do not regard students as having anything of value to contribute to critiquing educational practice or developing curricula. And, as we noted earlier, they often don't think teachers have much to contribute either.[152]

Taylor: Lawrence mentioned self-fulfilling prophecies. That idea may explain why we don't engage students in the way Peterson suggests. We don't think children are capable of controlling themselves or learning to conform to social norms without the governing influence of adults. We view children as inherently wild. This view of children, coupled with the view of education as information transfer, which results in insensitivity to children's questions and interests, leads to the type of stultifying classrooms we have today. When we create rigid, controlling classroom environments based on external rewards and punishments, we make classroom life so uninteresting and miserable that students are encouraged to either act out or do absolutely nothing with regard to schoolwork. And when they act in those ways, we take that behavior as confirmation of our view of them.[153]

NOTES

1. I conducted research to study efforts to transform traditional school mathematics practices. This research attempted to relate practices in individual classrooms to social, political, and cultural influences at the broader levels of school, community, and wider society. More specifically, the project consisted of two interrelated components. One component focused on the efforts of several teachers to implement an "inquiry approach" to mathematics instruction. It analyzed the problems and constraints that arose for the teachers, the sources of these problems and constraints, and the teachers' efforts to overcome or cope with them. The second component consisted of considering the impact of state and national education initiatives and policies on local school and classroom practices. The goal of the project was not to evaluate the performance of individual teachers or schools, but to attempt to understand the factors that influence how reform movements are interpreted and implemented at a local level.

The questions that guided data collection were the following:

1. How do participants' beliefs about mathematics and teaching mathematics, their knowledge of mathematics, and their understanding of the mathematics education reform initiative influence their conceptualization and enactment of their role in the reform effort? How do participants' interpretations of reform-related experiences influence their beliefs about mathematics and teaching mathematics, their knowledge of mathematics, and their understanding of the reform initiative?

2. How do classroom, school, and district structures (sets of social relations) enable and constrain the implementation of reform practices?

3. How are classroom, school, and district structures related to economic, political, and cultural influences at the local community, state, and national levels and to the accompanying notions of ideology, power, and history?

4. In the reform implementation process, what tensions and contradictions appear in participants' beliefs and actions and among sets of social relations at the various sociological levels of focus?

I spent one academic year conducting observations in three elementary and middle school teachers' classrooms in a suburban school district in a Midwestern state. Using a variation of the snowballing strategy described by Hornby and Simon (See Pat Hornby and Gillian Symon, "Tracer Studies," in *Qualitative Methods in Organizational Research: A Practical Guide*, ed. Catherine Cassell and Gillian Symon (London: Sage Publications, 1994), 167–186.), interviews with the three teachers led to and informed interviews with several of their colleagues and their principals. The interviews with the principals led to and informed interviews with district-level administrators, a representative of the publisher of the "reform" mathematics text used in the schools, and a university mathematics educator who conducted in-service professional development for the district. I also interviewed several sets of parents with children in the school system. These interviews all fed back into further interviews with the three teachers whose classrooms I was observing. In addition, the state in which the district resides undertook a statewide STEM education reform initiative. Again applying the snowballing strategy, an interview with the vice president of a venture capital firm supporting the initiative led to interviews with state university personnel and state department of education personnel involved in this initiative; these interviews led to interviews with the governor's policy director for education and the chair of the state senate's education committee. During this phase of data collection, the constant comparison method of Glaser and Strauss (See Barney G. Glaser and Anselm L. Strauss, *The Discovery of Grounded Theory* (New York: Aldine de Gruyter, 1967).) was used to review the data in relation to the guiding research questions, identify emerging themes, and develop questions for individual interviews. The interviews, classroom audiotapes, and fieldnotes were transcribed and coded, using the research questions and a critical socioconstructivist theoretical perspective as a guide for the generation of codes. A thematic category sort was then performed with these codes. These categories were organized into an outline, which formed the basis for the writing/analysis process. The data related to each category was used to identify tensions and contradictions in the reform process, provide triangulation, and serve as a source of examples for claims about the data. (In the ensuing notes, all names used to refer to interviewees from this research are pseudonyms.)

2. Diana Underwood, personal communication.

3. Interview with Ms. Roth, the vice president of a venture capital economic development initiative. With a state university as a partner to manage day-to-day operations, her firm launched the STEM project in an effort to improve K–12 math and science education in the state.

4. Interview with Ms. Roth.

5. Interview with Dr. Grant, the lead administrator at the managing-partner university for the statewide STEM initiative.

6. Interview with Ms. Palmer, chair of state senate's education committee.

7. Interview with Dr. Grant.

8. Jane Bentz, high school English teacher, personal communication.

9. Interview with Dr. Grant.

10. Interview with Dr. Grant.

11. Interview with Dr. Schultz, director of the statewide science, technology, engineering, and mathematics (STEM) project and professor of science education at the "managing partner" university for the project.

12. Interview with Dr. Schultz.

13. Interview with Ms. Roth.

14. Interview with Ms. Roth.

15. Interview with Dr. Quisenberry, a mathematics educator and administrator at one of the STEM network's regional partner institutions.

16. Interview with Dr. Schultz.

17. Interview with Ms. Roth.

18. Interview with Dr. Grant.

19. Interview with Mr. Novak, the associate director for mathematics curriculum at the state department of education.

20. Interview with Ms. O'Brien, the governor's policy director for education.

21. Interview with Ms. Roth.

22. See Robert J. Sternberg, "Giving Employers What They Don't Really Want," *The Chronicle of Higher Education*, June 17, 2013, https://www.chronicle.com/article/Giving-Employers-What-They/139877.

23. Interview with Ms. Palmer.

24. Diana Underwood, personal communication.

25. Quoted from Christopher Tienken, "Students' Test Scores Tell Us More about the Community They Live in Than What They Know," *The Conversation*, July 5, 2017, http://theconversation.com/students-test-scores-tell-us-more-about-the-community-they-live-in-than-what-they-know-77934.

26. Interview with Ms. Palmer.

27. Interview with Ms. Palmer.

28. Interview with Mr. Fry, the school district's director of curriculum and instruction and a former high school teacher.

29. Interview with Mr. Novak.

30. Indiana Department of Education, *Indiana's Academic Standards*. (Indianapolis, IN: Indiana Department of Education, 2000), http://www.math.iupui.edu/~jwatt/m457/forms/INMATHStandards.pdf.

31. Colleen E. Chesnut, Molly S. Stewart, and Anne Sera, *University Faculty Perceptions of Teacher Evaluation Law in Indiana* (Bloomington, IN: Center for Evaluation and Education Policy, Indiana University School of Education, 2015), http://ceep.indiana.edu/pdf/University_Faculty_Perceptions_CEEP_IB.pdf.

32. Quoted from Kevin G. Welner, "Obama's Dalliance with Truthiness," *Teachers College Record*, July 30, 2009, http://www.tcrecord.org/Content.asp?ContentID=15731.

33. Quoted from Arthur Costigan, review of *Teaching by Numbers: Deconstructing the Discourse of Standards and Accountability in Education*, by Peter Taubman,

Teachers College Record, November 30, 2009, https://www.tcrecord.org/books/abstract.asp?ContentId=15851.

34. Kohn, quoted in Carl B. Frederick, review of *The Nature and Limits of Standards-Based Reform and Assessments: Defending Public Schools*, by Sandra Mathison and E. Wayne Ross, editors, *Teachers College Record*, April 22, 2009, http://www.tcrecord.org/Content.asp?ContentID=15622.

35. Paraphrased from Mike Rose, *Why School? Reclaiming Education for All of Us*. (New York: The New Press, 2014), 49, 51.

36. Interviews with Ms. Hunziger, Mr. Iverson, and Ms. Jennings, elementary school principals.

37. Interview with Mr. Karch, middle school teacher.

38. Interview with Mr. Fry.

39. Interview with Ms. Borkowski, second-grade teacher.

40. Interview with Ms. Jennings, elementary school principal.

41. Paraphrased from Ted Dintersmith, *What School Could Be: Insights and Inspiration from Teachers across America* (Princeton, NJ: Princeton University Press, 2018), 64.

42. Quoted from Frederick, review of *The Nature and Limits of Standards-Based Reform and Assessments*.

43. Les Huddle, Scott Hanback, and Rocky Killion, "Op-ed: The Bad News Coming on ISTEP," *Journal and Courier*, June 4, 2015, http://on.jconline.com/1ImqeFm.

44. Paraphrased from Ted Dintersmith, "Venture Capitalist Visits 200 Schools in 50 States and Says DeVos is Wrong: 'If Choice and Competition Improve Schools, I Found No Sign of It,'" *Washington Post*, March 15, 2018, https://www.washingtonpost.com/news/answer-sheet/wp/2018/03/15/heres-what-our-secretary-of-education-needs-to-hear-by-a-venture-capitalist-who-visited-200-schools-in-all-50-states/?utm_term=.512e659329d8.

45. Quotes from Valerie Strauss, "Bill Gates Spent Hundreds of Millions of Dollars to Improve Teaching. New Report Says It Was a Bust," *Washington Post*, June 29, 2018, https://www.washingtonpost.com/news/answer-sheet/wp/2018/06/29/bill-gates-spent-hundreds-of-millions-of-dollars-to-improve-teaching-new-report-says-it-was-a-bust/?utm_term=.bf18bd9765b2.

46. Quoted and paraphrased from Valerie Strauss, "Statisticians Slam Popular Teacher Evaluation Method," *Washington Post*, April 13, 2014, https://www.washingtonpost.com/news/answer-sheet/wp/2014/04/13/statisticians-slam-popular-teacher-evaluation-method/?utm_term=.24cb73bde112.

47. Dr. Damian Betebenner, a statistical analyst who developed the system used in about thirty states to measure annual growth in students' test scores, quoted on p. 155 of Dale Russakoff, *The Prize: Who's in Charge of America's Schools?* (New York: Houghton Mifflin Harcourt, 2015). According to Betebenner, the system was designed to measure student gains and losses, not to assign blame or credit for them. He argues that the data should be used as a starting point for discussing with teachers the reasons underlying students' performance and he acknowledges that these reasons may include both in-school and out-of-school factors.

48. Paraphrased from Rose, *Why School?* 144–145.

49. Quoted from Gene V. Glass, "Why I Am No Longer a Measurement Specialist," web log post, August 17, 2015, http://ed2worlds.blogspot.com/2015/08/why-i-am-no-longer-measurement.html?m=1.

50. Quoted from Jonathan Groves, "Re: Introducing . . . the Corporate Reform Action Pack!," web log comment, October 15, 2010, http://groups.yahoo.com/group/MathTalk/message/3167;_ylc=X3oDMTM0NDQxYmNmBF9TAzk3M-zU5NzE0BGdycElkAzM0MDM0ODQEZ3Jwc3BJZAMxNzA1MDE2MDYxBG1zZ0lkAzMxODMEc2VjA2Z0cgRzbGsDdnRwYYwRzdGltZQMxMjg3MTI1NjEzB-HRwY0lkAzMxNjc-.

51. Quoted from David Rutter, "State Politicians Played Expensive ISTEP Joke on Schools," *Post-Tribune*, January 9, 2016, http://www.chicagotribune.com/suburbs/post-tribune/opinion/ct-ptb-rutter-on-istep-st-0110-20160108-story.html.

52. See "How Privatization of Schools (Charter Schools) Works: An Infograph" [Seattle Education web log posted August 8, 2016]. Retrieved from https://seattleducation2010.wordpress.com/2016/08/08/how-privatization-of-schools-works-an-infograph/.

53. See "Pence Headlining at ALEC Policy Summit; Promotes Corporate Takeover of Schools" [Indiana State Teachers Association web log posted December 2, 2013]. Retrieved from https://www.ista-in.org/index.php?p=pence-headlining-at-alec-policy-summit-promotes-corporate-takeover-of-schools&utm_content=buffer21156&utm_medium=social&utm_source=facebook.com&utm_campaign=buffer.

54. Quoted from Lee Fang, "Selling Schools Out," *The Investigative Fund*, November 17, 2011, https://www.theinvestigativefund.org/investigation/2011/11/17/selling-schools/.

55. Quoted from the American Legislative Exchange Council website. See https://www.alec.org/about/.

56. Diana Underwood, personal communication.

57. Interview with Ms. Palmer.

58. Interview with Ms. Palmer.

59. Quoted from John G. Nicholls and Susan P. Hazzard, *Education as Adventure: Lessons from the Second Grade* (New York: Teachers College Press, 1993), 176–177.

60. See p. 205 in Nicholls and Hazzard, *Education as Adventure*.

61. Ibid., 205.

62. Quoted from Frederick, review of *The Nature and Limits of Standards-Based Reform and Assessments*.

63. Mathison cited in Frederick, review of *The Nature and Limits of Standards-Based Reform and Assessments*.

64. Freeman cited in Frederick, review of *The Nature and Limits of Standards-Based Reform and Assessments*.

65. Paraphrased from Dintersmith, *What School Could Be*, 107.

66. Quoted from Seymour B. Sarason, *School Change: The Personal Development of a Point of View* (New York: Teachers College Press, 1995), 125–126.

67. Ibid., 126.

68. Paraphrased from Rose, *Why School?* 27, 28–29, 34.

69. Paraphrased from Dintersmith, *What School Could Be*, 69–70.

70. Ibid., 98.

71. Quoted from Alfie Kohn, "Encouraging Educator Courage," *Education Week*, September 16, 2013, https://www.edweek.org/ew/articles/2013/09/18/04kohn.h33.html.

72. Paraphrased from Dintersmith, *What School Could Be*, 173–174.

73. See Thomas Brucia, "In Your Opinion, What Should the Purpose of Education Be?" Message 9, December 16, 2011, https://www.ted.com/conversations/7491/in_your_opinion_what_should_t.html.

74. Following World War II, people began to raise questions about who was responsible for creating educational policy, how that policy was put into practice, and how policies were modified in the implementation process. What was the rationale behind the policies? How did administrators and teachers view the policies? Did they try to implement them faithfully? Did they ignore them? Change them based on their own purposes and beliefs? The questions weren't so much about education laws and published policy statements as they were about how those laws and policies were enacted and to what effect. These questions stemmed from a perceived failure of the educational system and from the questioning of authority that grew during the 1960s. "Undergirding all of these questions was a moral-political one: who *should* participate in educational decision making?" Paraphrased and quoted from Seymour B. Sarason, *The Predictable Failure of Educational Reform* (San Francisco: Jossey-Bass, 1990), 53.

75. Interview with Dr. Quisenberry.

76. Interview with Dr. Quisenberry.

77. Quoted from John Holt, *How Children Fail* (New York: Da Capo Press, 1982), 161.

78. Ibid., 193.

79. Ibid., 189.

80. Ibid., 166.

81. Ibid., 160.

82. Ibid., 160.

83. Ibid., 166.

84. Ibid., 220–221.

85. Ibid., 190–191.

86. Ibid., 145.

87. Quoted from Peter Gray, "Kids Learn Math Easily When They Control Their Own Learning," *Psychology Today*, April 15, 2010, https://www.psychologytoday.com/blog/freedom-learn/201004/kids-learn-math-easily-when-they-control-their-own-learning.

88. Quoted from Holt, *How Children Fail*, 135.

89. Paraphrased from Sarason, *The Predictable Failure of Educational Reform*, 88.

90. Quoted from p. 129 of Nicholls and Hazzard, *Education as Adventure*. Quote within the quote from p. 215 of John Goodlad's 1983 book, *A Place Called School*.

91. Quoted from p. 129 of Nicholls and Hazzard, *Education as Adventure*. Quote within the quote from p. 126 of Rosalind Driver's 1983 book, *The Pupil as Scientist*.

92. Quoted from Nicholls and Hazzard, *Education as Adventure*, 130, 146.

93. Quoted from Costigan, review of *Teaching by Numbers*.

94. Quoted from Holt, *How Children Fail*, 155.

95. Ibid., 155–156.

96. Ibid., 232.

97. Ibid., 232–233.

98. Ibid., 240–241.

99. Paraphrased from Holt, *How Children Fail*, 216.

100. Quoted from Holt, *How Children Fail*, 241.

101. Ibid., 240–241.

102. Diana Underwood, personal communication.

103. Quote attributed to the Chinese philosopher Chuang Tzu in Peter Gray, "What Einstein, Twain, & Forty-Eight Others Said about School," *Psychology Today*, July 26, 2011, https://www.psychologytoday.com/blog/freedom-learn/201107/what-einstein-twain-forty-eight-others-said-about-school.

104. Quoted from Nicholls and Hazzard, *Education as Adventure*, 41–42.

105. Ibid., 43–44.

106. Ibid., 157.

107. Ibid., 175.

108. Quoted from John Dewey, *Experience and Education* (New York: Simon and Schuster, 1938), 49.

109. Quoted from Holt, *How Children Fail*, 266–268.

110. Ibid., 281–282.

111. Ibid., 288–289.

112. Ibid., 293.

113. Ibid., 293–294.

114. Ibid., 294–295.

115. Ibid., 136.

116. Ibid., 296.

117. Quoted from Peter Gray, "Children Educate Themselves IV: Lessons from Sudbury Valley," *Psychology Today*, August 13, 2008, https://www.psychology-today.com/blog/freedom-learn/200808/children-educate-themselves-iv-lessons-sud-bury-valley.

118. Quoted from Peter Gray, "Forces Against Fundamental Educational Change," *Psychology Today*, August 27, 2008, https://www.psychologytoday.com/blog/free-dom-learn/200808/forces-against-fundamental-educational-change.

119. Paraphrased from Dintersmith, *What School Could Be*, 35.

120. Laura Sandefer, cofounder of Acton Academy, quoted in Dintersmith, *What School Could Be*, 37.

121. Kayla Delzer, elementary school teacher, quoted in Dintersmith, *What School Could Be*, 29.

122. Quoted from Peter Gray, "A Brief History of Education," *Psychology Today*, August 20, 2008, https://www.psychologytoday.com/blog/freedom-learn/200808/brief-history-education.

123. Ibid.

124. Quote attributed to Albert Einstein in Gray, "What Einstein, Twain, & Forty-Eight Others Said about School."

125. Quote attributed to Plato in Gray, "What Einstein, Twain, & Forty-Eight Others Said about School."

126. Quote attributed to the British philosopher, mathematician, and social critic Bertrand Russell in Gray, "What Einstein, Twain, & Forty-Eight Others Said about School."

127. Quote attributed to the American teacher Anne Sullivan in Gray, "What Einstein, Twain, & Forty-Eight Others Said about School."

128. Quote attributed to the American poet and writer Alice Duer Miller in Gray, "What Einstein, Twain, & Forty-Eight Others Said about School."

129. Quoted from Holt, *How Children Fail*, 231.

130. Ibid., 273–277.

131. Ibid., 289.

132. Paraphrased from Sarason, *School Change*, 132.

133. Ibid., 193.

134. Quoted from Gray, "Forces Against Fundamental Educational Change."

135. Sentiment expressed by Randy Dorn, former superintendent of public instruction in the state of Washington. See p. 172 of Dintersmith, *What School Could Be*.

136. Paraphrased from Bryan Caplan, *The Case Against Education: Why the Education System is a Waste of Time and Money* (Princeton, NJ: Princeton University Press, 2018), 240.

137. Quoted from Nicholls and Hazzard, *Education as Adventure*, 183.

138. Gray, "Children Educate Themselves."

139. Quoted from Holt, *How Children Fail*, 154.

140. Quoted from Nicholls and Hazzard, *Education as Adventure*, 173–174.

141. Paraphrased from Dintersmith, *What School Could Be*, 46.

142. Ibid., 127–128.

143. View expressed by Dr. Darryl Adams, superintendent of Coachella Valley Unified school district in California. See Dintersmith, *What School Could Be*, 137–138.

144. Quoted from Nicholls and Hazzard, *Education as Adventure*, 184.

145. Ibid., 185.

146. Ibid., 185.

147. Ibid., 184.

148. Ibid., 185.

149. Ibid., 118–119.

150. Ibid., 182.

151. Paraphrased from Dintersmith, *What School Could Be*, 104–105.

152. Paraphrased from Nicholls and Hazzard, *Education as Adventure*, 185–186.

153. Paraphrased from Sarason, *School Change*, 163.

Chapter Four

Authority Always Wins

ACCOUNTABILITY AND POWER RELATIONSHIPS.

Harris: So, the motivation problem, and by extension, the learning problem, is primarily a result of control issues in teacher-student classroom relationships?

Inglehart: It's more complex than that. There are control issues throughout the educational system. Teachers control students, administrators control teachers, school boards control administrators, and state politicians and bureaucrats control local school personnel through the establishment and enforcement of educational policies.

Blanchard: That hierarchical control is, to some extent, a reflection of scientific management principles designed to increase efficiency of operation.

Carpenter: Yes, it reflects a business approach to managing schools. Set numerical performance measures and hold those below you accountable for meeting them. If they fail, replace them. I can see how that approach might make sense in the production and sale of goods and services, but by what justification is its application to education appropriate? It doesn't seem right to hold teachers accountable for outcomes upon which schooling has been shown to have less influence than other variables.

Foster: I understand your point, but, again, we should be able to see some improvement in all students from the beginning of the year to the end of the year.

Carpenter: How much improvement is appropriate? Is it the same amount for all students? Should it be the same average amount for all groups of students? Perhaps for some students improvement is being able to come up out of the hole they have been trying to hide in, look around, and see that school can be a safe, nonthreatening place where it is okay to make mistakes, where they can say what *they* think.[1] Even though this may not show up as much improvement

143

on their standardized test score, it could be of much benefit in their future schooling.

Snepp: Only if they are in similar classrooms in the future.

Grable: How were teachers held accountable before the business mentality came to dominate?

Taylor: By talking to them about their hopes and concerns for students, their diagnoses of student difficulties, their ideas for helping students. By observing their classrooms.

Xander: It's a lot easier to just evaluate teachers by the numbers.

Van Houten: In today's data-driven approach to accountability, administrators may only have time to evaluate teachers by the numbers instead of by a more personal approach.

Walter: "The currently popular version of accountability . . . that holds classroom teachers and school administrators accountable for student achievement, with such high stakes consequences as increased pay or promotions on the one hand, or reduced pay, censure, or dismissal on the other hand . . . appears to be the centerpiece of the current reform movement." The Obama administration's Race to the Top program promoted this approach to accountability by making federal grants to states contingent on implementing such policies. Race to the Top had the support of education policymakers, politicians, philanthropists, and school superintendents. One might wonder, "How does something so one dimensional and toxic gain such adherence and enthusiasm?" One reason is that "it's something that can be measured with a fair degree of reliability—at least in such school subjects as reading, mathematics, and the sciences." Also, "this form of accountability can be readily employed by geographically distant policy overseers and regulators to make vexing decisions about how public money is to be divided and distributed.

 . . . Finally, and a good deal more speculatively, the current accountability movement is one of the many manifestations of the long-cherished value of individualism in American life. . . . In the context of the school, individualism is manifest as a focus on the student, taken one by one. With high stakes accountability, each student is considered separate and distinct from other students; each student is assigned scores on tests that the student completes alone. Where deficiencies are found, a plan may be devised for each student, with each student treated separately in an effort to raise his or her achievement scores. Let's call this 'aggressive individualism,' noting how readily it is sustained by high stakes accountability initiatives. Accountability rooted in aggressive individualism can be quite toxic, because it compels teachers to view their classrooms, not as small communities or settings . . . but merely as a collection of individuals. In so doing, high stakes accountability diminishes the teacher's opportunities to nurture social relationships that foster moral development, aesthetic sensibility, and democratic character. These three features of any education worthy of the name have almost no traction in the current reform climate. . . . The all-consuming attention to high stakes accountability [makes it] very difficult to treat the classroom as a setting where moral virtue, aesthetic sensibility, and democratic character are intentionally nurtured by teachers, and where the school administrators are rewarded for an organizational climate that encourages these prized educational ends. The pursuit of these ends requires classrooms that have the characteristics of a coherent community, where teacher-student and student-student relationships are fostered in ways that promote mutual regard, reciprocity of interests, and a shared pursuit of goals believed to be for the common good. It is in such settings that we can make significant contributions to moral, aesthetic, and democratic enlightenment. Alas, such settings are made ever so much more difficult to attain in the face of an aggressive individualism spawned by high stakes accountability."[2]

Ulrich: NPR recently reported that many businesses are doing away with the "rank-and-yank" approach to employee evaluation. That is, ranking employees numerically and firing those at the bottom of the list. Apparently, businesses have decided that the "by-the-numbers" approach focuses too much on outcomes and not enough on process, thereby missing employee insights and learning. Consequently, many employers have stopped using numerical rankings and are moving to more qualitative approaches to evaluation. According to one of the businesspeople interviewed for the story, the "rank-and-yank" approach employs the wrong psychology because it threatens employees and induces anxiety that causes them to focus on avoiding humiliation rather than actually improving their performance.[3]

Easton: In order to avoid humiliation, they should improve their performance.

Ulrich: Another person interviewed for the report indicated that most businesses that have done away with the ranking approach use monthly meetings between employees and supervisors instead. These evaluations tend to be less formal—there is no complicated rating process—and therefore are perceived as less threatening. He did note that this approach is more time consuming, however.[4]

Druley: I would like to return to Harris's and Inglehart's comments about hierarchical power relationships. These role relationships are now taken for granted. For example, very few question the "attitude that says: 'Students *need* to be governed, to be *given* the rules of governance, to *set aside* their diverse interests and curiosities, to learn what *we* know they need to learn, to conform *now* in order *later* in life to give expression to their interests and curiosities, to *respect* and *accept* the superior wisdom of their governors.' It is an attitude based on the fact (and it is a fact) that students are inexperienced, unsophisticated, and in need of guidance and direction. But it is not a fact that students are uninterested in governance, that they are indifferent to it, that they neither want nor need a voice in governance, that they do not relish a role of responsibility, that how they experience governance does not color their experience of subject matter, that their interests and curiosities are antithetical (or at least not relevant) to subject matter. . . . The idea that 'someday' far in the future they will be experienced, sophisticated, and responsible and until then we should regard them otherwise, is worse than nonsense. It is self-defeating of the purposes both of the governors and the governed."[5]

Snepp: And that attitude is essentially the same at every level of the hierarchy. The hierarchical relationship that puts teachers above students is mirrored by the hierarchical relationship that puts administrators above teachers. And to most people, this is the only way that such relationships could be structured.[6]

Inglehart: I can see that students in teacher education programs are viewed and treated in the way that Druley just described. But do school administrators treat practicing teachers that way?

Snepp: Increasingly, yes, in this era of strict accountability. The attitude is that teachers need to be given a prescription for what to cover and when to cover it. They must set aside their ideas and accept the superior wisdom displayed in their text's prepackaged teacher notes or in their district's curriculum guide. And by sticking to the teacher notes or the curriculum guide they are said to be "teaching with fidelity."

Ziegler: I believe a big part of the problem is trust. If we don't trust teachers and students, we cannot overcome the limitations imposed by strict hierarchical accountability. At schools like Sudbury Valley and Acton Academy, we may not be sure exactly when and how students are learning, and their learning may not be captured by traditional report cards or standardized tests, but we can see amazing growth when students pursue their interests and learn organically rather than by rote.[7]

Ulrich: School leaders who are successful at promoting and sustaining novel educational approaches don't try to micromanage teachers by dictating what should occur in classrooms. They establish work conditions in which teachers have the freedom to work with their students and principals to create learning activities that engage students and to evaluate student learning using means that go beyond traditional tests, for example, by using performance assessments. These school leaders do not view teachers as personnel to be controlled, but rather as collaborators in the effort to improve schools.[8]

Grable: Ziegler's and Ulrich's comments suggest that reform efforts that do not address power relationships within schools and school systems will not create any sustainable impact on school organization or school practice.[9]

Peterson: I agree. An examination of school reform efforts since World War II shows that the existing hierarchical power structure was regarded as the natural state of things. None of these efforts considered the possibility that a large part of the problem in schools and a major reason for the failure of previous reform efforts stemmed from a failure to redistribute power and change power relationships. These efforts assumed schools would be improved if their existing components were improved. Until we understand the constraining aspects of the hierarchical distribution of power in school systems and take steps to reconstruct those relationships, very little is going to change.[10]

Oates: I have heard calls for parents to have a greater say in their children's education. And, of course, teachers would like to have greater freedom to decide what they do in the classroom. But what about students? Enabling teachers' and parents' participation in decision-making may be an important, though difficult, step, but if teacher-student roles in the classroom remain unchanged, I don't think we will see improvement in students' experiences or their learning, however we measure it.[11]

Druley: Yes. We need to change existing power relationships among school personnel, but also between teachers and students. We need to ask, "What are the rules that govern student and teacher interactions and how are they formed?" Currently, the most common answer is that the teacher dictates the rules with no input from students. This stems from the view that students are inherently unruly and thus not capable of contributing to the negotiation of classroom rules. And, of course, students soon learn that there is no room for their opinions or their moral voice in the classroom.[12]

Peterson: I was not just advocating involving students in conversations about classroom governance, but in conversations about curriculum as well.

Van Houten: I am realizing that teacher education programs give no attention to the hierarchical power structure of schools. As a result, new teachers accept their place in the hierarchy as the natural state of things, as Peterson said. That's just the way it is. Unfortunately, this uncritical acceptance leads to problems for teachers and their students—prescribed content of little benefit to students, lack of trust in teachers' judgment, unmotivated students, discipline problems—and also hinders efforts to address these problems.[13]

Walter: School reformers often fail to acknowledge that aspects of the culture of a classroom—the social norms, role relationships, patterns of interaction, taken-for-granted beliefs—have a tremendous influence on how classroom activities are experienced. This is why attempts at implementing new curricula that make no effort to alter the traditional hierarchical social structure in the classroom result in little to no improvement in student interest and learning. Students' place at the bottom of the hierarchy guarantees that their ideas and interests will be disregarded as teachers are expected to feed them the new curriculum. Hence, students perceive the new curriculum as just as irrelevant and just as boring as the old curriculum.[14]

Blanchard: I have noticed a subtle way that power works in parent-school relationships. In particular, school personnel tell parents how they can help; they do not solicit parents' advice concerning matters of educational policy or practice. Just as students are not viewed as having anything worthy to contribute to such discussions, neither are parents.[15]

Yann: I know we discussed this before, but I just feel that allowing all these interested parties to have a say in classroom practices and school policy devalues the specialized knowledge teachers and administrators went to school to obtain.

Easton: If teachers and administrators aren't getting the job done, maybe we need input from outside parties.

Peterson: I prefer to look at it this way. As long as high-stakes testing dominates school practices, no one is going to get the job done. But what if schools were freed from that pressure? What if there were far fewer mandates about what must be "covered." (Now to Yann): You're a history professor, right? If you were invited to a discussion about the schools' social studies curriculum, I'll bet you would have some ideas you would like to share. Other parents might have ideas about business, social sciences, politics, community issues, health care, the arts, construction and engineering, writing, and so on. I don't think that inviting them to participate in a discussion is disrespecting teachers' expertise. It's involving the community in the education of the community's children.

Inglehart: What if a group of parents insists the school teaches "intelligent design?"

Easton: Majority rules.

Peterson: No. *That* would be an example of disrespecting teachers' expertise. It is ultimately up to teachers to evaluate suggestions and discard them or modify and integrate them.

Oates: What about students?

Peterson: What?

Oates: You advocated student involvement "in the formation of the purposes that govern their activities." You didn't mention them at all in what you just said.

Grable: "Unhierarching" a hierarchy is quite difficult.

Ross: To go back to what Blanchard said about the stance schools typically take toward parents (and I think this applies to their view of students as well), it is not all that different from the view most people held of the relationship between doctors and their patients. That is, doctors were the experts; it was solely up to them to decide a course of action. It was the patients' responsibility to comply with the doctors' orders. Why? Because no one, including patients, thought patients had anything of value to contribute to the decision-making process.[16]

Ross: I think that we need to examine the following questions: Who is making educational decisions in states and communities? How are the policies put into practice? What sense do they make to teachers and principals? How are the policies modified in the course of their implementation? Do the policies mandate specific practices or are they intended as general guidelines? How is the implementation of the policies monitored and assessed? Who is driving the implementation process? All of these questions are related to the one we asked before about who should decide the purpose of education. If you recall, we argued that anyone who would be affected in some way by educational policies and their consequences should have the opportunity to contribute to the formulation of those policies. However, examining school reform efforts, we see that although the jargon, and perhaps even the goals, of reform may have changed, the hierarchical power structure within which the reform was created and attempted never did.[17] As Grable noted, this is a recipe for failure.

MEETING TEACHERS'
NEEDS / "TEACHER-PROOFING" AND DESKILLING

Yann: I have been thinking about another connection between power relationships and why students experience schools as uninteresting places. Notice that when we state purposes for schools, it is always in terms of what schools should be for children. What's wrong with that, you ask? It is very different than purposes suggested for colleges and universities. Sure, they exist to further student learning and to prepare students for careers. But they also exist for faculty to further their learning and pursue their academic interests. We are concerned about making K–12 education interesting for students, but we ignore the question of whether it is fulfilling for teachers. Can we expect teachers to create stimulating educational experiences for students if they work in an environment that does not inspire and challenge them, that does not meet their intellectual needs?[18]

Snepp: My school district has tried to involve teachers in developing curricula. We are moving to an online curriculum—all materials available online. The director of curriculum and instruction formed groups of teachers to collect and create materials in each subject area. While this might seem to encourage teacher autonomy and show respect for teachers' judgment, there was really very little freedom for the teachers because the materials they developed had to address the state standards and they were still to be held accountable for students' performance on the state standardized test.

Grable: The "do whatever you want as long as the test scores are good" philosophy that we saw before.

Yann: The "teacher-proofing" of curricula that we mentioned earlier also illustrates inattention to teachers' needs. Some publishers' teaching materials specify how teachers are to introduce a lesson, how much time they are to allot for each part of the lesson, what questions they should ask and when they should ask them. End of unit tests are also provided. The underlying assumption is that as long as teachers follow the plan laid out for them, students will learn what they are supposed to learn. This results in the deskilling of teachers. They no longer need to plan lessons, create activities, or tailor instruction to specific students or groups of students based on their perception of student difficulties or difficulties with the lesson. Their detailed knowledge of individual students' understandings is largely irrelevant. Just follow the lesson plans, give the assessments in the teacher's edition of the text, and record the scores. The planning of all parts of lessons has been done by people external to the classroom. The teacher's role is to remain faithful to the prescribed plan. The teacher acts as a manager. And the skills teachers have lost have been replaced by managerial skills—enforcing rules, disciplining students, making sure everyone is on task.[19]

Newcomer: I am not sure it is correct to say that prepackaged curriculum materials illustrate inattention to teachers' needs. Some teachers welcome those materials and the guidance they give.

Druley: Because it helps them cope with what would otherwise be a nearly untenable situation given the external pressures they face. For example, if they follow the plan to the letter and their students still perform poorly, they can argue that the failure is not their fault.

Quinn: Today's "'data driven' education seeks only conformity, standardization, testing and a zombie-like adherence to the shallow and generic Common Core. . . . Creativity, academic freedom, teacher autonomy, experimentation and innovation are being stifled in a misguided effort to fix what is not broken in our system of public education. . . . In their pursuit of Federal tax dollars, our legislators have failed us by selling children out to private industries such as Pearson Education. . . . My profession is being demeaned by a pervasive atmosphere of distrust, dictating that teachers cannot be permitted to develop and administer their own quizzes and tests (now titled as generic 'assessments') or grade their own students' examinations. The development of plans, choice of lessons and the materials to be employed are increasingly expected to be common to all teachers in a given subject. This approach not only strangles creativity, it smothers the development of critical thinking in our students and assumes a one-size-fits-all mentality more appropriate to the assembly line than to the classroom. Teacher planning time has also now been so greatly eroded by a constant need to 'prove up' our worth . . . (through the submission of plans, materials, and 'artifacts' from our teaching) that there is little time for us to carefully critique student work, engage in informal intellectual discussions with our students and colleagues, or conduct research and seek personal improvement through independent study. We have become increasingly evaluation and not knowledge driven. Process has become our most important product, to twist a phrase from corporate America, which seems doubly appropriate to this case. . . . For the last decade or so, I have had two signs hanging above the blackboard at the front of my classroom; they read, 'Words Matter' and 'Ideas Matter.' While

I still believe these simple statements to be true, I don't feel that those currently driving public education have any inkling of what they mean."[20]

Druley: We now spend time in "data driven" meetings with our curriculum director. The problem with this is that the data—wrong answers on particular assessment questions—might indicate a problem, but it doesn't tell you what the solution to that problem should be.[21]

Ziegler: I think the deskilling that Yann mentioned is occurring in the field of medicine as well. With the increase in technology and especially with the increase in the number of specialists, diagnosing conditions is becoming much more technically oriented and family practitioners and internists have been reduced to triage doctors or even case managers. Additionally, insurance companies have taken more control of the practice of medicine by developing standards that specify what steps doctors must take in order to obtain a certain level of reimbursement. It almost seems as if they are trying to "doctor-proof" treatment.[22]

Harris: Don't you think technically-oriented diagnoses make sense in the field of medicine?

Snepp: Yes, but there is a drawback—the social or personal aspect of a patient's encounter with medicine, that is, their relationship with their family doctor is diminished.

Easton: I'd rather get well than be friends with my doctor.

Newcomer: Maybe part of getting well depends on your level of trust in or your relationship with your doctor.

Van Houten: I don't know about that, but I do know that sometimes children's interest to learn more about a specific topic or their development of a general love of learning stems from a special relationship they had with a teacher.

Druley: I don't think the level of control is as great for doctors, particularly doctors in private practice, as it is for teachers. They have to keep renewing their license and provide evidence of continuing education, but, as of yet, no one is standing over their shoulder reviewing their individual cases. They are accountable primarily to themselves and their patients. Whereas teachers are told to teach a certain curriculum, I think doctors have more freedom in terms of prescribing treatments and medications.[23]

Johnson: And more respect.

Carpenter: It is not just loss of respect and skills. Something more sinister is occurring. I go back to what Yann said about teachers' pedagogical skills being replaced by techniques for controlling students. "The notion of control and surveillance is pervasive these days. I believe that the consequence of scripted curriculum, teacher accountability, continuous monitoring of student performance, high stakes testing, and punishment for not reaching external standards is that schools become educational panopticons, that is, total control and surveillance communities dedicated to undermining the imagination, creativity, intelligence, and autonomy of students and teachers. . . . When I talk about an educational panopticon, I mean a system in which teachers and students are under constant scrutiny, allowed no choice over what is learned or taught, evaluated continuously, and punished for what is considered inadequate performance. In this context students and teachers are forced to live in a constant state of anxiety, self-doubt, wariness, anomie, and even suppressed rage. . . . Scripted curriculum turns teachers into mechanical delivery systems. Most teachers I know try to revolt against them, but they have to face what are called 'the Open Court police'—people who wander the halls of schools checking that teachers are on exactly the mandated page, asking set questions rather than discussing ideas or texts, and accepting only the answers provided by the teachers' booklet. Though those monitors obviously can't check all the classes at all the times they induce a state of anxiety since they can enter any classroom at any time without even knocking. This aspect of the panopticon contributes to the erosion of self-respect and pride in one's work by treating teachers as objects with no independent educational knowledge and judgment of their own. The irony is that even with the imposition of so-called 'teacher-proof' curriculum, teachers are evaluated on the effectiveness of their student's performance on tests relating to material they have no control over. No one evaluates Open Court or other such curriculum when students fail. It is the powerless 'proofed' teachers who take the hit. This is morally reprehensible and yet the question of the values underlying this kind of teaching and evaluation is neglected when experts discuss educational issues.

Teachers under surveillance are also the agents of surveillance since they are expected to do continuous monitoring of their students' progress. Continuous monitoring implies that learning takes place in measurable increments and that constant testing somehow contributes to enhanced performance. Whether it does or not, it reinforces educational practice which has no space for conversation, exploration, or the personalization of learning. The classroom becomes a humanly impoverished environment, a sanitized place where students' personality, charm, and ingenuity have no place. Morally it contributes to depriving the young of opportunities for the development of their minds. . . . Add high stakes testing and school-wide punishment for failure and you have even greater weapons of control and coercion. Student and parent anxiety is increased; teachers, being judged themselves by the results of the tests, have incentives to press and pressure their students to perform or even in some cases encourage them to be absent on testing days. Because of no tolerance and no exceptions policies, students who just can't do well because of disabilities that are no fault of their own, or students who don't speak English, are forced to take tests they know they will fail. Setting students up to fail is simply immoral, and yet there is surprisingly little outcry about this attack on these young people's very being.

When I bring up these moral issues to educators who consider themselves reformers in the spirit of No Child Left Behind, they usually acknowledge these 'unfortunate' things can happen but that they are unintended consequences of a program designed to get every child performing to high standards. That is not the case. These alienating immoral practices are intended consequences. People who make and administer high stakes tests know the moral and personal costs of subjecting all students to them. People who insult and denigrate teachers by forcing scripted curriculum on them are perfectly aware that they are forcing teachers to act against their conscience and students to close down their minds. What must be raised and answered for is the moral cost of creating joyless schools that resemble panopticons. I believe in high standards of literacy. I believe that students are capable of high and sophisticated levels of thinking and writing. I believe that children's imaginations and intelligence must be engaged in their learning. And I believe that respect for persons, for teachers and students, is at the core of good education. Consequently, it is up to those of us who care about the moral quality of life in the school to question the values at the core of current pseudo-school reform and refuse to accept dehumanizing, damaging, and morally questionable schooling."[24]

Quinn: "One of corporate school reform's many ironies is that its ideological justifications often yield their opposite. In the name of "raising standards" and holding educators accountable, teachers lose their professional autonomy and face an ever-increasing stream of new mandates. This leads to higher turnover. In order to fill the gaps, licensure rules are relaxed and 'supports' are provided for an increasingly amateur workforce—through prefabricated curriculum and assessments. And the cycle starts all over again. The demoralization of the American teacher is leading to the deskilling of their profession, which leads to teacher resignations, which leads to more demoralization, *ad infinitum*. . . . Such high turnover rates are disruptive to school culture and tend to concentrate the least experienced teachers in the poorest school districts."[25]

POLITICAL, CULTURAL, AND ECONOMIC INFLUENCES ON SCHOOLING

Lawrence: I think it's important to note that with the onset of the Cold War and the launch of Sputnik, the government was increasingly concerned with producing more scientists and engineers so as not to fall behind the Soviet Union. The way to do this was through schools. However, the academics in charge of developing new curricula to meet the government's demands did not trust teachers to implement the curricula correctly. Thus, the creation of "teacher-proof" curricula. The government encouraged school districts to adopt the new curricula, which was being sold by private textbook publishing companies, by providing monetary incentives as part of the National Defense Education Act.

Also, at this time, educational research and development was guided by the theory of behaviorism. The principles of behaviorism facilitated the construction of teacher-proof materials—anyone who can follow directions can provide the right stimuli. Furthermore, employing the theory of behaviorism enabled education to present itself as a scientific discipline that should rightfully be respected by both the government and the general public.[26]

Lawrence: It is important to note the political, cultural, and economic forces influencing education reform because, although I do think it is essential to consider power relationships, I believe our consideration of them to this point has been superficial. We have not examined the forces that enable and maintain existing power relationships. When Druley said, "We need to change existing power relationships . . . ," I cringed a little, not because I don't agree with that, but because the way it was said, regardless of intent, made changing power relationships seem as simple as flipping a switch. "Okay everyone, here's the new way we are going to organize schools." Similarly, Harris suggested that all that was needed to promote innovative school practices was a "shift in mindset." Grable was right to say that reform efforts must deal with the nature and allocation of power and that failure to do so will result in the failure of reform. This fits with our conclusion that blindness to historical and contextual factors is one of the chief reasons for reformers' lack of impact. This is especially true as it relates to power relationships. We need to understand the expectations and obligations that constrain and enable the hierarchical social relationships that characterize our system of schooling.

Xander: I agree. Unfortunately, political, cultural, and economic forces receive little attention in most educational researchers' studies. Traditional educational theory ignores the idea that certain knowledge is more valued in our society and those that possess or obtain that knowledge are more likely to wield power over others. In addition, a group may use knowledge as a "weapon" in an attempt to suppress a group it sees as a threat. Instead, traditional educational theory treats knowledge as value-neutral. Traditional educational theory also tends not to consider the differing customs, values, norms, and aspirations that characterize the various cultural groups that public schools serve and how these differences may impact the school experience of different groups.[27]

Anderson: So educational theory has assumed that school practices treat everyone equally and afford everyone the same opportunity.

Xander: Yes. Educational theory has focused on delivering content efficiently within schools viewed as value-neutral instructional sites where students are prepared to participate in society. The relationship between school knowledge and the principles, beliefs, and values of those in power is not considered. Those principles, beliefs, and values are accepted as the necessary and natural state of things. The possibility that schools legitimate certain knowledge and delegitimate other knowledge to the advantage of certain cultural groups and the disadvantage of others has never had a place in traditional educational theory.[28]

Blanchard: So, if we regard schools as knowledge transmission sites, clearly not all the knowledge possessed by the various cultural groups that make up a society can be included in the school curriculum. Thus, there is a bias in the selection of the knowledge that is included—those in control of the schools select the knowledge they deem most important to transmit to students. Some groups, namely those whose cultural background is most compatible with the knowledge, beliefs, ways of acting, and ways of thinking emphasized in school, will be advantaged while other groups will be disadvantaged.

Xander: Yes. In addition, traditional educational theory has tended to value the scientific method over other methods of inquiry such as historical analysis, ethnography, case studies, and clinical interviews. But the scientific method is not God-given; it has a history of development beginning in the 17th century and, as Karch noted earlier, was adopted by educational researchers in the early 1900s in part to enhance their prestige. Also, the scientific method is not value-free—it values experimentation that produces observable results and is governed by norms that have been socially constructed by members of the scientific community. I am not against the scientific method per se, but when applied to education its norms seem to have contributed to a decontextualized view of the relationship between knowledge and reality and a belief that the knowledge gleaned from educational experimentation matches the one true reality, that is, it is objective. The belief in objectivity and value-neutrality denies both ethical considerations and insights gained from historical analysis. Also discounted are the taken-for-granted beliefs and practices that function to preserve the existing power structure in society at large, and that also underlie the ascendance of the scientific method in the field of education. Traditional educational theory ignores historical and social contexts and cultural beliefs and practices that affect what occurs in classrooms and schools and thus fails to consider that not all participants in schools live the same reality. In particular, it fails to consider how those in power use that power to promote the beliefs, values, and ways of knowing that will keep them in power. One way this occurs is through what is taught in schools and how it is taught. The idea that certain knowledge may serve some groups' interests, but not others is not considered. Similarly ignored is the notion that schools are a place where different cultural and socioeconomic groups engage in struggle.[29]

Peterson: One can see what Xander describes also coinciding with the application of scientific management principles to schooling. Once scientific management became the guiding light of educational theory and practice, there was no place for consideration of the politics of power and struggle within schools.[30]

Xander: Yes. The "adoption and expansion of standardized, machine-readable exams was driven by technological advances in both the mechanical and psychometric sense of the word. The privileged position of science in modern society has focused attention toward the objective pursuit of what we can do and away from political questions such as where we should set performance standards, what should be included in content standards, and whether the benefits of testing outweigh the costs."[31]

Newcomer: Scientific management was "objective" because it was "scientific." Therefore, it should not be subject to the criticism of being biased in favor of this group or that.

Lawrence: That was the idea. But if one looks more deeply, scientific management or the more recent application of business management principles to schooling provides a means of technical control. The application of these principles in the practice of schooling allows schools to justify themselves to disparate groups. For administrators, accountability. For teachers, easy to use materials. For parents, the belief that their children are being prepared for college and/or jobs by learning crucial basic skills. For business and industry, workers to help them remain competitive. For government, efficient use of resources that keeps costs down. In this way schools are able to ensure buy-in from what could be a variety of competing groups.[32]

Ross: Lawrence's statement about how business management principles both control and legitimate schooling practices may help me make sense of a contradiction I have been thinking about. That is, "As we teachers continue to be subject to abuse, like torture victims, we turn to our victimizers for respite from the pain. We imagine that corporate lawyers and executives, accountants, millionaires and billionaires, men and women, although mainly men, who have championed the eradication of social security and unions, cutbacks in funding for social programs and the breaking of the New Deal have some insight into how we should educate the youth of this country. What they offer are practices culled from business and the logics of the marketplace. And out of shame, fear, fantasies of grandeur and worthlessness, and a profound sense of loss we are vulnerable to these."[33]

Carpenter: It seems to me that the reliance on test scores to evaluate educational outcomes is consistent with the emergence of "big-data analytics" to inform business practices. As a social scientist, I am afraid that universities have contributed to the elevation of these new methods of analyzing large data sets, often without sufficient attention to the quality of data we are analyzing, the quality of the results produced, and to the exclusion of other legitimate means of inquiry such as history and anthropology.[34] "Blind faith in big-data analytics can devolve into a belief that quantitative methods are the only way to investigate a problem. . . . Sometimes qualitative research methods are the only plausible way to fully grasp the obstacles that hinder student success."[35]

HISTORY, POWER, SCHOOL STRUCTURE, SOCIAL CONTEXT, AND SCHOOL REFORM

Peterson: If I may, I would like to propose a thesis that will connect our recent discussion of power relationships and the comments some have made about the organization of schools to our earlier discussion of the history of school reform efforts and their lack of impact. I apologize in advance for its length. School reform fails in part because reformers do not understand the effects on school practice of the organizational structure of schools, the power relationships therein, and the taken-for-granted beliefs and values that characterize the practice of schooling. When test scores decreased, the system itself and its way of operating were never questioned. It was assumed that test scores could be improved through new curricula, new teaching methods, better ways of preparing teachers, going back to the basics, setting rigorous standards, tightening accountability, doing more to involve parents, allocating money to preschool programs so that children were better prepared upon entering school. None of these proposed solutions questioned the way schools are governed, the way school policy is formed, the way schools are organized temporally and spatially, the way classroom norms and expectations for students inhibit student motivation and student questions. Schools have changed in superficial ways, not in ways that alter the underlying structure that inhibits reform efforts and makes the stated goals of school seem unrelated to students' real-life experience.[36]

"It is noteworthy, indeed symptomatic, that the proponents of educational reform do not talk about changing the educational system. They will couch their reforms in terms of improving schools or the quality of education. And if there is any doubt that they have other than the most superficial conception of the educational system, that doubt disappears when one examines their remedies, which add up to 'we will do what we have been doing, or what we ought to be doing, only we will now do it better.' In the past decade there have been scores of reports—by presidential and gubernatorial commissions, by foundation task forces—about how to improve educational outcomes. . . . None of them addresses interrelated questions: In what ways do our recommendations differ from those made by comparable groups twenty or even fifty years ago? How do we account for what seems to be the universal conclusion that there has been a marked deterioration in the climate and accomplishments of our schools? Why should the solutions we offer make a difference? . . . Commission members . . . think they know who the villains are: inadequate teachers, irresponsible parents, irrelevant or inadequate curricula, unmotivated students from whom too little is expected or demanded, an improvement-defeating bureaucracy, a lowering of standards for promotion and graduation, and a lack of competitiveness that would serve as a goad for schools to take steps to improve themselves. I use the word 'villain' advisedly because the assignment of blame allows them to pinpoint their recommendations for change. In a truly basic way, they indict the motivations of this or that group or practice, as if current conditions were willed. It is no wonder that implied in their recommendations is a 'shape up or ship out' attitude. Someone once said that it is hard to be completely wrong, and that is the case with these commission reports. There are kernels of truth in their criticisms, but these have been identified before and have led to actions that were obviously ineffective. Why should similar diagnoses and actions today be more effective?"[37]

Reformers accept the structure of the school system in its current form. They want to get better personnel in schools, but they do not question the nature of the relationships between school personnel. They do not consider how these relationships and other taken-for-granted beliefs about school—the purpose of school, for instance—may inhibit school personnel, no matter how well qualified, from enacting change.[38]

There are three ways of understanding educational reform. The first way ignores historical analysis. It seems to assume that study of previous reform efforts or of the development of school theory and practice in general has nothing to contribute to the design of current reform efforts. The second way assumes that historical analysis does have something to offer. The first approach can be seen in the slew of commission reports critiquing education and calling for change. The second approach informs the work of a small group of researchers in the history of education. This work is well-regarded in the field, but completely ignored by those who create school reform proposals. The third way of understanding reform situates schools not only in historical context, but also in the social context of the wider society in which they function. One consequence of this view is that we should expect that the norms, patterns of interaction, and conventions of interpretation that characterize a large social system will, when confronted with an attempt to change the system, serve to accommodate that change in a mostly superficial sense while largely preserving the system as is.[39]

Karch: School reform efforts must extend beyond the educational system itself if they want to have any chance of success. I am not saying we have to reform society in order to reform schools. But I am saying that school reform efforts must involve people and agencies who are not directly involved with schools, but who are directly involved in addressing social problems that underly problems arising in schools. For example, poverty, healthcare, housing policies, employment policies, college admission policies, and their attendant consequences. Many problems that occur in schools have ties to larger social problems. Consequently, they cannot be solved by tinkering with or even by completely overhauling the educational system. Unfortunately, this is the approach reformers have taken and continue to take. As Lawrence suggested before, perhaps educational researchers could undertake joint efforts with members from various groups to address educational and societal problems.[40]

Ziegler: Is this why the systemic reform efforts of the 1990s failed—they stayed within the system?

Karch: Yes, and although they did consider how proposed reforms would affect different parts of the system, they did little to address existing power relationships within the system.

Blanchard: It seems that "the characteristics, traditions, and organizational dynamics of school systems [are] more or less lethal obstacles to achieving even modest, narrow goals."[41] Once again, I am feeling pessimistic.

Oates: As I have learned more about human psychology, one thing that fascinates me is the idea that our actions are guided by certain taken-for-granted beliefs that both enable and constrain what we can imagine and what we can do. Of course, it must be this way; otherwise we would be paralyzed by overanalysis. Though we seldom, perhaps never, question these beliefs, that does not mean they cannot be questioned. One such belief about school that I believe we need to question is that education must occur within self-contained classrooms, which are contained within self-contained schools. The word "school" conjures up the image of a building or buildings in an isolated location. And those buildings are segmented into classrooms. That is where teaching and learning occur. Almost no one questions this assumption. And I have come to believe that reformers who do not question it, and who therefore only think about changing classrooms and schools, are well on their way to failure. The assumption is unfounded. For example, start to imagine how we could draw upon various organizations, businesses, and institutions within a community to engage students in learning that has real-life meaning.[42]

Xander: That is not the only axiom or taken-for-granted assumption that we need to consider. Educators need "to examine critically how their own views about knowledge, human nature, values, and society are mediated through the commonsense assumptions they use to structure classroom experiences. [Such reflection] provides a starting point for raising questions about the social and political interests that underlie many of the pedagogical assumptions taken for granted by teachers. Assumptions about learning, achievement, teacher-student relations, objectivity, school authority, and so on, all need to be evaluated critically by educators."[43]

Johnson: By social and political interests, do you mean remaining competitive in a global economy?

Xander: That would be one example.

Ziegler: What do you mean by assumptions about learning, achievement, and so on?

Xander: For example, the traditional view of learning is that it occurs by transmission from the learned to the unlearned. Whose interests does such a view serve?

Oates: It puts the "learned" in a position of authority over the "unlearned" and implicitly legitimizes the knowledge that the "learned" are trying to transmit.

Peterson: Because of the unequal power relationships between students and teachers, this view of learning also tends to encourage teachers to locate the source of learning failures as existing within students. Such attributions are not helpful for either students or teachers.

Xander: 'Achievement' is another good example. What do we mean when we talk about students' 'achievement' in school?

Taylor: Well, if we are measuring achievement by performance on a standardized test, then I guess we mean how well students have learned to spit back largely unrelated morsels of information.

Xander: Suppose the tests were changed to emphasize problem solving, analysis, and synthesis. What would achievement mean then?

Druley: In either case, school achievement means meeting goals *someone else has set*. Typically, when we use the term in everyday conversation, we refer to accomplishing goals *we have set for ourselves*.

Snepp: We also have to ask whose interests achievement tests serve? For what functions are they being used? Punitive? Diagnostic?

Xander: These are the sorts of things I meant by "evaluating taken-for-granted assumptions."

Ulrich: There are subtler "taken-for-granteds," too, that not only educators but also the general public needs to consider. I am thinking about the business mentality underlying the accountability/testing process in schools. I'm sure that approach makes perfect sense to most businesspeople and a large portion of the general public.

Grable: Also, it is taken for granted that science is objective and the scientific method is an appropriate way to solve all educational problems.

Lawrence: There are many more taken-for-granted subtleties. Schools refuse to acknowledge the cultural politics that legitimates certain knowledge, beliefs, values, social norms, and ways of acting and communicating within the school while delegitimating others. We assume schools provide an equal opportunity for all students. This assumption hides how rules for behavior, the emphasis on certain types of knowledge, and expectations for student motivation contribute to a system that discounts the needs and interests of students from lower cultural groups. This is not to say that students from these groups are powerless to resist their domination. They do resist, but the process is stacked in favor of the culture of those in power. Reformers need to study the clash between competing cultures in schools and the effect of this clash on the worldviews students are forming. They also need to identify the tensions and contradictions characterizing this cultural struggle, examine what these suggest about conflicts in underlying assumptions, and use this knowledge to argue for reform that will improve the education of all students.[44]

Foster: It sounds like you have a political agenda.

Grable: Doesn't everyone?

SCHOOLING AND THE STATE

Moderator: I would like to hear what Lawrence or others see as the implications of his statement for school reform, but first, does anyone else have anything to add to our discussion of school system structure and taken-for-granted assumptions?

Xander: Yes. I believe our discussion of structure, like our discussion of power relationships has been superficial. We need to consider the roles schooling plays in relation to other social institutions, the government, the economy. Schools are expected to provide workers with the knowledge that will enable them to fit into different slots in the labor market. Colleges and universities are expected to contribute to the growth of scientific and technical knowledge that will keep the U.S. ahead of its competitors. But education is also expected to foster the narrative of equal opportunity for all and the possibility of improving one's social standing. This narrative serves to insulate both schools and the government from criticism of policies that may actually contribute to inequality. Here is a contradiction that we touched upon before when discussing contradictory purposes of education. The economic function (the need for a stratified workforce)—I won't call it a purpose—conflicts with the "promise" of improved social class through more education. Even if everyone has more education, not everyone—in fact, not many—will move into a higher social class.[45]

Yann: Public schools assist governments by supporting the social narrative those in power want to tell and by producing workers and knowledge that will assist in the creation of wealth. But as Xander noted, as opportunities for obtaining credentials have increased and more workers have more credentials, the value of the credentials decreases. The wealth of a small number of people may increase, but most see little gain. The inability of the wealth-creation process to fit within the "more opportunities, more wealth for all" narrative may lead people to question the value of schools. The government is in a bind brought on by its own structure. It must promote wealth accumulation, but it also must maintain its legitimacy. If it becomes directly involved in addressing the failed promise of education, it runs the risk of being blamed for the problem. Instead, we have seen governments take a less direct approach by castigating public schools and supporting charter schools and voucher programs as alternatives.[46]

Grable: The "bind brought on by its own structure" you refer to arises because of a taken-for-granted belief that the purpose of school is to prepare students for jobs and thereby sustain the country's economic competitiveness. So, I'm not sure it's really "structurally" generated. What happens if we reject that purpose of education?

Yann: You and I may reject that purpose. The vast majority of the general public doesn't even question it anymore.

Karch: The view that schools are value-neutral institutions whose sole purpose is to instill students with knowledge has contributed to a narrow focus in educational research on ways to make the transmission of knowledge more efficient. Better teaching strategies, better curricula, better classroom management strategies—this is what most educational research has focused on. But the purpose of schools, at least in the view of those in power, goes beyond simple knowledge transmission. Schools are viewed as an integral part of the economic production process. Any crisis in the economy will impact the schools because the government will step in to promote the production and distribution of knowledge it considers essential to address the economic problem. It will do this by creating programs, offering grants, and establishing positions to further the knowledge production it desires.[47]

Ziegler: We can see this in the recent emphasis on STEM education. We frequently hear that we are losing ground to our economic competitors, that we are lagging in innovation, and that there is a shortage of qualified workers in STEM fields.

Xander: "In order for the economy to continue generating profits and employment and in order for capital [that is, wealth] accumulation to go on, the consumer must be stimulated to purchase more goods *individually*. This is a primary way markets expand. That is, the ideology of what might be called possessive individualism needs to be strengthened. . . . By stimulating an ideology of possessive individualism, the economy 'creates' a crisis in the school. The school, which under current financial and ideological conditions cannot meet the stimulated needs of competing individuals and interest groups, loses its legitimacy. [Education cannot guarantee that everyone will move up a rung on the social ladder.] The state [that is, the government], in order to maintain its own legitimacy, hence, must respond in a way that both continues to expand capitalist social relations *and* an individualistic market at one and the same time. This is exactly the place of voucher plans and tax credit systems. The contradiction is relatively clear. A crisis is caused in part by the fact that the economy needs to sponsor an ideology of consumption on an individual not a collective level. In this way, more goods are produced and consumed. At the same time, however, this sets loose social forces that impact on nearly every sphere of social life. Individual groups will then focus on the consumption of *all* goods and services, including education, in a less collective way. General collective needs over, say, education will be seen in the light of what it can do for my own specific group, family, or self, as an individual right. To the extent that schools cannot meet these needs—and they really can't in many ways—the state apparatus will be caught in a crisis of legitimacy."[48]

Blanchard: This is happening in our schools now.

Xander: Yes.

Yann: I would like to expand on what Xander said about voucher plans. These plans provide a way for the government to relieve pressure on itself by handing over control of schools to private companies—charter school companies—that are responsible for the management of the schools. The schools become another element in the "marketplace." In this way the state can deflect criticism about schools and about the unequal benefits they provide students of differing class backgrounds. The façade of choice masks the lack of change in the underlying processes of the economy and the educational system that perpetuate inequality. On one hand, it is possible that charter or voucher plans could provide schools with the freedom to take risks in organization, curricula, and teaching. On the other hand, the focus on individual consumption to which Xander referred, the "what can it do for me?" mentality, may result in the more common pattern of the differential benefits of government policies that address social problems going disproportionately to the wealthy.[49]

Easton: This sounds like a conspiracy theory.

Yann: Deleterious effects of social and educational practices don't have to be the result of a conscious conspiracy.

Grable: It seems like at the root of most problems associated with schools are issues of control.

Lawrence: The fact that governments are turning schools over to the free market may actually indicate a loss of control by government. It has run out of ways to address the criticisms of racial, gender, and ethnic groups traditionally underserved by schools. So, it ships out the problem to the free market. This is a brilliant solution. Earlier, Grable sarcastically suggested that the scientific method could be applied to solve any problem. Similarly, there is a large segment of our individualistic, consumerist society that believes the free market can cure all economic and social ills. We need to find ways to take advantage of this loss of control. I agree with Yann that voucher plans and charter schools might be used by progressives to create alternative models of education. Preferably ones that emphasize a communal rather than an individualistic perspective.[50]

Foster: I knew you had a political agenda!

CRITICAL PEDAGOGY

Moderator: Please tell us about these "alternative models of education" that follow from the critique you offered, Lawrence. I have a feeling that Xander and several others may also have ideas to share.

Lawrence: Teachers need to examine the dominant school culture with a critical attitude that tries to unearth the beliefs and practices that schools treat as necessary and natural, as objective and neutral. Whose interests do these beliefs and practices serve? How are they communicated and maintained within the school culture? How do they fit with the beliefs and practices of students from different socioeconomic groups and what are the consequences of conflicts between the culture of different groups and the dominant school culture? This is not easy—it involves trying to identify what appear to be universal truths in school and holding them up for questioning. "Why do we do it that way?" "How did this way of doing things come about?" "What are the consequences of doing it this way?" "Whose interests does doing it this way serve?" "What are the ethical implications of doing it this way?" What tensions and contradictions underlie the routine beliefs and practices in the school?" How do our guiding beliefs and practices enable and constrain our actions?" "What alternatives exist and what might be the consequences of pursuing them?"[51]

Xander: Yes, the dominant culture of schools is not immutable. We need to understand that school organization, school structure, school rules and practices are the products of human actions. The relationship between social rules and norms and human action is a dialectical one. Human actions give rise to the social rules and norms that guide their actions. Alternately, social rules and norms guide the human actions that create social rules and norms. This means, for instance, that different social classes are both the products and the creators of the society in which they exist. It also means that there is always the possibility for change through organized struggle. Teachers and students need to identify those actions that serve to maintain the dominant school culture and those actions that might productively challenge it.[52] "To work with working-class students, for instance, under the purported impetus of a radical pedagogy would mean not only changing their consciousness, but simultaneously developing social relations that sustain and are compatible with the radical needs in which such a consciousness would have to be grounded in order to be meaningful."[53]

Grable: "Changing their consciousness?" That doesn't sound very constructivist.

Yann: It is not just teachers that need to critically examine the dominant school culture. No change can take place unless students also understand how aspects of that culture work against their needs and interests. Students need to consider how their class and family backgrounds both fit with and clash with the dominant school culture and analyze the implications of those fits and clashes for their future experiences both in school and out of school.[54]

Harris: In order to understand how they are being repressed?

Yann: In order to understand how the dominant school culture both enables and constrains their activity and their prospects for the future.

Xander: "Conflicts and contradictions must be studied and analyzed by teachers as issues to be problematized and used as points for classroom discussion and vehicles for connecting classroom practices to larger political issues. . . . If citizenship education is to be emancipatory, it must begin with the assumption that its major aim is not 'to fit' students into the existing society; instead, its primary purpose must be to stimulate their passions, imaginations, and intellects so that they will be moved to challenge the social, political, and economic forces that weigh so heavily upon their lives. In other words, students should be educated to display civic courage, i.e., the willingness to act *as if* they were living in a democratic society. . . . First, the active nature of students' participation in the learning process must be stressed. This means that transmission modes of pedagogy must be replaced by classroom social relationships in which students are able to challenge, engage, and question the form and substance of the learning process. . . . Second, students must be taught to think critically. . . . Not only must they learn to understand their own frame of reference, they must also learn how the latter has developed and how it provides a 'map' for organizing the world. . . . Third, the development of a critical mode of reasoning must be used to enable students to appropriate their own histories, i.e., to delve into their own biographies and systems of meaning. That is, a critical pedagogy must provide the conditions that give students the opportunity to speak with their own voices, to authenticate their own experiences. . . . Fourth, students must learn not only how to clarify values, they must also learn why certain values are indispensable to the reproduction of human life. Moreover, they must comprehend the source of their own beliefs and action. They must learn how values are embedded in the very texture of human life, how they are transmitted, and what interests they support regarding the quality of human existence. Fifth, students must learn about the structural and ideological forces that influence and restrict their lives. . . . Students must be taught how to act collectively to build political structures that can challenge the status quo."[55]

Anderson: How could anyone do that to kids?

Quinn: What do you mean?

Anderson: It seems to me that this is no different than when Van Houten, Walter, Yann, and Xander asked this question earlier. They were reacting to adults' efforts to control children's learning to achieve various purposes, primarily economic. Now Lawrence, Xander, and Yann are attempting to use students to achieve their own political agenda. They don't like various aspects of our social and economic life and they are going to use schools to change them.

Blanchard: You want schools to be neutral?

Anderson: Yes. They should be.

Moderator: The neutrality or non-neutrality of schools raises an important question—"the question of the nature and extent of the influence which the school should exercise over the development of the child."[56]

Carpenter: "I believe firmly that a critical factor must play an important role in any adequate educational program. . . . An education that does not strive to promote the fullest and most thorough understanding of the world is not worthy of the name. Also, there must be no deliberate distortion or suppression of the facts to support any theory or point of view. On the other hand, I am prepared to defend the thesis that all education contains a large element of imposition, that in the very nature of the case this is inevitable, that the existence and evolution of society depend upon it, that it is consequently eminently desirable, and that the frank acceptance of this fact by the educator is a major professional obligation. I even contend that failure to do this involves the clothing of one's own deepest prejudices in the garb of universal truth and the introduction into the theory and practice of education of an element of obscurantism. . . . [It is a] fallacy that the school should be impartial in its emphases, that no bias should be given in instruction. . . . [The] individual is inevitably molded by the culture into which he or she is born. In the case of the school a similar process operates and presumably is subjected to a degree of conscious direction. My thesis is that complete impartiality is utterly impossible, that the school must shape attitudes, develop tastes, and even impose ideas. It is obvious that the whole of creation cannot be brought into the school. This means that some selection must be made of teachers, curricula, architecture, methods of teaching. And in the making of the selection the dice must always be weighted in favor of this or that. . . . Dewey states in his *Democracy and Education* that the school should provide a *purified* environment for the child. . . . I am sure, however, that this means stacking the cards in favor of the particular systems of value which we may happen to possess. It is one of the truisms of the anthropologist that there are no maxims of purity on which all peoples would agree."[57]

Foster: In this country we can't agree on what attitudes and values should be instilled in children.

Carpenter: "Opponents of educational imposition unblushingly advocate the 'cultivation of democratic sentiments' in children or the promotion of child growth in the direction of 'a better and richer life.' The first represents definite acquiescence in imposition; the second, if it does not mean the same thing, means nothing. I believe firmly that democratic sentiments should be cultivated, and that a better and richer life should be the outcome of education, but in neither case would I place responsibility on either God or the order of nature. I would merely contend that as educators we must make many choices involving the development of attitudes in boys and girls and that we should not be afraid to acknowledge the faith that is in us or the forces that compel us. . . . [It is also a] fallacy that education is primarily intellectualistic in its processes and goals. Quite as important is that ideal factor in culture which gives meaning, direction, and significance to life. I refer to the element of faith or purpose which lifts man out of himself and above the level of his narrower personal interests. Here, in my judgment, is one of the great lacks in our schools and in our intellectual class today. We are able to contemplate the universe and find that all is vanity. Nothing really stirs us, unless it be that the bath water is cold, the toast burnt, or the elevator not running; or that . . . we miss the first section of a revolving door. Possibly this is the fundamental reason why we are so fearful of molding the child. We are moved by no great faiths; we are touched by no great passions. We can view a world order rushing rapidly towards collapse with no more concern than the outcome of a horse race; we can see injustice, crime and misery in their most terrible forms all about us and, if we are not directly affected, register the emotions of a scientist studying white rats in a laboratory. And in the name of freedom, objectivity, and the open mind, we would transmit this general attitude of futility to our children. In my opinion this is a confession of complete moral and spiritual bankruptcy. We cannot, by talk about the interests of children and the sacredness of personality, evade the responsibility of bringing to the younger generation a vision which will call forth their active loyalties and challenge them to creative and arduous labors. A generation without such a vision is destined, like ours, to a life of absorption in self, inferiority complexes, and frustration. The genuinely free man is not the person who spends the day contemplating his own navel, but rather the one who loses himself in a great cause or glorious adventure."[58]

Anderson: My concern is that you want to impose a certain type of "critical" attitude and a particular cause. You want to use schools to shape society in the way *you* see fit.

Lawrence: Isn't using schools to prepare students for college and jobs and to maintain the United States' standing in the world using schools to shape society in the way *you* see fit?

Van Houten: I look at it this way: "Public education does not serve a public. It *creates* a public. And in creating the right kind of public, the schools contribute toward strengthening the spiritual basis of the American creed. That is how Jefferson understood it, how Horace Mann understood it, how John Dewey understood it. And, in fact, there is no other way to understand it. The question is not, Does or doesn't public schooling create a public? The question is, What kind of public does it create? A conglomerate of self-indulgent consumers? Angry, soulless, directionless masses? Indifferent, confused citizens? Or a public imbued with confidence, a sense of purpose, a respect for learning, and tolerance? The answer to this question has nothing whatever to do with computers, with testing, with teacher accountability, with class size, and with the other details of managing schools. The right answer depends on two things, and two things alone: the existence of shared narratives and the capacity of such narratives to provide an inspired reason for schooling."[59]

Karch: Perhaps it would be helpful to understand the three approaches to citizenship education that have been implemented in schools. I will refer to them as the citizenship transmission model, the citizenship-education-as-social-science model, and the reflective inquiry approach to citizenship education. In the citizenship transmission model, knowledge is considered objective. Therefore, questions about where knowledge comes from and how it is legitimated are not considered in the classroom. Knowledge in this model is viewed as something to be absorbed and then applied to achieve goals that others have already established. The facts of the social order are simply transmitted to students along with rules for behavior whose justification is regarded as either transparent or unnecessary. There is no room for freedom of thought in this model. The arbitrariness of social constructs and the ideas that they have a history and that they serve to maintain the power of certain groups are hidden behind the notion of objectivity. The goal of the approach is to transmit the beliefs and values revered by the society to students for the purpose of maintaining the social order. Not only does this put students in a passive role in the classroom, but it tends to produce passive, unquestioning citizens.

The citizenship-education-as-social-science model employs pedagogical techniques that emphasize inquiry and discovery. However, rather than focusing on the construction of knowledge through social interaction and negotiation, this approach deteriorates into the "discovery" of what is treated as objective knowledge legitimated by experts. Thus, this model also precludes questioning the origins of knowledge and the way in which knowledge functions as a means of social control. That is, there is little room to question whose interests certain knowledge serves. In both this model and the citizenship transmission model, knowledge ends up being regarded as ahistorical, apolitical, valueless, and purely technical in nature. As a result, both of these approaches ignore students' backgrounds and their interpretations of their experiences.

In contrast to the first two models of citizenship education, the reflective inquiry approach views knowledge as a social construction. Students' beliefs, values, and real-life experiences take center stage in classroom discussions. This model emphasizes the development of students' decision-making skills. In this way, it is expected that students will be educated to take an active role in the maintenance and transformation of government. Unfortunately, this model tends to ignore how the knowledge, beliefs, and values deemed legitimate by the state can constrain discussions in schools that might critically analyze the social and economic interests that such knowledge, beliefs, and values support. In other words, this model offers students an overly optimistic view of their decision-making power by failing to consider social, political, and economic factors in the wider society that constrain what decisions citizens may participate in and that constrain the parameters of those decisions. In part, this problem with the reflective inquiry model stems from a solely psychological definition of critical thinking, much like that Ross offered earlier. Such a definition does not address how the organization of a society and its "taken-for-granteds" impinge on classrooms and schools to limit critical thought.[60]

Xander: Citizenship education needs to rethink its purpose. It needs a multidisciplinary approach that entertains social and political questions. "Should society be changed?" "In what way?" "How free are we in this society?" "What are the political consequences of our day-to-day actions?" "Who should be educated?" "What knowledge, beliefs, and values are appropriate in the domain of school?"

"How should schools be organized and what structure of social relationships is appropriate within schools?"[61]

Johnson: I think it is also important to point out that "moral education has generally been taken to refer to the promotion of the moral values and knowledge of individual students. In moral education programs, such as those inspired by Lawrence Kohlberg, who saw his efforts as continuous with those of John Dewey, there is also a democratic emphasis on student responsibility for the ethos of the school community. Discussion, inquiry, and action are concerned with creating and sustaining a just community, not merely with developing moral individuals. Yet these moral development programs and schools stop short of fostering active negotiation of the rules that govern the conduct of the school's intellectual work. It hardly needs to be pointed out that few schools promote discussions of such matters. When open discussion of ethical issues does occur in schools, it is likely to focus on other topics such as stealing, property damage, drug use, and disruptive behavior. The real stuff of citizenship in a democracy—the question of how we should conduct our daily work—is left out."[62]

Snepp: "Teachers and schools tend to mistake good behavior for good character. What they prize above all is docility, suggestibility; the child who will do what he is told; or even better, the child who will do what is wanted without even having to be told. They value most in children what children least value in themselves. Small wonder that their effort to build character is such a failure."[63]

Yann: In regard to Anderson's concern, I would say that the relationship between educational theory and practice should not be one where academics develop "solutions" and provide them to administrators, teachers, and students to implement. That approach has been tried many times and failed many times. Rather, those groups and individuals concerned about education need to come together, much as we have come together here today, to discuss the purpose and potential of education. We need to try to understand each other's varied histories and points of view and work together to develop a more humane model of schooling that benefits all involved.[64] It is important to stress that simply working with administrators and teachers will be insufficient. Students, parents, workers, and other community members have something to contribute to the development and analysis of alternative proposals for schooling, including curriculum and teaching. Students, parents, workers, community members, teachers, and administrators can draw on their domains of expertise and learn from each other during this process. This is not to deny that teachers know a great deal about what works and what doesn't work in classrooms. But in a reimagined schooling environment, it is not clear what classrooms might be. Input from others could spur teachers' imagination in this regard.[65]

Harris: What influence have the ideas of "critical" or "radical" educators had on educational practice?

Taylor: Very little.

Grable: If they had had much influence, Henry Giroux wouldn't be living in Canada.

Inglehart: There are two aspects of radical pedagogy that puzzle me. First, why do they accept the label "radical"? They seem to revel in it. But by doing so they essentially ensure their failure—they marginalize themselves. Second, Lawrence criticized the progressives' conception of power, calling it superficial. Clearly, the radical educational theorists have a much more detailed understanding of power relationships between schools and economic and social structures in the wider society. I know that radical educators talk about teachers as transformative intellectuals and they promote curricula that, for example, would engage students in mathematics by having them examine how certain economic policies and practices constrain their social mobility. But from what I have seen, most of their proposals accept the existing structure of schools. That is, they are intended to fit within encapsulated classrooms in encapsulated schools in a system of hierarchical power relationships. And the progressives had just about convinced me that any attempt at reform in such a system was certain to fail.

Harris: Maybe that's why radical educators have had little impact on school practices.

Ziegler: I know that many radical educators draw upon various forms of Marxism in their critiques of schooling. And just like Marx was on target with many of his criticisms of capitalism, so too are they on target with their criticisms of schooling. However, perhaps it is also the case that just as Marx's proposed alternative to capitalism turned out to be disastrous when put into practice, radical educators' proposals are, if not disastrous, at least inadequate.

Grable: The leaders of the radical pedagogy movement are mostly college professors and "although college professors, if not too numerous, perform a valuable social function, society requires great numbers of persons who, while capable of gathering and digesting facts, are at the same time able to think in terms of life, make decisions, and act. From such persons will come our real social leaders."[66]

NOTES

1. Paraphrased from John Holt, *How Children Fail* (New York: Da Capo Press, 1982), 190.

2. Quoted and paraphrased from Gary D. Fenstermacher and Virginia Richardson, "What's Wrong with Accountability?" *Teachers College Record*, May 26, 2010, https://www.researchgate.net/publication/325181686_What%27s_Wrong_with_Accountability.

3. Yuki Noguchi, "Yay, It's Time for My Performance Review! (Said No One Ever)," web article accompanying report on NPR's *All Things Considered*, Sep-

tember 28, 2016, https://www.npr.org/2016/09/28/495795876/yay-its-time-for-my-performance-review-said-no-one-ever.

4. Ibid.

5. Quoted from Seymour B. Sarason, *School Change: The Personal Development of a Point of View* (New York: Teachers College Press, 1995), 185.

6. Paraphrased from Sarason, *School Change*, 166.

7. Paraphrased from Ted Dintersmith, *What School Could Be: Insights and Inspiration from Teachers across America* (Princeton, NJ: Princeton University Press, 2018), 42–43.

8. Ibid., 169.

9. Paraphrased from p. 73 and p. xiii of Seymour B. Sarason, *The Predictable Failure of Educational Reform* (San Francisco: Jossey-Bass, 1990).

10. Ibid, 28.

11. Ibid, 5.

12. Paraphrased from Sarason, *School Change*, 165–166.

13. Ibid., 166.

14. Ibid., 170–171.

15. Ibid., 187.

16. Ibid., 187.

17. Paraphrased from Sarason, *The Predictable Failure of Educational Reform*, 53.

18. Paraphrased from Sarason, *School Change*, 211.

19. Paraphrased from Michael W. Apple, *Education and Power* (Boston, MA: Routledge & Kegan Paul, 1982), 146–147.

20. From a letter of resignation submitted to a superintendent and school board in Syracuse, New York, by Gerald J. Conti. Quoted in Claire Gordon, "Teacher's Epic Resignation Letter: Profession 'No Longer Exists'," web log post, April 10, 2013, https://www.aol.com/2013/04/10/gerald-conti-teacher-resignation/.

21. Diana Underwood, personal communication.

22. Interviews with Dr. Eggleston, family practitioner, and Dr. Kinsey, pediatrician.

23. Interviews with Drs. Kinsey and Eggleston.

24. Quoted from Herbert Kohl, "The Educational Panopticon," *Teachers College Record*, January 8, 2009, http://www.tcrecord.org ID Number: 15477.

25. Quoted from Kevin Prosen, "'The Teacher Shortage' is No Accident—It's the Result of Corporate Education Reform Policies," *In These Times*, August 25, 2015, http://inthesetimes.com/working/entry/18344/the_teacher_shortage_isnt_an_accidentits_the_result_of_corporate_education.

26. Paraphrased from Apple, *Education and Power*, 150–151.

27. Paraphrased from Henry A. Giroux, *Theory and Resistance in Education* (South Hadley, MA: Bergin & Garvey, 1983), 73.

28. Ibid., 73.

29. Ibid., 73–74.

30. Ibid., 170.

31. Quoted from Carl B. Frederick, review of *The Nature and Limits of Standards-Based Reform and Assessments: Defending Public Schools*, by Sandra Mathison and E. Wayne Ross, editors, *Teachers College Record*, April 22, 2009, http://www.tcrecord.org/Content.asp?ContentID=15622.

32. Paraphrased from Apple, *Education and Power*, 151.

33. Peter Taubman, quoted in Arthur Costigan, review of *Teaching by Numbers: Deconstructing the Discourse of Standards and Accountability in Education*, by Peter Taubman, *Teachers College Record*, November 30, 2009, https://www.tcrecord.org/books/abstract.asp?ContentId=15851.

34. Eric Klinenberg, "What Trump's Win Compels Scholars to Do," *The Chronicle of Higher Education*, November 11, 2016, https://www.chronicle.com/article/What-Trump-s-Win-Compels/238389.

35. Quoted from Mark Salisbury, "Big Hopes, Scant Evidence," *The Chronicle of Higher Education*, April 9, 2017, https://www.chronicle.com/article/Big-Hopes-Scant-Evidence/239710.

36. Paraphrased from Sarason, *The Predictable Failure of Educational Reform*, 4–5 and Sarason, *School Change*, 132.

37. Quoted from Sarason, *The Predictable Failure of Educational Reform*, 13–14.

38. Paraphrased from Sarason, *The Predictable Failure of Educational Reform*, 14.

39. Ibid., 34–35.

40. Ibid., 35–36.

41. Quoted from Sarason, *The Predictable Failure of Educational Reform*, 12.

42. Paraphrased from Sarason, *School Change*, 190–191, 193 and Sarason, *The Predictable Failure of Educational Reform*, 112.

43. Quoted from Giroux, *Theory and Resistance in Education*, 67.

44. Paraphrased from Giroux, *Theory and Resistance in Education*, 66.

45. Paraphrased from Apple, *Education and Power*, 58.

46. Ibid., 120–122.

47. Ibid., 60.

48. Quoted from Apple, *Education and Power*, 122.

49. Paraphrased from Apple, *Education and Power*, 125–127.

50. Ibid., 127.

51. Paraphrased from Giroux, *Theory and Resistance in Education*, 64–65.

52. Ibid., 115.

53. Quoted from Giroux, *Theory and Resistance in Education*, 149–150.

54. Paraphrased from Giroux, *Theory and Resistance in Education*, 150.

55. Quoted from Giroux, *Theory and Resistance in Education*, 200–203.

56. Quoted from George S. Counts, *Dare the School Build a New Social Order?* (Carbondale, IL: Southern Illinois University Press, 1978), 9–10.

57. Ibid., 16–17.

58. Ibid., 17–20.

59. Quoted from Neil Postman, *The End of Education: Redefining the Value of School* (New York: Vintage Books, 1995), 18.

60. Paraphrased from Giroux, *Theory and Resistance in Education*, 179, 182–183, 186–187, 189.

61. Ibid., 193.

62. Quoted from John G. Nicholls and Susan P. Hazzard, *Education as Adventure: Lessons from the Second Grade* (New York: Teachers College Press, 1993), 50.

63. Quoted from Holt, *How Children Fail*, 234.

64. Paraphrased from Giroux, *Theory and Resistance in Education*, 240.

65. Paraphrased from Apple, *Education and Power*, 175.

66. Quoted from Counts, *Dare the School Build a New Social Order?* 19.

Chapter Five

Crystal Visions, No Surrender

VISIONS FOR EDUCATION:
ANYBODY HERE SEEN MY OLD FRIEND JOHN? (PART I)

Oates: I go back to something John Dewey said: "'School is not a preparation for life, it is life.' School is not a preparation for democratic living after schooling stops; it is the site for experiencing democratic living now."[1] [2] Engaging students in mathematics so that they will understand how economic policies constrain them is not engaging in democratic living; it is trying to prepare students to be a certain type of citizen—a citizen who will challenge the status quo. And while I am all for citizens who challenge the status quo, I believe that employing schools to produce this type of citizen is not only futile, but also unethical.

Peterson: "Dewey sought a theory of experience that would guide education. He strove to avoid experience that increases specific skills, but confines life to a narrow course. He also sought to avoid experience that is exciting or fun but does not strengthen the disposition for increasingly complex and meaningful experience. The educative experience he sought would foster interest and excitement, strengthen skills and widen horizons, and make knowledge more coherent. This experience would involve 'an organic connection between education and personal experience.'[3] It would start with personal concerns and expand these to encompass wisdom, knowledge, and skills of the child's culture. These should truly become the child's property, that she might enhance its value. Not inert property, but material from which to fashion new experiences—intellectual adventure for the child and for society."[4] For example, "learning to read and write means exploring the place that books, reading, and writing play in the ongoing complex conversation that is our culture. When reading is dominated by workbooks and achievement tests that measure children's comprehension of words and sentences, this world is sometimes easy and predictable. At other times it is difficult, but it is rarely an exploration. Literature can be a challenging object of interest and making sense of literature means asking the questions that renew social life while examining its connections to the places we have been and the people we have known."[5]

Ross: "Our education system has mined our minds in the way that we strip-mine the earth: for a particular commodity. And for the future, it won't serve us. We have to rethink the fundamental principles on which we're educating our children."[6]

Quinn: The focus on filling students with knowledge and information obscures any consideration of what they are curious about. Of course, there is much that they are curious about, but we treat that as unrelated, perhaps even a hindrance, to what we think they need to learn. In this way, we disrespect the knowledge, interests, and ability to think that students bring to school with them. We act as if it is solely up to us to mold them into our predetermined image of what they should be.[7]

Newcomer: "Whether or not we acknowledge it, students are curriculum theorists and critics of schooling. If they are drawn into the conversation about the purposes and practices of education, we may all learn useful lessons."[8]

Quinn: "The absence of student experience from current educational discourse seems to be a consequence of systematic silencing of the students' voice."[9]

Oates: Why aren't there any students on this panel?

Moderator: As one of the organizers of this panel, I will own that mistake. We should have invited several students.

Taylor: I think "teachers have been taught to view students as having few resources relevant to the attainment of educational goals."[10]

Peterson: There is no more important emphasis than that of "the participation of the learner in the formation of the purposes which direct his [or her] activities in the learning process."[11]

Foster: Anarchy again. You are trapped in the 1960s. You want children to be free and happy and do whatever they want to do as long as it makes them feel good.

Peterson: No. Of course, I want children to be free and happy, but I do not support "unimpeded self-expression." I am not advocating "individualistic conceptions of freedom as untrammeled choice, [but] rather envisioning school as part of a culture that draws strength from and contributes to social diversity. . . . The only freedom of enduring value [is] freedom of intelligence, 'the power to frame purposes and to execute purposes so framed. Such freedom is in turn identified with self-control; for the formation of purposes and the organization of means to execute them are the work of intelligence.'"[12]

Oates: "Every education system in the world is being reformed at the moment and it's not enough. Reform is no use anymore, because that's simply improving a broken model. What we need . . . is not evolution, but a revolution in education. This has to be transformed into something else. One of the real challenges is to innovate fundamentally in education. Innovation is hard, because it means doing something that people don't find very easy, for the most part. It means challenging what we take for granted, things that we think are obvious. The great problem for reform or transformation is the tyranny of common sense. Things that people think, 'It can't be done differently, that's how it's done.' . . . There are ideas that all of us are enthralled to, which we simply take for granted as the natural order of things, the way things are. And many of our ideas have been formed, not to meet the circumstances of this century, but to cope with the circumstances of previous centuries. But our minds are still hypnotized by them, and we have to disenthrall ourselves of some of them. . . . We have to change metaphors. We have to go from what is essentially an industrial model of education, a manufacturing model, which is based on linearity and conformity and batching people. We have to move to a model that is based more on principles of agriculture. We have to recognize that human flourishing is not a mechanical process; it's an organic process. And you cannot predict the outcome of human development. All you can do, like a farmer, is create the conditions under which they will begin to flourish."[13] [14]

Quinn: Parents well know how curious and adventurous young children are. Children want to explore everything. Parents often exclaim how hard it is to keep up with their children. But this doesn't mean they follow their children around letting them do whatever they want. Of course, parents provide guidance, but the guidance follows their observation of children's interests. There is a huge difference between allowing children to do anything they want and supporting and guiding them in their efforts to explore their interests. The same is (or could be) true in schools. Parents and educators talk about honoring children's individuality. But it is just talk. The current structure and organization of schools, the social norms, the expectations for teachers and students override any efforts to attend to children's individuality. We have already discussed that schools evolved this way largely in response to the large influx of immigrants in the late nineteenth and early twentieth centuries. The factory model of schooling worked (at least in some sense) then. It is not working now, and we cannot continue to pretend that it does. We must give more than lip service to respecting students' individuality.[15]

Blanchard: The purpose of education . . .

Anderson: What?

Blanchard: I have been thinking. When the moderator first posed the question, "What is the purpose of education?," it seemed of utmost importance that we answer it. I am beginning to wonder if that question is inappropriate.[16] [17]

Easton: Are you serious?! How could anyone do that to kids? You would put students in a school with no purpose?

Oates: In spite of all of the purposes we listed, traditional schooling serves no ethical purpose that I can see.

Easton: What do you mean by "ethical purpose?"

Oates: Schools provide individuals with credentials and thereby provide society with a stratified workforce. So school is not really about learning anything, and schools reproduce existing inequalities in the social order. I find those functions, or lack of functions, of schools unethical.

Easton: You want everyone to come out of school being equal?

Inglehart: Do schools "reproduce" existing inequalities or simply "mirror" them?

Grable: What's the difference?

Druley: I think Blanchard is on to something. "The debate about *the* purpose of education ignores the elephant in the classroom. We have wrapped up our schools in rote memorization, low-level testing, and misguided accountability—preventing them from achieving *any* real purpose. It's a fool's errand to debate whether students are better off memorizing and forgetting Plato's categorization of the three parts of a human's soul, the quadratic equation, or the definition of the Cost of Goods Sold. If classroom 'learning' is a mirage, it doesn't matter whether it's based on *The Odyssey*, a biology textbook, AP History flashcards, or a phone book."[18]

Ross: From thinking about our discussion, I have concluded that "real reform is not going to occur within the established school system."[19] Traditional schooling "waste[s] the ingenuity, initiative, and collaborative spirit of students. . . . It [is] an exercise in endurance, waiting, and remembering—not a journey of discovery or an artistic production."[20]

Snepp: I agree. "The idea of special learning places where nothing but learning happens no longer seems to me to make any sense at all. The proper place and best place for children to learn whatever they need or want to know is the place where until very recently almost all children learned it—in the world itself, in the mainstream of adult life. If we put in every community, as we should (perhaps in former school buildings), resource and activity centers, citizens' clubs, full of spaces for many kinds of things to happen—libraries, music rooms, theaters, sports facilities, workshops, meeting rooms—these should be open to and used by young and old together. We made a terrible mistake when (with the best of intentions) we separated children from adults and learning from the rest of life, and one of our most urgent tasks is to take down the barriers we have put between them and let them come back together."[21] [22] [23]

Van Houten: Snepp's statement fits into many questions our discussion has raised for me. Is it possible that the knowledge we try to convey to students in schools could be better learned outside of schools in real-life contexts that could prompt the construction of that knowledge? What if we forbade the teaching of literature, math, science, and history in school classrooms? Such a question may seem bizarre, but it is only by considering such a question that we may hope to entertain alternatives to traditional schooling. If we believe that significant change will not occur as long as the current organizational structure of schools remains in place and if we truly appreciate the descriptions of learning that occurs when students are confronted with challenging, real-life problems, then such questions are not bizarre, but necessary. We need to shake the traditional image of classrooms that any mention of "school" conjures up in our minds. And then we need to imagine what alternative educational settings might look like.[24]

Walter: It does seem wildly impractical. Any attempt to dismantle or circumvent traditional schooling will meet with tremendous pushback from publishers of educational materials, from testing companies, from schools of education, from school administrators, and probably from teachers. As Taylor pointed out earlier, education is a big business.

Ziegler: I believe that "fundamental change in education is . . . occurring outside of the traditional school system. It is occurring among groups of families who decide to 'unschool' their children (that is, to home school them in a free way, where there is no curriculum or evaluation) and among people who start nonschool schools, such as those modeled after the Sudbury Valley School. People in these movements establish among themselves new sets of social norms, which allow them to overcome the barriers to behaving in ways that seem abnormal to others. Their observations of children who are educating themselves lead them to perceive education in a new light, as something to admire and enjoy in children but not to control."[25]

Quinn: Well, now it's my turn: How could anyone do that to kids?

Peterson: I thought you would be in favor of that type of education.

Quinn: Who can afford to home-school their children? Who can afford to send their children to a private school? I understand that the Sudbury Valley School operates at relatively low cost and that school vouchers may help parents send their children to private schools, but to advocate home-schooling as a solution to the problems of public education is unconscionable. Do you know how many families simply could not afford to do that? You are advocating education that only the wealthy can take advantage of.

Carpenter: I agree with your view of home-schooling. That aside, funding for alternative schools is problematic. Must they be private schools? When Ross said that real reform will not occur within the established school system, might he as well have said that it will not occur within public schools? Earlier, when Newcomer said that local communities should have the greatest influence in deciding the purpose of education for their schools, I found myself nodding in agreement, yet wondering about the feasibility of that suggestion. Local schools receive the majority of their funding from the state and we know that whoever controls the purse strings tends to control the decision making.

Ross: I want to clarify that I was not suggesting, as Anderson did earlier, that privatization and competition is the route to real reform. Our state has been moving in that direction for the last 10 years or so, but the results have been inconclusive at best.

Moderator: Let's save the funding issue for another time. Does anyone else have something to add regarding alternatives to traditional schools?

Ulrich: I understand your inclination to treat funding as a separate issue and focus on what occurs in classrooms. However, given the current emphasis on privatization, school choice, charter schools, and vouchers, I think we should consider what effect, if any, these ideas may have on classrooms. After all, they are "alternatives to traditional schools."

Moderator: I agree with you. Let's explore those reform ideas.

VISIONS FOR EDUCATION: CORPORATE EDUCATION REFORM

Taylor: School choice is definitely a priority of the current Secretary of Education, Betsy DeVos. She believes that parents should control how their money is used for their children's education.

Snepp: "In Michigan, she led the push to use public dollars to pay for private school tuition through vouchers and other means. That experiment has been a success for banks and hedge funds, and a resounding failure for many students. A 2016 report by the Education Trust-Midwest, a nonprofit, concluded that under the model shaped by DeVos, 'Michigan's K–12 system is among the weakest in the country and getting worse. In little more than a decade, Michigan has gone from being a fairly average state in elementary reading and math achievement to the bottom 10 states . . . '"[26]

Johnson: What worries me about the idea of school choice is that "the more that people begin to see education as a consumer choice, the more they will be unwilling to pay for other people's children. And if they have no children in school, then they have no reason to underwrite other people's private choices. The basic compact that public education creates is this: The public is responsible for the education of the children of the state, the district, the community. We all benefit when other people's children are educated. It is our responsibility as citizens to support a high-quality public education, even if we don't have children in the public schools. But once the concept of private choice becomes dominant, then the sense of communal responsibility is dissolved. Each of us is then given permission to think of what is best for me, not what is best for we."[27]

Blanchard: How do voucher programs work?

Foster: "Voucher programs offer publicly funded financial aid to parents for private schools. Tax credit programs usually offer individuals or corporations tax credits if they donate to a scholarship granting organization, which in turn offers private school scholarships based on various criteria, including income."[28]

Anderson: So, the state gives parents a voucher, which they can use to pay their child's tuition at a private school. They "give parents an alternative to low-performing public schools."[29]

Peterson: "About 75 percent of voucher schools across the country are religious—usually [Protestant] or Catholic, with about 2 percent identifying as Jewish and 1 percent identifying as Muslim. . . . Many of the private schools that participate in these state-led programs are run by evangelical Christian churches. They are sometimes unaccredited and . . . the ideas in [their] textbooks often flout widely accepted science and historical fact. . . . No state or federal organization tracks the curriculum being used in private school choice programs. The religious affiliations of schools that participate in these programs are also not always tracked. . . . Most states have little oversight on the curriculum used in schools that participate in private school choice programs. Some states have zero regulations on the topic. Others require private schools to follow the state's broad-based content standards but specify little else. . . . Additionally, private schools that participate in these programs are not typically subject to the same accountability and transparency rules as public schools, although rules vary on a state-by-state basis. . . . The leaders of [Abeka, Bob Jones University Press, and Accelerated Christian Education (ACE), three publishers of textbooks for evangelical Christian schools] subscribe to an authoritarian vision of education in which students are taught not to question their elders. . . . [A former ACE vice president wrote], 'Our material is not written with conventional viewpoints in mind. We do not believe that education should be nondirective or speculative, or that the final interpretation of facts and events should be left up to immature, inexperienced minds as mainline secular curricula do.'"[30]

Grable: Whether you are five years old, 15, 35, or 95, "the final interpretation of facts and events" can only be made in your own mind!

Ross: I think the point is that they would not be in favor of an "inquiry" approach that said, "Discuss this topic, argue about it, and draw your own conclusions." They are going to tell you what conclusions to draw.

Walter: To be fair we need to acknowledge that "Abeka and Bob Jones and other biblically-based curricula try to approach academics from a biblical standpoint and from a moral, ethical view, which does not necessarily push any agenda outside of an understanding of God and who Christ is."[31] You know, secular textbooks also have their own point of view.

Oates: That is certainly true, as Carpenter argued earlier, even if our former governor does not believe it. A point of view, a bias if you will, is established simply by the choice of what to include and what not to include in the book and how much space to allot to various topics.

Newcomer: What I wonder about is that "with taxpayers footing the bill for religious private schools, the separation of church and state, a cornerstone of American democracy, becomes a murky line."[32]

Anderson: But earlier you argued that local communities should have the greatest voice in determining the purpose of their schools. If a community, or a group within a community, decides that they want their schools to teach a Christian-oriented curriculum, shouldn't they be able to use their tax dollars to support that school?

Newcomer: Hmm. I'm going to have to think about that. (Now to Johnson) This is what you meant by "education as a consumer choice," isn't it?

Ziegler: Can someone provide a little historical background so that we can understand how the school choice movement arose?

Karch: Yes.

Ziegler: I figured you would be able to do that, Karch.

Karch: Government funding for education does not bother "school choice" reformers, but government control of schools does. They want consumers—parents and students—to be able to choose from an array of schools that are privately managed, but that receive public funding. (This same view underlies the push for privatization of prisons.) When compulsory public education first arose in the nineteenth century, government played a large role in schooling. Not only were state and local governments responsible for school funding, but also for school curricula, personnel, policies, and procedures. The public expected schools to prepare students for adult life and work, to create productive citizens, and to promote social mobility.

However, political economics began to change in the 1980s. Rather than believing that government should regulate markets, favor shifted to free markets based on competition and choice. The idea was that competition and choice would result in more efficient production and higher quality products. Government regulation created too much inefficient bureaucracy and gave too much influence to special interests. A free market came to be seen as the remedy for any problem in the economy, be it slow growth, unemployment, or inflation. This view of the relationship between the economy and government is often called "neoliberalism." "Neoliberalism led logically to specific policies such as cutting taxes and government spending, deregulating the economy, and transferring as much government activity as possible to the private sector, including education. And when government funding is necessary to get something done, turning management over to the private sector."

In 1955, the economist Milton Friedman suggested that government should not be involved in running schools at all. He argued that governments should provide students with vouchers that they could use to pay for a private school of their choice. These schools could be for-profit, non-profit, or religious schools. Friedman allowed that a democracy required a certain amount of knowledge in its citizens and therefore that it made sense for government to require and subsidize a minimum amount of education of all citizens, but he did not believe government-run schools were appropriate in a free-market economy. In his view, in a free-market competition between schools, schools of low quality would not survive. Thus, competition would improve the quality of schooling. What typically happens instead in an unregulated free market is that consumers buy what they can afford; therefore, poorer families will still purchase inferior quality schooling because it is the only option that fits their budget. For free-market education reformers, the existence of a few government schools is tolerated because they are viewed as at least giving the poor access to some education. The racial segregation that results when private schools enter into competition with public schools does not seem to be of concern to these reformers. At least it does not seem as important as transferring the responsibility for education out of the hands of government and to private entities.

One last thing to note: we have discussed the impact of *A Nation at Risk* in launching a steady stream of reform efforts. Some commentators have offered a more sinister interpretation of this report, namely that it was an attempt by the Reagan administration to convince people that public schools were failing and thus lay the groundwork for the push for privatization and the attempts to weaken teachers' unions.[33]

Xander: In 1991 a federally funded research center produced a report questioning the claims in *A Nation at Risk* and concluding "that policymakers and pundits who bemoan a system-wide crisis are both overstating and misstating the problem."[34] But few paid attention to it.

Karch: Thanks largely to its coverage by the media, *A Nation at Risk* led to panic about the quality of America's public schools. Both Democrats and Republicans called for more rigorous curricula, improved standardized test scores, and more accountability from educators. At the same time, politicians' interest in racial integration of schools waned. Schools attended mostly by poor students of color were grossly underfunded in comparison to schools attended mostly by white students of higher socioeconomic backgrounds. But with the market now in control, the government was able to absolve itself of this problem with a "separate but improved" rationale by which politicians convinced themselves that higher standards, accountability, and competition would result in an improved education for all students, even those low-income minority students who remained in segregated schools. Parents and students would be free to choose their schools. If schools ended up being segregated, it wouldn't be the government's fault. And if a school was doing very poorly, it would be closed, and students would be given a voucher to use at another school of their choice. It is these views and policies that set the stage for the market-based education reform we have witnessed over the past few decades.

The Improving America's Schools Act, signed by President Clinton in 1994, paved the way for the creation of charter schools. These schools would be funded by the government but operated by private companies. Because, under the law, these schools would have more freedom than traditional public schools, the claim was that they would be able to experiment with and adopt more innovative educational practices. In 1999, Florida, under Governor Jeb Bush, enacted the country's first voucher plan. Students in schools deemed to be failing according to their standardized test score performance were given vouchers from the state to be used to pay for tuition at private schools.

Philanthropists, foundations, venture capitalists, politicians, and business leaders in finance and technology all jumped on the school privatization bandwagon. Their approach to reform has been almost exclusively top-down. Parents, students, teachers, even school administrators have had little voice in the movement. But with the support of wealthy donors, the school privatization movement has created its own education reform industry. This industry consists of "organizations employing same-thinking researchers, program designers, consultants, lobbyists, campaign organizers, and media producers. A cadre of super-wealthy donors regularly gives millions of dollars to pro-education-reform candidates for state and local offices; they fund ballot initiatives around the country and pour hundreds of thousands of dollars into local school board races. The right-wing American Legislative Exchange Council (ALEC), which drafts model legislation for conservative state lawmakers, has been an important ally of the education-reform movement. Some states have adopted ALEC model education legislation verbatim. Help also came from the White House. President George W. Bush advanced both charter schools and vouchers. His signature education law, 'No Child Left Behind' (signed in 2002), established that students in low-testing, low-income public schools could transfer within their district to another public school or to a charter school."[35] "[No Child Left Behind (NCLB)] mandated standardized testing, incentivized charter schools and demanded schools be held accountable."[36]

Yann: "Susan Neuman, an assistant secretary of education during the roll-out of NCLB, admitted that others in Bush's Department of Education 'saw NCLB as a Trojan horse for the choice agenda—a way to expose the failure of public education and 'blow it up a bit.'"[37]

Karch: President Obama and his Secretary of Education, Arne Duncan, were big supporters of charter schools. Their education program, "Race to the Top," offered competitive grants to states that submitted education reform plans addressing issues laid out by the Department of Education.[38] "To win [Race to the Top] monies, states had to agree to enact Common Core State Standards (or their equivalent), evaluate teachers and schools based on testing results and open a path for more privatized schools (charter schools)."[39] In particular, states could not restrict the growth of charter schools and they were to allow charter schools to use public facilities for free or at least at reduced cost. Because in many states money for public education follows the students, these policies severely reduced public-school education budgets, many of which were already insufficient. Of course, this led to backlash from supporters of public schools. But most states were as sorely in need of money as their public-school systems; only four states declined to enter the Race to the Top competition. The end result was that the charter school movement gained a great deal of momentum from the Obama administration's policies.[40]

Lawrence: I would like to add a little to that. We have referred to the "school privatization movement." But that is not the way reformers present charter schools and voucher plans to the general public. Rather, they present them as ways that will expand schooling choices for parents and students. Choice, not privatization, is their mantra. They advertise that all students and parents will have better schools to choose from, including low-income, minority students currently languishing in poorly rated schools. In this way, they make it sound like a plan that will benefit everyone.[41]

Karch: "The earliest charters were expected to serve as laboratories for innovative practices that district schools would adopt and spread. In fact, there has been little cross-pollination."[42]

Lawrence: Yes, and in spite of the fact that classroom practices in many charter schools do not differ substantially from those in district public schools, advocates of market-based reform have been able to gain support for their ideas by pushing the concept of "choice." The most conservative politicians pushing market-based school reform want to transfer control of schools to the private sector. More moderate politicians supporting these reforms are less concerned with privatization than with getting students into higher-performing schools. They see choice and competition as the way to do that. "Both conservatives and moderates call school choice 'the civil rights issue of our time.'"

It is also important to note that charter school advocates portray these schools as public schools because they receive money from the government and ostensibly are supervised by some entity appointed by the state. In reality, though, the day-to-day operations of charter schools, including their finances, are managed by a private company. Some charter management organizations are for-profit, others are non-profit. In either case, the fact that these organizations are private typically results in their not being subject to the same level of scrutiny as public schools. In addition to charter schools, supporters of market-based education reform have begun promoting private, for-profit online schools as well. There is a lot of money to be made in this emerging education market.[43]

Yann: "In April 2011 the Pearson and Gates Foundations formed a partnership to design online reading and math courses. According to [a New York State] Attorney General's report, Pearson executives wanted to market the material and predicted potential profits would be worth tens of millions of dollars."[44]

Lawrence: As Karch noted, the market-based education reform movement emphasizes accountability using standardized test scores. Based on this measure, there is little difference in performance between charter schools and district public schools. Approximately one-half of charter schools perform the same as their district school counterparts, one-fourth perform worse, and one-fourth perform better, although sometimes only marginally better. Beyond this, there is a great deal of fraud associated with charter schools and voucher programs. Public money handed over to private companies with insufficient oversight procedures in place. What could go wrong? Another problem both charter schools and voucher programs contribute to is an increase in segregation in schools, both racial and socioeconomic. "According to a 2016 comprehensive report by the Brookings Institution, 'charter schools enroll more black and poor students than traditional public schools in the same areas and are more likely to be at one extreme or the other of the racial and economic demographic spectrum than traditional public schools.'" With all of these problems associated with charter schools and voucher programs, you might wonder why so many people are still supporting them and calling for more of them.[45]

Grable: Let me guess. Money.

Lawrence: Yes. Businesspeople and investors have figured out that there is a lot of money to be made from the market-based education reform movement. The government is handing out huge sums of money to companies to manage charter schools, create online materials, conduct professional development, and develop charter school and voucher program advocacy campaigns. Before this, a few textbook companies had the corner on the education market. But the introduction of charter schools and private management companies opened up the education market to more players. Another reason support for charter schools and voucher programs remains steadfast in the face of less than compelling evidence of their effectiveness is that, for many of their supporters, ideology is more important than results. These are the ideologues who believe the free market can solve any social and economic problem. For them, there is no other way. It remains to be seen how these people will react to stories such as the one out of Washington, D.C. in 2018 that reported that school officials had allowed one-third of the senior class to graduate in 2017 without meeting all necessary requirements. This was a blow to the charter school, voucher program movement because reformers had held up Washington, D.C. as a model of reform success due to its voucher program and large percentage of charter schools.[46]

Taylor: So "by declaring schools 'failures,' public monies were increasingly diverted to private corporations. Yet, after a half-century of trials, there is no body of evidence that shows privatized schools are better or less expensive. . . . The plain fact is that privatization, even at its best, does not have sufficient power to close the achievement gap—but it segregates. It imperils the unity of schools and society. This proposed solution works against the very democratic and equity principles for which public systems were formed."[47]

Xander: Your comment about the proposed solution working against democratic principles made me think of something else we should add to Karch's and Lawrence's background of the school choice movement. During the 1960s, established social norms and institutions in the United States came under attack. The civil rights movement, protests against the Vietnam War, and the "sex, drugs, and rock-and-roll" culture illustrate this. Both conservative and liberal elites reacted negatively to these attacks. On the conservative side, the view was that college campuses were breeding grounds for these attacks. Because colleges and universities were largely funded by tax revenue and contributions from businesses and because the trustees of colleges and universities came primarily from the business community, the conservative view was that "the oppressed business people who have lost all influence should organize and defend themselves instead of idly sitting by while fundamental freedoms are destroyed by the Marxist onslaught from the media, universities and the government." The reaction from the liberal side was more surprising. The Carter administration produced a study titled "The Crisis of Democracy" that concluded there was *too much democracy*. According to this view, there were too many special interest groups making demands on the government. In order for government to run smoothly and effectively, the population should "sit obediently while the intelligent minority runs things in the interest of everyone." Their conclusion was that schools needed to do a better job indoctrinating children in order to prevent the kinds of uprisings that occurred in the 1960s. Crucially, "there [was] one group omitted in the lament of the liberal internationalists: the corporate sector. That's because they don't comprise a special interest; they represent the national interest. Therefore, their dominant influence in what we call democracy is right and proper and merits no mention or concern."[48]

Harris: I agree that charter schools have not proven to be a cure-all for education's ills. However, I think some of the critique we have just heard that intimates that reformers are motivated by greed is unfair. If one reads about the history of the recent reform effort in Newark, it is certainly the case that the politicians and "venture philanthropists" driving the initiative aimed to expand charter schools, apply business-style, data-driven accountability, reduce tenure protections and weaken unions, and reward and punish teachers based on students' standardized test scores. But I don't think Mark Zuckerberg gave $100 million for the effort because he was looking to make more money. Many of the venture philanthropists and education reformers genuinely hoped to improve education for the nation's poorest children. They had made their money by introducing disruptive business models in established industries and they assumed the same approach would work in education. But their top-down approach did not engender trust among the community—they did not engage the community in conversation about local problems and needs. Thus, they failed to overcome local political resistance. They also grossly overestimated the ability of a new system to overcome the effects of poverty, violence, and broken homes.[49]

Snepp: What bothers me about the top-down approach employed in Newark and elsewhere is that the reformers claim to be motivated to do what is best for students, but they don't involve students in any way.

Grable: That's because "doing what is best for students" means doing what they think will ultimately be most beneficial to businesses and the U.S. economy. They view schools as service organizations that produce human capital.

Blanchard: Well, what's happened in our state?

Quinn: In our state, "lawmakers originally promoted the state's school voucher program as a way to make good on America's promise of equal opportunity, offering children from poor and lower-middle-class families an escape from public schools that failed to meet their needs. But five years after the program was established, more than half of the state's voucher recipients have never attended Indiana public schools, meaning that taxpayers are now covering private and religious school tuition for children whose parents had previously footed that bill."[50] Our governor from 2005 to 2013 earned national recognition "for his methodical and persistent undermining of public schools and their teachers in the name of reform. . . . After his election, [the governor] quickly laid the groundwork for creating a system based on the belief that the market principle of competition would improve education outcomes and drive down costs. Under the guise of property tax reform, [he] seized control of school funding by legislating that the state would pay the largest share of district costs known as the general fund, while giving localities the responsibility for paying for debt service, capital projects, transportation and bus replacement. [The governor] and the legislature also made sure that districts would be hamstrung in raising their local share by capping property taxes so that they could not exceed 1 percent of a home's assessed value. The poorer the town, the less money the district could raise.

. . . A . . . change to the grading system by the legislature favored 'innovation schools,' many of them charters, by grading them with a less exacting standard, thus making them look more successful than they are. If the grading system was designed to prove that public schools were the dismal failure that [the governor] claimed, the cure for failure was not school improvement through research-based strategies and support, but rather through ramping up competition and choice. On May 5, 2011, [the governor] signed HB 1003 into law, which was the broadest voucher program in the country. . . . A tax credit program for private school 'scholarships' was doubled, and parents who home-schooled or sent their children to private schools could receive a $1,000 tax deduction. Charters were greatly expanded by legislation that allowed for more charter sponsors, including private religious colleges. The law also permitted public schools to become charter schools and increased funding for the charter sector. By the end of his term, [the governor's] rhetoric regarding public education was openly hostile. Public schools were called government schools. He referred to attending a public school without the ability to have a voucher as an incarceration. He had created the conditions that spawned a dizzying array of vouchers, voucher-like schemes, for-profit and not-for-profit charters and virtual charter schools. . . . Each child educated in [the state's] public schools is paying the price for a reform system built not to ensure his or her personal success, but rather to maximize the number of students who leave the 'government' schools they attend."[51]

Harris: Well, from the reformers' point of view, leaving "government" schools should contribute to students' personal success.

Walter: "If you want to privatize something and destroy it, a standard method is first to defund it, so it doesn't work anymore; people get upset and accept privatization. This is happening in the schools. They are defunded, so they don't work well. So, people accept a form of privatization just to get out of the mess. There's no improvement in education, but it does help to instill the new spirit of the age: 'Gain wealth, forgetting all but self.'"[52]

Ulrich: Based on my travels to schools I do not think that charter schools are more innovative than public schools. Some charter schools had implemented innovative curricula and teaching practices, but just as many public schools had done so as well. Many charter schools, just like public schools, are focused on raising test scores. Their innovation is nothing more than "cute test-prep jingles." I was somewhat surprised by this because, with fewer regulations to follow, I had been led to believe that one of the raison d'êtres of charter schools was to develop innovative models of practice. But many seemed so concerned about preparing their students to appear attractive to colleges that they were just offering more of the same old traditional approach to schooling. One more thing: "Business principles aren't the key to improving U.S. education. If choice and competition improve schools, I found no sign of it. Pitting schools against each other in a test-score 'Hunger Games' drags everyone down. I saw no sign of union status affecting a teacher's dedication or effectiveness."[53]

Lawrence: I should have also noted that enrollment in teacher education programs in the state has declined. "[This] downward trend in education enrollments can be traced directly to the policies promoted [by the governor and the superintendent of public instruction]. Between 2000 and 2012 constant-dollar teacher salaries in [our state] decreased by 10 percent, outpaced nationally only by North Carolina's 14 percent decrease. At the same time, the . . . Rules for Educator Preparation and Accountability policies promoted by [the governor and the schools' superintendent] increased regulation of education schools and licensure requirements for teacher education students while lowering standards of preparation for nontraditional teacher prep programs. Coupled with the equally flawed testing and test-based teacher evaluation policies implemented in the state, these rules have driven out experienced, effective teachers while discouraging new teachers from entering the field. Unless [the state] changes course, its public education system is headed for disaster. Already teacher shortages are being felt across the board, not just in traditional shortage areas. The answer to this problem lies in getting back to treating teachers and school leaders as professionals, increasing standards of educator preparation for everyone, not just those who attend education schools, and paying teachers in a manner commensurate with the important work they do. Any other talk about teacher education reform is just empty rhetoric."[54]

Taylor: "There's a prevailing attitude that the legislature is trying to choke public education. . . . I can say that there's that feeling out there in our school community."[55]

Easton: Why would anyone do that to kids?

Taylor: Do what?

Easton: Why would legislators purposely try to damage schools that serve the vast majority of children in this state? "During the 2011 session, our legislature delivered a series of changes to K–12 education that . . . will result in a profound difference in the lives of [the state's] children while greatly improving the prospects of our state. This breakthrough came in the form of four pieces of landmark legislation emphasizing teacher quality, administrative flexibility, school accountability, and parent and student choice.

Prior to [that] session, 99 percent of Indiana's teachers were annually rated 'Effective.' If that rating were actually true, 99 percent—not just one-third—of our students would be passing national tests. [Now], because of the diligence and fortitude of our reform-minded legislators, teachers [are] promoted and retained based on performance rather than seniority. Teacher evaluations, which [are] locally formulated . . . rely on student improvement. Successful educators [are] rewarded, while those whose students lag behind [are] asked to find work elsewhere. Additionally, schools [are] now . . . graded on an A–F scale and they, too, [are] held accountable for student advancement; and the state [does] not hesitate to intervene in those schools that fail repeatedly. While collective bargaining has its place, teacher contracts are too often filled with provisions that hinder learning. Some contracts, for example, stipulate that instructors can spend only a limited amount of hours with their students, while others mandate they can only be observed in the classroom with prior notice from principals. Collective bargaining [is] now . . . limited to wages and benefits and . . . no longer stand[s] in the way of effective school leadership or student progress. Lastly, and perhaps most importantly, we . . . now honor parents. We . . . trust them and respect them enough to decide when, where, and how their children can receive the best education, and therefore the best chance in life. To accomplish this, we [have ended] all restrictions on charter school creation and increasing non-governmental school options through what is now the nation's largest voucher program. . . . [N]o . . . family will be denied the opportunity to choose an appropriate school, including having the ability to direct government dollars toward their school's tuition.

. . . These are not partisan reforms: Our ultimate goals are shared by President Obama and find favor across a broad ideological and political spectrum. . . . [Our state's] historic breakthrough proves that change is within reach, if the debate is focused on the children. Each reform must be tested against the obvious—yet often overlooked—criteria of what is best for the child and most likely to lead to his or her progress, and ultimately, success."[56]

Snepp: I'm trying to make sense out of the statement that if 99 percent of teachers are effective, then 99 percent of students should be passing national tests. First of all, equating teachers' effectiveness solely with students' scores on national tests is absurd and offensive. But let's forget that and focus on the statistics. Would you say then that because only 33 percent of students pass, only 33 percent of teachers are effective? It's not a situation where all the students in some teachers' classrooms pass and all the students in other teachers' classrooms fail. It's much more likely that the pass rate in many teachers' classrooms is around 33 percent, with some having higher pass rates and some having lower pass rates—in other words, the pass rates are normally distributed. For the sake of argument, suppose every teacher had a 33 percent pass rate. By your reasoning, I'm guessing that means every one of those teachers should be rated as ineffective. Or, let's assume for simplicity that all teachers have the same number of students in their classrooms. Then, out of 100 teachers, if 95 have a pass rate of 34 percent and 5 have a pass rate of 14 percent, the average pass rate for the 100 teachers is 33 percent. Granted, that's not a normal distribution, but from your point of view, who's effective now? Are 95 percent effective because they are higher than average? Or are they all still ineffective? Don't try to answer that because that conception of effectiveness is nonsense. Furthermore, your understanding of statistics seems to be, to put it charitably, unknowledgeable. Finally, you mentioned teacher evaluations relying on student improvement. But your 99 percent vs. 33 percent argument does not consider improvement at all.

Anderson: I agree with most of what Easton said and, in addition, I think we need to end teacher unions' "dominance over K–12 education policy." They haven't done anything to fix the system. It's stuck in a rut. The collective-bargaining reform that Easton mentioned will help public schools compete with charter schools and private schools that accept vouchers because public school administrators will no longer be constrained by those aspects of teachers' contracts that hindered learning. Low-performing schools will have to improve if they want to remain in existence. Competition is going to result in improved performance for all schools.[57]

Quinn: Since when have unions dominated K–12 education policy?

Anderson: For example, their insistence on seniority-based placements hampered administrators from getting the best people in the right positions.

Quinn: Unions have had little influence on curriculum or school structure. You say they haven't done anything to fix the system, but that is not their job; their job is to make sure their members are treated fairly.

Easton: Market forces and competition are what is needed to promote innovation and improvement in schools. We can't allow unions to interfere with that.

Foster: At root, this is a question of what public money should be used for. Education is the principal determinant of earnings. We need to pay attention to that. "You can't be a lifelong learner if you're not a lifelong earner."[58] Families should have options and the ability to spend their money in a way that best meets their needs.

Snepp: Well which is it, public money or their money?

Oates: You can't be a lifelong earner if you're not a lifelong learner.

Quinn: I would say that "choice and the attack on public education, at its root, is about decreasing government spending and lowering taxes."[59]

Ulrich: As we have just heard, it's also about destroying teachers' unions. Corporate leaders and their political cronies have been trying to destroy unions for some time. With unions out of the way, the corporate world will have nearly total control of economic policy in this country. Teachers' unions form one of the largest and more powerful blocs of labor. So corporate education reformers are trying to weaken them by lobbying for policies that favor union-free charter schools and policies that give public monies to union-free private schools. Corporate education reformers actually don't want to find areas of agreement with unions because they want to eliminate the unions.[60]

Van Houten: Here's what bothers me about the business approach to reform. "Today's education reformers believe that schools are broken and that business can supply the remedy. Some place their faith in the idea of competition. Others embrace disruptive innovation, mainly through online learning. Both camps share the belief that the solution resides in the impersonal, whether it's the invisible hand of the market or the transformative power of technology. Neither strategy has lived up to its hype, and with good reason. It's impossible to improve education by doing an end run around inherently complicated and messy human relationships. All youngsters need to believe that they have a stake in the future, a goal worth striving for, if they're going to make it in school. They need a champion, someone who believes in them, and that's where teachers enter the picture. The most effective approaches foster bonds of caring between teachers and their students.

Marketplace mantras dominate policy discussions. High-stakes reading and math tests are treated as the single metric of success, the counterpart to the business bottom line. Teachers whose students do poorly on those tests get pink slips, while those whose students excel receive merit pay, much as businesses pay bonuses to their star performers and fire the laggards. Just as companies shut stores that aren't meeting their sales quotas, opening new ones in more promising territory, failing schools are closed and so-called turnaround model schools, with new teachers and administrators, take their place. . . . Merit pay invites rivalries among teachers, when what's needed is collaboration. Closing schools treats everyone there as guilty of causing low test scores, ignoring the difficult lives of the children in these schools—'no excuses,' say the reformers, as if poverty were an excuse. . . . While these reformers talk a lot about markets and competition, the essence of a good education—bringing together talented teachers, engaged students and a challenging curriculum—goes undiscussed. . . . While technology can be put to good use by talented teachers, they, and not the futurists, must take the lead. The process of teaching and learning is an intimate act that neither computers nor markets can hope to replicate. Small wonder, then, that the business model hasn't worked in reforming the schools—there is simply no substitute for the personal element."[61]

Ulrich: The ironic thing about U.S. education is that people far removed from schools and classrooms—politicians, billionaire philanthropists, corporate executives (especially of textbook and testing companies), federal and state education bureaucrats, and college admissions officers—have more influence on education policy and practice than teachers and school administrators. These influencers, with their focus on standardized test scores, ensure that students spend their time memorizing (and then forgetting) irrelevant facts and learning to imitate low-level procedures that they won't be able to apply to real-life problems. Students are being forced to learn facts and skills that are easy to measure, but they are not being prepared to participate in an economy that requires the ability to innovate. It is not even clear that they are being prepared for college; they are being prepared to have an impressive college application. They are engaged in very little hands-on work. Additionally, non-academic skills and the students who possess them receive scant attention. The result is that students leave school without the knowledge or skill set that could help them forge their own path in the world.[62]

Xander: Yes, "unless a testing and accountability program is part of a larger effort that includes educational enrichment and teacher professional development we get, instead, a focus on scores, rankings, and an elaborate technology of calibration and compliance. . . . The model of change has to be built on deep knowledge of how the organization works, its history, its context, its practices. The model of change in Race to the Top seems to be drawn from ideas in the air about modern business, ideas about competition, innovation, quick transformation, and metrics—an amalgam of the economistic and the technocratic. This is not a model of change appropriate for schools . . . they are more than a business and have as their ultimate goal the development of children."[63]

Oates: Foster said that what is at issue for the business reformers is what public money should be used for. Perhaps the issue is simply money. When one reads or hears about corporate education reform in the media today, the story is most often told in terms of two competing groups: teachers' unions and the corporate reformers. The teachers' unions are typically portrayed as the bad guys, fighting reform efforts in order to preserve their cushy contracts. They are not fighting them because they are concerned about the impacts of the reforms on student learning. The good guys are the corporate elites including Rupert Murdoch, the Walton family, Mark Zuckerberg, and various venture capitalists and hedge fund managers who, we are to believe, don't care about making money in education, but just want to see all children—rich, poor, white, black, brown—get a good education. The fact that they make their living on Wall Street and have intimate acquaintance with privatization schemes designed to bleed money from public institutions for their own profit is just a coincidence. "No, in the standard fairy tale sold as education journalism, these 'reformers' are presented as having had an honest, entirely altruistic 'epiphany' that led them to discover that the reforms that are necessary (i.e., only the policies Wall Street deems acceptable) comprise 'the civil rights issue of this era.' In this framing, millionaires and billionaires trying to eviscerate traditional public education from their Manhattan office suites are the new Martin Luther Kings—even though the empirical data tell us that their schemes to charter-ize and privatize schools have been a systemic failure, often further disadvantaging the most economically challenged students of all (one example: see Stanford's landmark study showing more than a third of kids whom reformers ushered into charter schools were educationally harmed by the move). The truth, of course, is that for all the denialist agitprop to the contrary, corporate education 'reformers' are motivated by self-interest, too."[64]

Inglehart: What are their self-interests?

Oates: Money is the biggest one. Private companies supply the standardized tests and sell alternatives to traditional school curricula to charter schools. Beyond that, there is a lot of money to be made by investors. For example, Rupert Murdoch gave $1 million to a reform effort in New York City that aimed to increase standardized testing and re-route money from teachers, textbooks, and school maintenance into technology for assessment. Simultaneously, Murdoch purchased an educational technology company. This company had just signed a large contract with the New York City schools. The New York City school official responsible for the contract, Joel Klein, then went to work for Murdoch. Investors profit, testing companies and technology companies profit, charter school management organizations profit.

There is also a significant tax break, called the New Markets Tax Credit, for banks and investors who lend money to finance the construction of new charter schools. Also, the reallocation of money for public schools to finance voucher programs has been a gold mine for the for-profit charter school industry. According to PBS Frontline, Wall Street has been trying to capitalize on the charter school industry for some time. It seems that in the eyes of corporate reformers, the purpose of education is not to educate students, but simply to make money. They spend millions of dollars advertising the reforms and supporting candidates who will legislate the reforms because the enactment of the reforms will mean huge payoffs for their investments in education. "In light of all the money that's already being made off such 'reforms' (and that could be made in the future), pretending that businesspeople who make their living on such transactions are not applying their business strategies to education is to promote the fallacy that the entire financial industry is merely a charitable endeavor."[65]

Ulrich: The schools in our state capital are now managed by a portfolio model.

Blanchard: Like a stock portfolio?

Ulrich: Yes. "The operational theory behind portfolio districts is based on a stock market metaphor—the stock portfolio under the control of a portfolio manager. If a stock is low performing, the manager sells it. As a practical matter, this means either closing the school or turning it over to a charter school or other management organization. When reopened, the building is generally reconstituted, in terms of teachers, curriculum and administration. In theory, this process of closing, rebidding and reconstituting continues until the school and the entire portfolio is high performing. These approaches have been described (positively) as 'creative destruction' or (negatively) as 'churn.'"[66]

Ross: "While the Mind Trust [a venture capital fund and charter school incubator] and Stand for Children [an education advocacy group] would have [city] residents believe these reforms are community-driven, in essence, the influence they wield over [the school district] and the school board is not dissimilar to what happens when a state takes over a school district. The Mind Trust and its web of connections in the statehouse, the mayor's office, the Chamber of Commerce and countless other high-level organizations, institutions and foundations, both around the city and nationally, determine much of what happens in [the district]. But the longer the Mind Trust operates in the city, the clearer it becomes that these forces are focused on turning [district] schools over to private operators, and often the operators selected by the Mind Trust fail to demonstrate levels of student success higher than the schools they are tapped to replace."[67]

Xander: 2011 was a good year for lobbyists pushing online education. Several states enacted laws to permit the expansion of online or virtual education. The success stemmed from the combination of corporate backers dangling large amounts of money and think tanks and foundations supporting privatization of education. Though the reforms passed into law would clearly increase the profits of education-technology companies, they were presented as efforts to improve students' education through the use of technology. With the use of technology expanding everywhere, who was going to argue with that? The increase in laws authorizing virtual education attracted even more investors to the education reform market. Corporate education reformers typically claim their primary concern is improving learning opportunities for children. However, at a 2011 conference for education start-up companies and potential investors, investment banker Michael Moe touted the enormous opportunity the education reform market presented investors. Moe had been working for over a decade to find ways to turn the K–12 education system into a source of profit for investors. He oversees an investment group and consulting firms that help businesses obtain a slice of the $1 trillion pie of tax revenues spent each year across the country on education. At the conference, Moe called education "the next big 'undercapitalized' sector of the economy, like healthcare in the 1990s."[68]

Walter: "Educating the young, like protecting them from serial killers, should be regarded as a social responsibility, not as a matter of profit."[69]

Xander: Moe believes that the school privatization movement will grow even faster following the legislative successes of 2011. In the wake of the Great Recession, as schools around the country try to get by with substantially reduced budgets, online education is an attractive cost-saving alternative to traditional schools. At one virtual school in Florida, the cost is almost $2500 less per student than at traditional public schools. Idaho, Indiana, and Florida passed laws that will allow expansion of online education options and for-profit K–12 schools. Some students may complete their entire education online via a public school managed by a for-profit online education provider. In some cases, this will mean entrusting the education of students to online education providers who have little or no experience. Essentially, students will be guinea pigs in an online learning experiment.[70]

Druley: Students are guinea pigs in any new approach.

Oates: Students are guinea pigs in any new approach that views education as something that is *done to* children.

Karch: This is not to say that all online education is bad. Adaptive programs for students with special needs, online AP classes for rural schools where no teacher is available, virtual labs—these are areas where online education can be useful. But there is little evidence that students are well-served when they complete the entire curriculum online. In fact, a Stanford University study of virtual schools in Pennsylvania found that students in online schools performed significantly worse than students attending school in traditional school buildings. Additionally, a study by the University of Colorado published in 2010 showed that 30 percent of for-profit virtual schools met the minimum progress levels set by No Child Left Behind whereas 54.9 percent of traditional schools reached these levels.[71]

Easton: Wait a minute! I thought you didn't care what the numbers say.

Karch: I did not say that. I believe Grable made a comment to that effect.

Grable: I did. This whole discussion of corporate education reform is making me feel sick to my stomach and like I want to bang my head against the table at the same time. I may have a comment in a little while if I can compose myself.

Ziegler: "Why are our legislators rushing to jump off the cliff of cyber charter schools when the best available evidence produced by independent analysts show that such schools will be unsuccessful?"[72]

Quinn: The legislators, both Democrat and Republican, are doing the bidding of their corporate sponsors and for the corporate sponsors it's not about education—it's about money.

Newcomer: It seems that venture capitalists and philanthropists have figured out a way to create and fund for-profit virtual school companies that essentially use philanthropy as a Trojan horse to reap profits.[73]

Druley: You know, we discussed how educators' initial rationale for inquiry-oriented reforms was swept aside by politicians' mantra of preparing students to compete in the global economy. It seems to me that Harris's firm's rationale for their STEM reform effort was swept aside by a broader rush for profits. And, in contrast to what Newcomer just said, perhaps the philanthropists' good intentions were taken advantage of by charter school managers and testing and textbook companies.

Yann: Corporate education reformers may not like to hear this, but one thing educational research has shown us is that socioeconomic status has a stronger relationship to student achievement than any other factors, including the quality of teachers, the prevalence of unions, and the organizational structure of schools. An article in *The Nation* reported on research showing that socioeconomic background accounts for 60 percent of student achievement while teaching accounts for 15 percent. Reviewing data from the U.S. Department of Education, *Dissent* magazine found that students from public schools with a poverty rate below 10 percent scored higher on an international test than students from the other eight participating countries with poverty rates below 10 percent. In other words, U.S. students from low-poverty schools perform quite well on international tests. But the United States' overall scores are much worse because we have more poverty than other advanced nations and students from high-poverty schools tend to score much worse on these tests. The Great Recession exacerbated these problems. As the middle class shrinks, fewer families can afford to live in wealthy districts where school funding is based on property taxes.

A study by the University of Kansas showed how property tax-based funding essentially allows wealthy school districts to "hoard" public money for their schools while poorer districts naturally have to make do with much less. This disparity in money is associated with disparity in test scores between wealthy and poor districts. "This structure is hugely beneficial to the super-rich—but the poverty question poses a potential political problem for them. As the *New York Times* recently put it, if America realizes that 'a substantial part of the problem [is] poverty and not bad teachers, the question would be why people like [Wall Streeters] are allowed to make so much when others have so little.'" In recent years wealth inequality has become a topic in political discussions. Some politicians are calling for a return to more regulations on Wall Street, increasing taxes on the wealthy, and modifying school funding formulas so that more money is directed to schools in high-poverty districts. Of course, neither corporations nor the wealthy are fond of such policies. To protect their interests, they have formed groups such as "Democrats for Education Reform," which try to steer the discussion away from public policies that contribute to poverty. They do this by continually denigrating the quality of schools and teachers. They criticize the structure of public schools. Also, they reject the argument that we need to raise taxes on the wealthy in order to provide more funds for schools by saying that "we can't throw money at the problem." Of course, this ignores the data I cited earlier that suggests that combating poverty could narrow the achievement gap. But by claiming that school choice is the "civil rights issue of this era," corporate education reformers create a narrative that makes it appear they are concerned about the plight of the poor, but at the same time that narrative inhibits discussion about the economic policies that enable the top 10 percent of the population to continue to get richer at the expense of the bottom 90 percent.[74]

Newcomer: Well, as we discussed, there are problems with the "structure of public schools." But still, that's twisted—they're basically taking advantage of poverty to make money.

Carpenter: "We treasure the occasional story about a child who climbs out of poverty, graduates from a prestigious university, and goes on to success. Since it's possible for a handful, we cling to the view that nothing is broken in America. But it is. Education has become the modern American caste system. We fuzz up the issue in a sea of statistics about test-score gaps, suggesting social inequity is a classroom issue. We bemoan the achievement gap but dwell on the wrong "achievement" and the wrong "gap." Achievement should be based on challenging real-world problems, not standardized tests that amount to little more than timed performance on crossword puzzles and sudoku. The gap we need to face is how much more we spend to educate our rich children than our poor."[75]

Grable: I am amazed (appalled) at the arrogance and ignorance of education reformers. The business reformers seem to have ignored the history of school reform efforts. If we give them the benefit of the doubt and assume that they are not motivated only by making money, they seem to believe that they can step in and apply business principles to fix the problems with education that no one else has been able to fix. The free market, choice, test-based accountability, application of "big data analytics"—these will fix everything. Trust us; we know what we're doing. Don't take this the wrong way. I believe many educational researchers are equally arrogant and ignorant when it comes to education reform. They have created an insulated community of academics with norms for educational theory and practice that virtually ensure they will have little impact on what occurs in school classrooms. If they remain unwilling to engage in social and political analysis of factors that impinge on classroom practices and unwilling to engage in political action, their research will remain ineffective in fostering change. Schools of education are not much better. Our former governor may have been a blockhead, but his critique of schools of education was not entirely misplaced. To see this, one only needs to ask graduates of these schools how their teacher education program was relevant to the daily classroom reality they experience. Schools of education have not questioned the traditional structure of schools that Peterson discussed, nor have they questioned their place in that structure. Thus, their efforts, however well-intentioned, have little effect on school reform.

Foster: Do you have anyone else you would like to criticize?

Yann: I see a similarity between the current corporate education reform we have been discussing and the scientific management reforms of the early twentieth century. As we noted, back then ideas about efficiency influenced the language and, to some extent, the practice of education. To paraphrase Grable, the view seemed to be that "scientific management" could solve any problem. Today, it is business science—a combination of economic theories, statistical data analysis, and technology—that reformers offer as the cure-all to education's ills. The language of business science, precise and authoritative, breeds confidence that it is the path to success. Playing into this framework is the fact that almost no one questions anymore that the purpose of school is economic—to prepare students for jobs that will enable them to make a living and that will help the U.S. compete in a global economy. This focus on job preparation together with business people's faith in the business science framework and their general ignorance about the complexities of teaching and learning have led reformers to discount the importance of teachers' classroom knowledge. In spite of what corporate reformers may think, "teaching and learning are not simply technical and management problems. Reformers need to incorporate rather than disregard the rich wisdom of the classroom, for the history of policy failure is littered with cases where local knowledge and circumstance were ignored. . . . Business-school alliances will not result in fundamental, long-range educational change if the terms of the alliances essentially have the powerful passing judgment and bestowing dollars on beleaguered classrooms. . . . [The American philosopher George Santayana said], 'Those who cannot remember the past are condemned to repeat it.' If Santayana wanted a textbook-perfect illustration of his aphorism, he could find it in both the approach and the rhetoric of contemporary school reform."[76]

Harris: I believe that "what we need is to learn the discipline of business without the short-term orientation. Markets are amoral. A competitive market will determine a fair price whether for cocaine or cocoa, but not necessarily the enduring social value. A one-year increase of 25 percent in the price of a house does not reveal the underlying forces causing the price increase, or its real value. Markets do not know the worth of a mature forest three generations hence. Nor can a market accurately determine the lifetime value of thoughtful exposure to the classics or art or music. Enduring acts of civility are not bought and sold. The qualities that professional educators worry about often do not lend themselves to short-term market valuation. We can learn from business to allocate resources responsibly, have transparent and disciplined budgets, and plan for a more secure financial future. At the same time, we need to avoid the hubris of business 'success.'"[77]

Newcomer: Snepp, Ziegler, Ulrich, and several others have highlighted the importance of trust in reform efforts. Perhaps this is not a common concept in business, but the ideas of W. Edwards Deming are an exception. Deming was a statistician and management consultant. He "based his quality management philosophy on two seemingly disparate ideas: The use of statistical tools to measure and improve systems and the conviction that those closest to any given process are best equipped to identify problems and opportunities for improvement. What made Deming's ideas controversial was his insistence that meaningful employee input only works if it is based on trust. Deming opposed punitive employee evaluations and individual bonus systems on the grounds that they foster fear and undermine teamwork. Deming's ideas about process measurement were embraced throughout industry, but his exhortations on the importance of building a culture of trust were not. . . . [However, a school district in Leander, Texas recently implemented both of Deming's primary ideas.] The school district adopted Deming's ideas about using statistical analysis and teamwork to improve classroom pedagogy and school design, and even to jump-start a student-led anti-bullying campaign. But to sustain its strategy and build a trust-based culture of the kind Deming advocated, Leander [had to obtain] a waiver from the state's teacher-evaluation system."[78]

Blanchard: I'm glad we discussed corporate education reform and perhaps there are some business ideas, as Newcomer just mentioned, that could benefit education, but I see very little in the broader corporate education reform movement that's going to improve educational experiences for students. Learning occurs in interactions between teachers and students, in interactions between students, and in activities that engage students with literature, history, science, mathematics, etc. The reforms proposed by the corporate reformers are so far removed from the micro, interpersonal level at which learning occurs that they will have no effect on learning. They may have negative effects such as increasing the segregation of school populations and increasing the reliance on online learning, results which will decrease the quality and frequency of conversations between teachers and students. Lawrence noted that vouchers and charter schools might provide an opportunity to create schools very different from traditional schools. But so far it seems the vast majority of the private companies administering these schools are giving us more of the "same old, same old."

Newcomer: Perhaps that is one reason why Mike Petrilli, the president of the Thomas B. Fordham Institute, which has been a leading advocate of corporate education reform, recently stated that "the 2017 results from the National Assessment of Educational Progress indicate a 'lost decade' of academic achievement. . . . Trends [in education] have left policymakers and philanthropists feeling glum about reform, given the growing narrative that, like so many efforts before it, the modern wave hasn't worked or delivered the goods, yet has produced much friction, fractiousness, and furor."[79]

VISIONS FOR EDUCATION: WE NEED LESS EDUCATION

Inglehart: I have a proposal. "Most critics of our education system complain we aren't spending our money in the right way. . . . These critics miss what I see as our educational system's supreme defect: *there's way too much education*. . . . Think about all the classes you ever took. How many failed to teach you *any* useful skills? . . . From kindergarten on, students spend thousands of hours studying subjects irrelevant to the modern labor market. How can this be? Why do English classes focus on literature and poetry instead of business and technical writing? Why do advanced math classes bother with proofs almost no student can follow? When will the typical student use history? Trigonometry? Art? Music? Physics? "Physical Education"? Spanish? French? Latin! . . . The class clown who snarks, 'What does this have to do with real life?' is on to something."[80]

Van Houten: Is the only purpose of education to teach useful skills?

Inglehart: Good question. A common argument for keeping some of the subjects I mentioned is that they help form well-rounded citizens. Or they provide enrichment. If that was true, why do so many students find these subjects to be so boring? I'm not saying that all learning has to have a practical use. It is also true that not all learning has to be inspiring. But if it has neither a practical use nor is it inspiring, it is nothing but a waste of time (and money). "Education definitely *can* be good for the soul. But that hardly shows actually existing education achieves this noble end. In practice, education often turns out to be a neglectful or abusive mother rather than a nourishing one."[81]

Johnson: I agree that many of the courses I took in high school and college were a waste of time. But why then are college admissions officers and employers so concerned about applicants' education?

Inglehart: Lawrence has already identified the reason: credentials. Admissions officers and employers aren't actually interested in applicants' education—they're interested in their educational record. I refer to this as 'signaling.' One's educational record provides useful signals about one's ability and character. It doesn't matter that what students learn in school is of no practical use in the labor market; their educational record provides information about what type of workers they will be. The stronger their academic record, the more likely they will be productive workers. Employers have figured this out and their pay scales are based on it. Employees aren't paid for the useless knowledge they learned in school (and probably have long since forgotten). They are paid because the fact that they mastered this knowledge and got good grades says something about their character. In particular, a strong academic record signals intelligence, conscientiousness, and conformity. Employers know school is boring, but if you had the stick-to-it-iveness to grind through the boredom and get good marks, that tells them something about your work ethic. Also, if you were a model student, that tells employers that you are likely to be a model worker who will conform to social and company expectations. In other words, succeeding in a school environment tells employers you are likely to succeed in a work environment, irrespective of what you may or may not have learned in school. Couldn't something else signal a worker's potential to employers? In theory, yes, but in practice, no. Although there are alternatives to traditional education, our society has elevated the standard path—K–12 followed by college or university—to such a status that, for most jobs, nothing else is deemed acceptable.[82]

Anderson: So, the signaling system works efficiently for colleges and employers. Add that to the list of factors inhibiting reform efforts.

Blanchard (to Inglehart): This makes sense, but what do you propose to do about it?

Inglehart: If education was all about developing worthwhile skills, a decrease in the amount of education people receive would be a bad thing. Less skilled workers would mean less production. But if education is all about acquiring credentials, then a decrease in the amount of education would have no effect on the skills workers possess and therefore no effect on production. In this case, a decrease in education would actually save society money because less would be wasted on irrelevant learning. This is why I am against government subsidies for education. It is a waste of money to help students acquire even more useless knowledge. It would be better for society if education was less affordable. Of course, education is not all signaling. Students do learn some useful skills—reading, writing, and basic mathematics. But it is more signaling than skill development. If education was less affordable, employers wouldn't expect prospective employees to possess as much. However, that would not be a problem because the employees don't need this extra education anyway. "Ultimately, I believe the best education policy is no education policy at all: the separation of school and state."[83]

Anderson: In other words, leave education to the free market?

Inglehart: Yes. It is certainly to employers' advantage to be able to rank prospective workers. This ranking results in greater productivity for businesses and thus more wealth for society as a whole. The ranking of students has social value. But if everyone had one less degree, the ranking system would still produce the same results.[84]

Easton: As several others have argued, we need to educate students so that they have the knowledge and skills needed to be innovative. How are you going to accomplish that with less education?[85]

Inglehart: That "sounds plausible—until you recall the otherworldliness of the curriculum. In high school, students spend only about a quarter of their time on math and science. In college, about 5 percent of students major in engineering, 2 percent in computer science, and 5 percent in biology and biomedical science."[86]

Druley: And all other school subjects are worthless?

Inglehart: Most other school subjects are worthless. Certainly, companies would rather have weak readers than employees who can't read at all. But for subjects that students forget after graduation and never use, it would be a good idea to impose very high standards that most students cannot meet. Music is a good example. Many students who will never have a career in music fritter away years on it in school. If music teachers set their standards so high that only the top 20 percent of the class could pass, much waste would be eliminated and those students who are able to remain in the class might actually be able to forge a career in music. In my view, an even better approach is to simply cut such impractical classes from the curriculum. They are a waste of taxpayer money. "There really is no need for K–12 to teach history, social studies, art, music, or foreign languages. This is especially clear if you recall how much students forget: despite years of schoolwork, American adults can't date the Civil War, name their congressman, draw, sing, or speak French." Now you might argue that we need to try to do a better job teaching these subjects so that students retain more. But the chance of this actually working seems slim—educational researchers have been working on this problem for years—and the cost of professional development for teachers and reteaching of students will be high.

A similar argument applies at the college level. Eliminate impractical majors at public colleges; at private colleges, students in impractical majors should not be eligible for government grants or loans. We need to raise tuition at public colleges. We need to get rid of government subsidies and grants. Grants should become loans that charge market interest rates. Taxpayers should not be bearing the cost of education. Students and their families should. Even public high schools should charge some tuition. If we increase the cost of education, students will be less inclined to pursue majors that will be of no use to them or to society. "Common sense insists the best way to discover useful ideas is to search for useful ideas—not to search for whatever fascinates you and pray it turns out to be useful."[87]

Harris: "But we need to invest in people!"

Inglehart: "We usually rely on the free market to provide crucial investments. We can do the same for education."

Newcomer: "Nothing is more important than education!"

Inglehart: "Food's more important, and we rely on the free market for that."

Quinn: "Government has to make sure even the poorest children receive a good education!"

Inglehart: "Means-tested vouchers can cheaply handle this problem. There's no need for government to run schools or subsidize tuition for kids who *aren't* poor."[88]

Inglehart: Granted, most people abhor the idea of increasing the cost of education for students and their families. For one thing, we believe that the poor will be hurt most by such a policy. Quinn's argument is a common one. It is based on social justice rather than social return. And it would be correct if education was primarily job skill development. In that case, raising tuition would result in less education for all and a less skilled workforce. The poor would be especially hard hit; they can afford the least education so they will have the least skills and earn the lowest wages. However, because education is mostly signaling, the poor really won't be disadvantaged by shifting the cost of education to students. Why? One poor student can be helped greatly by a scholarship. But if all poor students receive scholarships, the value of their credentials is diluted, and wealthier students will just purchase more credentials. This is inflation in the world of academic credentials. It serves to maintain social inequality. Government subsidies for education actually work against social justice. In the early part of the 20th century, you didn't need a high school diploma to get a good job. By mid-century you did, but you didn't need a college degree. Now you do. As levels of education have risen, people have needed to acquire more credentials in order to obtain well-paying jobs. "The hundreds of billions our society fritters away on education every year could make a giant dent in these [other] dire [social] problems. . . . Taxing people to fund programs with modest or debatable social benefits strikes me as deeply wrong." In my view, government should not use tax revenue to support education in any way. The only sources of school funding should be tuition and donations from private foundations and individuals. I am not a fan of charter schools, vouchers, and school choice. As I have argued, the credential inflation problem stems not from poor quality education, but from too much education. Having more choices isn't going to address this problem. We don't need more choices; we need much less education. Leaving education to the free market, with no government subsidies, could go a long way to achieving this goal.[89]

Druley: Instead of arguing for less education, why not work to try to fix the education system we have?

Inglehart: You mean, "let's transform our schools from time sinks to skill factories"? As I noted, educational researchers have been trying to find ways to improve the learning of basic skills for years with little success. "The logical inference is either (a) pinpointing ways to improve basic skills is elusive or (b) schools spurn the methods that work."[90]

Grable: Skill factories?

Yann: Well, if you examine the purpose of education and the conception of teaching and learning underlying Inglehart's argument, that's the best schools could hope to be. For him, the sole purpose of schools is to prepare students to get a job. Teaching consists of transmitting facts, which students "learn" by memorizing. In his view, history is equated with knowing names and dates. The idea that by studying history, philosophy, and literature one might develop ways of looking at the world, interpreting events, and approaching social, political, and economic problems that could be equally, or, in some cases, perhaps more beneficial than the methods STEM disciplines provide seems not to occur to him.

Quinn: Inglehart's argument about forgetting doesn't hold up. Yes, students forget facts from history and social studies. They forget much of what they learn about foreign languages. You could say the same thing about math. Students forget a great deal. Why is there so much repetition in the mathematics curriculum from year to year? Maybe the problem is with the way history and social studies (and math) are taught, not that they are taught.

Ross: The statement about music was particularly telling. The only reason to study music is so you will have a career in it? I'm pretty sure my kids know they will not be professional musicians, but I believe their experience in band and choir will enable them to enjoy singing and playing instruments for the rest of their lives. But for Inglehart, education is all about productivity; nothing else has value.

Grable: I was curious by what rationale he believes students are searching for "useful" ideas or view their future in as strictly utilitarian terms as he does.

Oates: Inglehart thinks that taxing people to fund education that has debatable social benefits is deeply wrong. I find his view of the purpose of education and the conception of "social benefits" that follows from it deeply wrong.

Easton: I will admit that I have some qualms about Inglehart's proposal, but I do like the "separation of school and state" idea. Parents have the right to control their children's education; the government should not control it.

Grable: There's that word "control" again.

Blanchard: I wonder why the critical theorists don't support separation of school and state. They argue that government is using schools to promote beliefs and attitudes that maintain the status quo and keep the current class of elites in power.

Carpenter: The government, and therefore schools, are largely controlled by big-business elites. Separating school and state would only give big business more direct control of schooling. The critical theorists don't want that.

Yann: That's the irony in Easton's view. He seems to think that separation of school and state means more freedom for parents and students when the more likely result is it means even greater control of schools by the business sector. Where's the freedom in that?

Easton: A free market in education is not controlled by the business sector. It's controlled by consumers—parents and students. As a result of increased competition, only schools that meet consumers' needs will survive.

Druley: That seems naïve or idyllic or both. Through advertising and control of the options provided, business influences what consumers believe they need.

And if you don't believe this, consider why you are referring to parents and students as "consumers" and, by inference, to education as a commodity. If views like this are the consequence of Inglehart's "separation of school and state," I am not in favor of such a proposal.

Inglehart: Let's be clear. I don't expect educational decision makers to implement my ideas any time soon. Our society is too enamored with a romantic vision of the benefits education supposedly provides. As a consequence of this deeply held cultural belief, even separation of school and state may not result in improved education. I was advocating the idea primarily because I don't think government should waste tax dollars on education that provides little to no benefit to individuals or society. When educators talk about our traditional curriculum "broadening horizons," it is really just a tack to quell the question, "Why do we have to learn this stuff?" Succeeding in suppressing this question is not the same as engaging students in education that they find intrinsically interesting. Broadening horizons would allow students to explore, not force them to study the same curricula everyone else has been forced to study for decades. "Regimentation may be a good way to mold external behavior, but it's a bad way to win hearts and minds—and a terrible way to foster thoughtful commitment."[91]

VISIONS FOR EDUCATION: ANYBODY HERE SEEN MY OLD FRIEND JOHN? (PART II)

Walter: "I have a proposal. We think of schools as places where the young are prepared for life. I say we discard that idea and instead think of them as full-blown, rich, fascinatingly complex, real-world slices of life. Let's treat schools themselves as powerful learning resources, as things to poke, prod, measure, examine, investigate, analyze, describe, take apart, and put back together differently to see if they work better. . . . Let's use the schools we have to operationalize the schools we need, call it 'The Project,' and make it the only universally required course. . . . No other project will more thoroughly engage emotion. Challenging kids and their teachers to put The Project to real-world use by continuously improving their own school shows a respect for firsthand experience and those who have it that's presently non-existent. It maximizes autonomy—the engine of imagination, creativity, ingenuity, and successful adaptation to social change. It puts our actions where our mouths are when we talk about liberty, democracy, and individual worth. It replaces top-down mandates (which have never, ever improved classroom instruction), with the only kind of innovation that works and sticks—bottom up. . . . If you're concerned about all that material you studied in school that you don't think The Project would 'cover,' accept the fact that 'covering the material' isn't educating. It's ritual. Covering the material is what has brought education to crisis. It's what drives mile-wide-inch-deep 'learning' that evaporates as soon as tested. It's why adults retain so little of what they were once 'taught.' It's what underlies the institution's fad-prone but static nature. . . . We have to get past the assumption that rigorous math, science, language arts, and social studies instruction add up to a quality education; past the notion that educating is mostly a matter of transferring information; past the denigrating idea that the point of it all is just to prepare the young for college or work. Humanness has far more to offer than that . . .

One more thing: accountability. Those hostile to public schooling have blown it far out of proportion, so the public demands that the matter be addressed. Because The Project will trigger thought processes far too complex and idiosyncratic to be evaluated by standardized tests, contracts will have to be cancelled. Period. There's no way that test items written in cubicles at McGraw-Hill, Pearson, Educational Testing Service, or at any other remote site, can cope. But that's no problem. The job can be returned to those who had it before corporate heads, rich philanthropists, and politicians undermined respect for and confidence in them—classroom teachers. They're on top of the problem. They talk to their students every day, read their papers, watch their body language, listen to their dialogue, laugh at their jokes, cry at their misfortunes, look over their shoulders as they work. No one else is more qualified than teachers to say how well students are doing. And using the already employed will save taxpayers billions of dollars."[92][93]

Newcomer: "Though they are rare at present, there have been a variety of schools where students chose what and how to study. Schools where students routinely discuss the nature and point of what they are learning seem rarer still. Matters of personal conduct and social rules are negotiated by the community in some alternative schools, but questions about the nature of knowledge, about what knowledge is useful, and whether a topic should be studied in a manner consistent with the principles that governed its choice are rarely matters for students' dialogue. Yet these questions are central to any community committed to democratic life. [It is not clear to me that the] Sudbury Valley School . . . provoke[s] inquiry about what knowledge is worthwhile. . . . Students must take responsibility for the nature of their work and become not mere choosers but curriculum theorists. This might promote reflection and discourse on the significance of the work done in school. Without this, the participation of learners in the formation of the purposes that govern their learning is incomplete."[94]

Ulrich: There are more than 500 "Deeper Learning" schools across the United States. Though there are differences among them, they share some common ideas about education. In particular, they emphasize encouraging students to draw on their own experiences and take charge of their own learning. Teachers are not expected to lecture, but to provide guidance based on their own experiences and interests. The skills deemed essential in these schools are "collaboration, communication, creativity, and critical analysis." They emphasize project-based learning and when students complete a project their work is put on public display. Another innovative approach, The Future Project, is transforming schools by encouraging students to create and pursue projects related to their own goals. In the process of completing their projects, students acquire useful skills (including "writing, public speaking, project management, collaboration, and math skills"), learn relevant concepts, and develop solid work habits. Students in these schools become self-motivated and learn to appreciate the assistance of their teachers. Their outlook for the future changes: they start to believe that they can make a difference in the world. "So back to that purpose question. Maybe, in the end, the purpose of school is to help our kids find their *own* sense of purpose." Following the practical and moral failure of the accountability through standardized testing approach, we need an approach to education that will inspire students and teachers. An approach in which students can pursue goals they set for themselves, not goals someone else has set for them.[95]

Druley: This may seem to be off topic, but the turn our discussion has taken has prompted me to think about the relationship between schooling and democracy. "'Democracy is a way of life controlled by a working faith in the possibilities of human nature . . . by faith in the capacity of human beings for intelligent judgment and action if proper conditions are furnished.'[96] . . . [Unfortunately, we live] in a time when scores on the [standardized tests] seem to be the only thing that matters in Washington and the state capitals, a time when legislators regularly appear on television, lengthening the school year, shortening the time for teaching by announcing new tests, declaring standards for graduation from each grade, withdrawing benefits from families of students who do not attend regularly, berating the schools, and ignoring the complex, recalcitrant details of daily life in classrooms. Democracy may not be something that takes place in state capitals, but the seeds of its destruction may be growing there."[97]

Taylor: "We need all we can get in the way of diverse perspectives on education. We do not need researchers or other authorities who circumvent conversation about the ends and means of education by assigning destinations and specifying travel schedules. Rather than trying only to discern whether authorities are speaking *truths* about education, we could put their suggestions to a different test: Do they promote fruitful conversation?"[98]

Newcomer: "We need more conversation across the lines between students and teachers and through the walls that divide them from academic researchers, administrators, legislators, and parents. In the shadow of the quest for certainty, of generalizations about education, and of state and national testing programs, conversation may appear mundane and weak. As Dewey argued, however, the only solution to the problem of education is education: that form of conjoint communicated experience which enables us to extract meaning from experience and promotes the desire for more such experience. That, in the end, is democracy: a rich, adventurous conversation. This is the point and the process of education."[99]

Druley: Yes. "Mutual respect and the making of different perspectives into intellectual and social challenge, even adventure, are, as Dewey hoped to persuade us, the essence of democratic education and democratic life."[100]

Ross: [I have observed that] "students who seek understanding also see collaboration as an effective way to succeed in school. . . . The preoccupation with superiority and the tendency to see much of school as a test both work against this, but the students' ability to address these issues in open discussions is a source of hope. . . . The importance of these discussions does not reside only in the conclusions that emerge from them. It is in the quality of these discussions that the spirit of democracy is most clearly evident and most soundly defended."[101]

Van Houten: We have been discussing how schools might be different, how the teacher-student relationship might be different. What does this mean for teacher education programs? Would they be irrelevant? Or how would they need to change?

Ziegler: I was wondering about that, too. Is a specialized degree even required? Can any intelligent adult teach? Lawrence argued for increasing standards of educator preparation. But what would those standards be if schools change in the ways we have just been discussing?

Peterson: I think prospective teachers "should learn their craft the way a surgeon learns to operate: by intense supervision in a real setting with expert mentors. Student-teachers are usually observed only twice during a semester and then given a written evaluation. But young teachers, like young doctors, should work side by side with skilled mentors, getting plenty of feedback, having plenty of opportunities to observe and taking on greater and greater responsibility as they improve. . . . Therapists spend a great deal of time watching videotapes of themselves in action, reflecting on their sessions and discussing the most difficult moments with senior therapists to explore other ways they might have responded. In much the same way, young teachers need to record their daily encounters with their classrooms and then, with mentors and peers, have serious, open-minded conversations about what's working and what isn't. Teachers must also learn far more about children: typically, teaching students are provided with fairly static and superficial overviews of developmental stages, but learn little about how to watch children, using research and theory to understand what they are seeing. As James Comer, a professor of child psychiatry at Yale, has argued for years, if we disregard the developmental needs of our students it's unlikely we'll succeed in teaching them. . . . To fix our schools, we need teaching programs that are as rich in resources, interesting, high-reaching and thoughtful as the young people we want to attract to the profession. Show me a school where teachers are smart, well-educated, skilled and happy to be there, and I'll show you a group of children who are getting a good education."[102]

Taylor: I think we need to figure out what schools will be before we can figure out what teacher education should be.

Ross: I think it is the opposite. How are you going to change schools if teacher education programs are still producing the same type of teachers?

Grable: Producing?

Carpenter: Maybe they need to evolve together.

Druley: "Evolve" suggests a gradual change. Johnson argued earlier that the type of change we have been discussing cannot be done gradually.

Harris: Perhaps we need to ask, "What is the purpose of teacher education?"

Foster: Good lord!

Moderator (chuckles): The teacher education question seems very important. However, that will have to be a discussion for another time. Our time is up for today. Thank you all for participating. (Now to Blanchard): Are you still feeling pessimistic?

Blanchard: No. Concerned and puzzled, but not so pessimistic. Full of questions, really. "Can schooling become a collaborative quest for excitement and meaning? . . . Might schooling become an adventure, with attendant risks and difficulties, wherein the participants negotiate the nature, direction, and details of the ongoing journey? . . . Can the energy, critical consciousness, and sense of fairness of these [young] people and their peers be engaged in education? Might we create classrooms where social solidarity and moral responsibility coexist with intellectual excitement and adventure?"[103]

Moderator: I know we haven't solved any major problems. But I hope that in our consideration of these problems we touched upon ideas that you will think about and continue to discuss with others who are interested in education—including children.

NOTES

1. Quoted from Seymour B. Sarason, *The Predictable Failure of Educational Reform* (San Francisco: Jossey-Bass, 1990), 73.

2. Upon encountering a section titled "Visions for Education: Anybody Here Seen My Old Friend John . . . ," many people would probably think of John Dewey. And several participants in this roundtable have cited his ideas. But there are two other "Johns" whose writing transcends the staid arrogance and insipid recommendations found in so much writing on education. John Holt was an elementary school teacher (primarily fifth grade) who drew upon his experiences to explain how prevailing beliefs about the purpose of schooling, the organization and methods of schooling, teacher and student roles, and the nature of children combine to make school an uninteresting, confusing, and sometimes threatening place for students. John Nicholls was a university professor and researcher whose focus was achievement motivation. In education circles, he was probably best known for his distinction between ego-involvement (engaged in order to look good or avoid looking bad) and task-involvement (engaged in order to learn). Both of these writers convey a deep, abiding empathy for children, particularly for the underdogs in school. But it is more than empathy. Respect. And a conviction that *all* children are intelligent, are thinkers, are problem

solvers, can contemplate challenging ideas and communicate their responses, and that they can and should participate in the formulation of purposes that guide their education. One gets the feeling that both of these writers have actually listened to children, conversed with them, like them, and care about them. (And although his name is not John, I would include Seymour Sarason in the same group.)

3. Quoted from John Dewey, *Experience and Education* (New York: Simon and Schuster, 1938), 25. This quote appeared in John G. Nicholls and Susan P. Hazzard, *Education as Adventure: Lessons from the Second Grade* (New York: Teachers College Press, 1993), 84.

4. Quoted from Nicholls and Hazzard, *Education as Adventure*, 84.

5. Ibid., 122.

6. Quoted from a transcript of a TED talk given by Sir Ken Robinson. See Ken Robinson, "Do Schools Kill Creativity?," transcript of TED talk, February 2006, https://www.ted.com/talks/ken_robinson_says_schools_kill_creativity/transcript.

7. Paraphrased from Seymour B. Sarason, *School Change: The Personal Development of a Point of View* (New York: Teachers College Press, 1995), 162.

8. Quoted from Nicholls and Hazzard, *Education as Adventure*, 8.

9. Quoted from Frederick Erickson and Jeffrey Shultz, "Students' Experience of the Curriculum," in *Handbook of Research on Curriculum*, ed. Phillip W. Jackson (New York: Macmillan, 1992), 481.

10. Quoted from Sarason, *School Change*, 184.

11. Dewey, *Experience and Education*, 67, quoted in Nicholls and Hazzard, *Education as Adventure*, 100.

12. Quoted from Nicholls and Hazzard, *Education as Adventure*, 100–101. Quote within the quote from Dewey, *Experience and Education*, 67.

13. Quoted from a transcript of a TED talk given by Sir Ken Robinson. See Ken Robinson, "Bring on the Learning Revolution!," transcript of TED talk, February 2010, https://www.ted.com/talks/sir_ken_robinson_bring_on_the_revolution/transcript.

14. Dintersmith also argues that the structure of today's educational system is based on model that is no longer suitable. He describes how, in 1893, the Committee of Ten outlined a new model of education in response to the large number of immigrants and the change from an agricultural society to a manufacturing society. The factory school model that resulted from the work of the Committee of Ten and Charles Eliot of Harvard was perfectly suited for training students for assembly-line work that required rapid repetition, but no creativity. And it worked. Both individuals and the country profited from this model of schooling. The middle class grew, and the United States became the most powerful country in the world. The problem is that we still use this model of schooling. There have been warnings that is was no longer working, going back at least as far as 1983's *A Nation at Risk*. But instead of developing a new model, like the Committee of Ten did, we continue to tinker with the old one. We add content, create new standards, put even more emphasis on tests of low-level skills, but we leave the basic structure of the system untouched. Even the countries we are trying to catch up with in terms of test scores have concluded that the old model is no longer adequate in an information-age, technology-based society

that thrives on creativity and entrepreneurship. See Ted Dintersmith, "A Venture Capitalist Searches for the Purpose of School. Here's What He Found," *Washington Post*, November 3, 2015, https://www.washingtonpost.com/news/answer-sheet/wp/2015/11/03/a-venture-capitalist-searches-for-the-purpose-of-school-heres-what-he-found/?utm_term=.8c7e18bd30a1.

15. Paraphrased from Sarason, *School Change*, 140.

16. "In the end, then, much of the value of studying the history of education lies not in providing us with answers, but in daring us to challenge the questions and the assumptions that our intellectual forebears have bequeathed to us. The key problem, often, is not to find an answer to a question but to get past it. John Dewey (1910) touched on this point in one of his most brilliant essays: 'Old ideas give way slowly; for they are more than abstract logical forms and categories. They are habits, predispositions, deeply ingrained attitudes of aversion and preference. Moreover, the conviction persists—though history shows it to be a hallucination—that all the questions that the human mind has asked are questions that can be answered in terms of the alternatives the questions themselves present. But, in fact, intellectual progress usually occurs through sheer abandonment of questions together with both of the alternatives they assume—an abandonment that results from their decreasing vitality and a change of urgent interest. We do not solve them: we get over them.'" (p. 19) [Note that this view is remarkably consistent with Thomas Kuhn's description of paradigm changes in the book *The Structure of Scientific Revolutions*.] "Conceivably, some of the questions that are most imbedded in contemporary thinking [about education] may be the very ones that are meaningless and need to be abandoned. . . . [One such example is:] What should be the goals that define the curriculum of schools? . . . Questions such as what the objectives of schooling are or how to prepare children for their adult lives or how to meet their needs have acquired over the years such a taken-for-granted quality that we almost automatically proceed to try to answer them rather than hold them up to critical examination. Somehow seeing those questions played out in a different time and under different social circumstances serves the purpose of casting them as something less than normal and natural. As Dewey argued, real advances are rarely made by doggedly pursuing the answers to questions that in effect have no answers; and one effect of casting those questions in historical perspective is to begin to see them in a fresh light, leading, perhaps, even to abandoning them. In the end, we might as well admit that historical inquiry will not provide a solution to any urgent educational problem. The lessons of the history of education are obviously not lessons in the ordinary sense. Instead, history invites us to reinterpret old questions and sometimes to cast them aside in order to pave the way for new ones. At its best, history provides us with a record of our cumulative experience and suggests how that experience may be interpreted. The renditions of certain traditional questions provided here are undoubtedly subject to other interpretations that may lead to quite different conclusions; nevertheless, if the study of the history of education unearths old and often-buried assumptions imbedded in the questions we ask and thereby exposes them to critical scrutiny, it could be of some real use after all." Quoted from Herbert M. Kliebard, "Why history of education?" *Journal of Educational Research* 88, no. 4 (1995): 194–195, 198.

17. Thanks to Paul Cobb for once posing the question, "What are the foundations of mathematics?" to our graduate seminar.

18. Quoted from Dintersmith, "A Venture Capitalist Searches for the Purpose of School."

19. Quoted from Peter Gray, "Forces Against Fundamental Educational Change," *Psychology Today*, August 27, 2008, https://www.psychologytoday.com/blog/freedom-learn/200808/forces-against-fundamental-educational-change.

20. Quoted from Nicholls and Hazzard, *Education as Adventure*, 5–6.

21. Quoted from John Holt, *How Children Fail* (New York: Da Capo Press, 1982), 296–297.

22. Similarly, Counts argued that it was a mistake to separate children's education from the activities of adults. See George S. Counts, *Dare the School Build a New Social Order?* (Carbondale, IL: Southern Illinois University Press, 1978).

23. Postman also concurs, writing, "The strict application of nurturing and protective attitudes toward children has created a paradoxical situation in which protection has come to mean excluding the young from meaningful involvement in their own communities." Neil Postman, *The End of Education: Redefining the Value of School* (New York: Vintage Books, 1995), 102.

24. Paraphrased from Sarason, *School Change*, 193–194.

25. Quoted from Gray, "Forces Against Fundamental Educational Change."

26. Quoted from Amanda Terkel, "How Betsy DeVos Became the Most Hated Cabinet Secretary," *Huffington Post*, October 24, 2017, https://www.huffingtonpost.com/entry/betsy-devos-most-hated-secretary_us_59ee3d3be4b003385ac13c9b.

27. Quoted from Diane Ravitch, "How Choice May Kill Public Education," web log post, June 24, 2012, http://dianeravitch.net/2012/06/24/how-choice-may-kill-public-education/.

28. Quoted from Rebecca Klein, "Voucher Schools Championed by Betsy DeVos Can Teach Whatever They Want. Turns Out They Teach Lies," *Huffington Post*, December 7, 2017, https://www.huffingtonpost.com/entry/school-voucher-evangelical-education-betsy-devos_us_5a021962e4b0e96f0c6093c.

29. Ibid.

30. Ibid.

31. Stephen Lindahl, assistant director of Calumet Christian School in Griffith, Indiana, quoted and cited in Klein, "Voucher Schools."

32. Quoted from Klein, "Voucher Schools."

33. Paraphrased and quoted from Joanne Barkan, "Death by a Thousand Cuts: The Story of Privatizing Public Education in the USA," *Washington Post*, May 30, 2018, https://www.washingtonpost.com/news/answer-sheet/wp/2018/05/30/what-and-who-is-fueling-the-movement-to-privatize-public-education-and-why-you-should-care/.

34. Quoted from Thomas Ultican, "Destroy Public Education (DPE) for Dummies," web log post, February 22, 2018, https://tultican.com/2018/02/22/destroy-public-education-dpe-for-dummies/.

35. Paraphrased and quoted from Barkan, "Death by a Thousand Cuts."

36. Quoted from Ultican, "Destroy Public Education."

37. From a 2008 article in *Time* by Claudia Wallis, quoted by Alfie Kohn, and requoted in Ultican, "Destroy Public Education."

38. Barkan, "Death by a Thousand Cuts."

39. Quoted from Ultican, "Destroy Public Education."

40. Paraphrased from Barkan, "Death by a Thousand Cuts."

41. Ibid.

42. Quoted from Dale Russakoff, *The Prize: Who's in Charge of America's Schools?* (New York: Houghton Mifflin Harcourt, 2015), 46.

43. Paraphrased and quoted from Barkan, "Death by a Thousand Cuts."

44. Quoted from Alan Singer, "Pearson Caught Cheating, Says Sorry, But Will Pay," *Huffington Post*, December 13, 2013, https://www.huffingtonpost.com/alan-singer/pearson-caught-cheating-s_b_4439043.html.

45. Paraphrased and quoted from Barkan, "Death by a Thousand Cuts."

46. Paraphrased from Barkan, "Death by a Thousand Cuts."

47. Quoted from William Mathis, "Losing Our Purpose, Measuring the Wrong Things," web log comment, September 1, 2017, https://dianeravitch.net/2017/09/01/william-mathis-what-is-the-purpose-of-school-and-what-do-we-measure/.

48. Paraphrased and quoted from Noam Chomsky, "Chomsky: The Corporate Assault on Public Education," *AlterNet*, March 8, 2013, https://www.alternet.org/education/chomsky-corporate-assault-public-education.

49. See Russakoff, *The Prize*.

50. Quoted from Emma Brown and Mandy McLaren, "How Indiana's School Voucher Program Soared, and What It Says about Education in the Trump Era," *Washington Post*, December 26, 2016, https://www.washingtonpost.com/local/education/how-indianas-school-voucher-program-soared-and-what-it-says-about-education-in-the-trump-era/2016/12/26/13d1d3ec-bc97-11e6-91ee-1adddfe36cbe_story.html.

51. Quoted from Carol Burris, "A Telling Story of School 'Reform' in Mike Pence's Home State, Indiana," *Washington Post*, December 21, 2017, https://www.washingtonpost.com/news/answer-sheet/wp/2017/12/21/a-telling-story-of-school-reform-in-mike-pences-home-state-indiana/?utm_term=.8cb9b39614d3.

52. Quoted from Chomsky, "Chomsky: The Corporate Assault on Public Education."

53. Paraphrased and quoted from Ted Dintersmith, "Venture Capitalist Visits 200 Schools in 50 States and Says DeVos is Wrong: 'If Choice and Competition Improve Schools, I Found No Sign of It'," *Washington Post*, March 15, 2018, https://www.washingtonpost.com/news/answer-sheet/wp/2018/03/15/heres-what-our-secretary-of-education-needs-to-hear-by-a-venture-capitalist-who-visited-200-schools-in-all-50-states/?utm_term=.512e659329d8.

54. Quoted from an article written by Gerardo Gonzalez, Dean of the Indiana University School of Education. See Gerardo Gonzalez, "Indiana Education Headed for Disaster," *The Indianapolis Star*, June 1, 2015, https://www.indystar.com/story/opinion/readers/2015/06/01/indiana-education-headed-disaster/28316527/.

55. Quote attributed to Scott Hanback, Tippecanoe School Corporation superintendent, in Dave Bangert, "Bangert: Ed Reform's Next Trick? Teacher Shortage," *Journal and Courier*, August 1, 2015, http://on.jconline.com/1IaDKcC.

56. Quoted from the foreword to the American Legislative Exchange Council's "Report Card on American Education," written by Mitch Daniels in 2012. See "Report Card on American Education," American Legislative Exchange Council, retrieved July 22, 2018, from https://www.alec.org/publication/2012-education-report-card/.

57. Paraphrased and quoted from American Legislative Exchange Council, "Report Card on American Education."

58. The first part of Foster's statement here is attributed to Anthony Carnevale, Georgetown University professor and director of the Center on Education and the Workforce, in Patricia Cohen, "A Rising Call to Promote STEM Education and Cut Liberal Arts Funding," *New York Times*, February 21, 2016, https://www.nytimes.com/2016/02/22/business/a-rising-call-to-promote-stem-education-and-cut-liberal-arts-funding.html.

59. Quoted from Ultican, "Destroy Public Education."

60. Paraphrased from David Sirota, "The Bait and Switch of School 'Reform'," *Salon*, September 12, 2011, https://www.salon.com/2011/09/12/reformmoney/.

61. Quoted from David L. Kirp, "Teaching is Not a Business," *New York Times*, August 16, 2014, https://www.nytimes.com/2014/08/17/opinion/sunday/teaching-is-not-a-business.html.

62. Paraphrased from Dintersmith, "Venture Capitalist Visits 200 Schools in 50 States."

63. Quoted from Mike Rose, *Why School? Reclaiming Education for All of Us* (New York: The New Press, 2014), 64, 65.

64. Paraphrased and quoted from Sirota, "The Bait and Switch of School 'Reform.'"

65. Ibid.

66. Taken from a 2016 paper on the portfolio model from the National Education Policy Center at the University of Colorado at Boulder's School of Education and quoted in Valerie Strauss, "What's Really Going on in Indiana's Public Schools," *Washington Post*, July 12, 2018, https://www.washingtonpost.com/news/answer-sheet/wp/2018/07/12/whats-really-going-on-in-indianas-public-schools/?noredirect=on&utm_term=.34b69aec7197.

67. Quoted from Darcie Cimarusti, "What's Really Going on in Indiana's Public Schools," *Washington Post*, July 12, 2018, https://www.washingtonpost.com/news/answer-sheet/wp/2018/07/12/whats-really-going-on-in-indianas-public-schools/?noredirect=on&utm_term=.34b69aec7197.

68. Paraphrased and quoted from Lee Fang, "Selling Schools Out," *The Investigative Fund*, November 17, 2011, https://www.theinvestigativefund.org/investigation/2011/11/17/selling-schools/.

69. Quoted from Terry Eagleton, "The Slow Death of the University," *The Chronicle of Higher Education*, April 6, 2015, https://www.chronicle.com/article/The-Slow-Death-of-the/228991.

70. Paraphrased from Fang, "Selling Schools Out."

71. Ibid.

72. Quote attributed to Ed Fuller, an education researcher at Penn State University, in Fang, "Selling Schools Out."

73. Fang, "Selling Schools Out."

74. Paraphrased and quoted from Sirota, "The Bait and Switch of School 'Reform'."

75. Quoted from Ted Dintersmith, *What School Could Be: Insights and Inspiration from Teachers across America* (Princeton, NJ: Princeton University Press, 2018), 124–125.

76. Paraphrased and quoted from Rose, *Why School?* 69–73, 75, 82.

77. This quote is from William Keep, Dean of the School of Business at the College of New Jersey. See William Keep, "The Worrisome Ascendance of Business in Higher Education," *The Chronicle of Higher Education*, June 21, 2012, https://www.chronicle.com/article/The-Worrisome-Ascendance-of/132501.

78. Andrea Gabor, author of the book *After the Education Wars: How Smart Schools Upend the Business of Reform*, quoted in Diane Ravitch, "Andrea Gabor: Will One of the Nation's Most Innovative Districts Survive a Change in Leadership?," web log post, May 15, 2019, http://dianeravitch.net/2019/05/15/andrea-gabor-will-one-of-the-nations-most-innovative-districts-survive-a-change-in-leadership/.

79. Petrilli, quoted in Diane Ravitch, "Mike Petrilli: In the Face of So Many Setbacks, Where Does Reform Go from Here?," web log post, July 20, 2018, https://dianeravitch.net/2018/07/20/mike-petrilli-in-the-face-of-so-many-setbacks-where-does-reform-go-from-here/.

80. Quoted from Bryan Caplan, *The Case Against Education: Why the Education System is a Waste of Time and Money* (Princeton, NJ: Princeton University Press, 2018), 1–2, 10.

81. Paraphrased and quoted from Caplan, *The Case Against Education*, 2, 239.

82. Paraphrased from Caplan, *The Case Against Education*, 3, 13–14, 17–21.

83. Paraphrased and quoted from Caplan, *The Case Against Education*, 5–6.

84. Paraphrased from Caplan, *The Case Against Education*, 167.

85. Ibid., 175.

86. Quoted from Caplan, *The Case Against Education*, 175.

87. Paraphrased and quoted from Caplan, *The Case Against Education*, 175, 204–207, 210.

88. The exchange between Harris, Newcomer, Quinn, and Inglehart here is taken from Caplan, *The Case Against Education*, 196.

89. Paraphrased and quoted from Caplan, *The Case Against Education*, 213–214, 216.

90. Ibid., 225.

91. Ibid., 256, 260.

92. Quoted from Marion Brady, "Improving Schools With 'The Project'," *Washington Post*, September 9, 2011, http://www.marionbrady.com/articles/2011-Washington%20Post9-9.pdf.

93. Postman offers a similar proposal in the form of an educational fable in which a deteriorating city's students undertake to save their city. Of the students, he says, "They will find their education in the process of saving their city." He notes that "It is not written in any holy book that an education must occur in a small room with chairs in it." And he acknowledges that "it would be foolish to deny that there were not

certain problems attending this whole adventure. For instance, thousands of children who would otherwise have known the principal rivers of Uruguay had to live out their lives in ignorance of these facts. Hundreds of teachers felt that their training had been wasted, because they could not educate children unless it were done in a classroom. As you can imagine, it was also exceedingly difficult to grade students on their activities, and after a while, almost all tests ceased. This made many people unhappy, for many reasons, but most of all because no one could tell the dumb children from the smart children anymore." See Postman, *The End of Education*, 95, 96, 99.

94. Quoted from Nicholls and Hazzard, *Education as Adventure*, 102–103.

95. Paraphrased and quoted from Dintersmith, "A Venture Capitalist Searches for the Purpose of School."

96. Dewey (1940, 223), quoted in Nicholls and Hazzard, *Education as Adventure*, 51.

97. Quoted from Nicholls and Hazzard, *Education as Adventure*, 51–52.

98. Ibid., 191.

99. Ibid., 192–193.

100. Ibid., 52.

101. Ibid., 51.

102. Quoted from Susan Engel, "Teach Your Teachers Well," *New York Times*, November 1, 2009, https://www.nytimes.com/2009/11/02/opinion/02engel.html.

103. Quoted from Nicholls and Hazzard, *Education as Adventure*, 4–5, 7.

Bibliography

Adams Jr., Jacob E. "Education Reform–Overview." Retrieved July 11, 2018. http://education.stateuniversity.com/pages/1944/Education-Reform.html.

American Legislative Exchange Council. "Report Card on American Education." Retrieved July 22, 2018. https://www.alec.org/publication/2012-education-report-card/.

Apple, Michael W. *Education and Power*. Boston, MA: Routledge & Kegan Paul, 1982.

Associated Press. "Panel: Upgrade Schools." *Post-Tribune*, December 15, 2006. https://www.chicagotribune.com/suburbs/post-tribune/.

Ball, Deborah L., and Hyman Bass. "Interweaving Content and Pedagogy in Teaching and Learning to Teach: Knowing and Using Mathematics." In *Multiple Perspectives on Mathematics Teaching and Learning*, edited by Jo Boaler, 83–104. Westport, CT: Ablex Publishing, 2000.

Bangert, Dave. "Bangert: Ed Reform's Next Trick? Teacher Shortage." *Journal and Courier*, August 1, 2015. http://on.jconline.com/1IaDKcC.

Barkan, Joanne. "Death by a Thousand Cuts: The Story of Privatizing Public Education in the USA." *Washington Post*, May 30, 2018. https://www.washingtonpost.com/news/answer-sheet/wp/2018/05/30/what-and-who-is-fueling-the-movement-to-privatize-public-education-and-why-you-should-care/.

Bartscht, Jan. "In Your Opinion, What Should the Purpose of Education Be?" Message 29, December 12, 2011. https://www.ted.com/conversations/7491/in_your_opinion_what_should_t.html.

Bass, Randall V. "The Purpose of Education." *Educational Forum* 61, no. 2 (1997): 128–132. https://doi.org/10.1080/00131729709335242.

Becker, Jerry P., and Bill Jacob. 2000. "The Politics of California School Mathematics: The Anti-Reform of 1997–99." *Phi Delta Kappan* 81, no. 7 (2000): 529–537.

Berliner, David. "Education Professor: My Students Asked Who I Would Vote For. Here's What I Told Them." *Washington Post*, October 22, 2018. https://www.washingtonpost.com/education/2018/10/22/education-professor-my-stu-

dents-asked-who-i-would-vote-heres-what-i-told-them/?tid=ss_mail&utm_term=.
d0ad82c5a7c2.

Bidwell, Allie. "The History of Common Core State Standards." *U. S. News & World Report*, February 27, 2014. https://www.usnews.com/news/special-reports/ articles/2014/02/27/the-history-of-common-core-state-standards.

Brady, Marion. "Improving Schools With 'The Project.'" *Washington Post*, September 9, 2011. http://www.marionbrady.com/articles/2011-Washington%20Post9-9. pdf.

Brooks, David. "The Biggest Issue." *New York Times*, July 29, 2008. https://www. nytimes.com/2008/07/29/opinion/29brooks.html?mtrref=www.google.com&gwh= 9391F281242608C604C227943465E32C&gwt=pay&assetType=opinion.

Brotherton, David C. Review of *Corridor Cultures: Mapping Student Resistance at an Urban High School*, by Maryann Dickar. *Teachers College Record*, March 3, 2009. http://www.tcrecord.org/library/Abstract.asp?ContentId=15586.

Brown, Emma, and Mandy McLaren. "How Indiana's School Voucher Program Soared, and What It Says about Education in the Trump Era." *Washington Post*, December 26, 2016. https://www.washingtonpost.com/local/education/how-in-dianas-school-voucher-program-soared-and-what-it-says-about-education-in-the-trump-era/2016/12/26/13d1d3ec-bc97-11e6-91ee-1adddfe36cbe_story.html.

Brucia, Thomas. "In Your Opinion, What Should the Purpose of Education Be?" Message 9, December 16, 2011. https://www.ted.com/conversations/7491/in_ your_opinion_what_should_t.html.

Bruni, Frank. "College, Poetry and Purpose." *New York Times*, February 18, 2015. https://www.nytimes.com/2015/02/18/opinion/frank-bruni-college-poetry-and-purpose.html.

Bruni, Frank. "How and Why You Diversify Colleges." *New York Times*, May 14, 2016. https://www.nytimes.com/2016/05/15/opinion/sunday/how-and-why-you-diversify-colleges.html.

Burk, Adam. "In Your Opinion, What Should the Purpose of Education Be?" Message 1, November 2011. https://www.ted.com/conversations/7491/in_your_opin-ion_what_should_t.html.

Burris, Carol. "A Telling Story of School 'Reform' in Mike Pence's Home State, Indiana." *Washington Post*, December 21, 2017. https://www.washingtonpost. com/news/answer-sheet/wp/2017/12/21/a-telling-story-of-school-reform-in-mike-pences-home-state-indiana/?utm_term=.8cb9b39614d3.

Bykerk-Kauffman, Ann. "Phases and Eclipses of the Moon." Retrieved June 1, 2018. https://serc.carleton.edu/sp/library/guided_discovery/examples/moon_phases. html.

Camins, Arthur H. "What's the Purpose of Education in the 21st Century?" *Washington Post*, February 12, 2015. https://www.washingtonpost.com/news/answer-sheet/ wp/2015/02/12/whats-the-purpose-of-education-in-the-21st-century/?utm_term=. e532a78f8698.

Caplan, Bryan. *The Case Against Education: Why the Education System is a Waste of Time and Money*. Princeton, NJ: Princeton University Press, 2018.

Carey, Kevin. "The Kludging of Higher Education." *The Chronicle of Higher Education*, November 25, 2013. https://www.chronicle.com/article/The-Kludging-of-Higher/143215.

Carnoy, Martin, and Richard Rothstein. *What Do International Tests Really Show about U.S. Student Performance?* Washington, D.C.: Economic Policy Institute, 2013. https://steinhardt.nyu.edu/scmsAdmin/media/users/sl1716/IGEMS/PISA-TIMSS_paper.pdf.

Carter, Gene. "What's the Purpose of School in the 21st Century?" *Good*, March 19, 2012. https://www.good.is/articles/what-s-the-purpose-of-school-in-the-21st-century.

Castle, Kathy. "In Your Opinion, What Should the Purpose of Education Be?" Message 59, December 22, 2011. https://www.ted.com/conversations/7491/in_your_opinion_what_should_t.html.

Catanzano, Matteo. "In Your Opinion, What Should the Purpose of Education Be?" Message 41, December 28, 2011. https://www.ted.com/conversations/7491/in_your_opinion_what_should_t.html.

Cheek, Karen. 1996. "Education in the Southern Colonies." Last modified 1996. http://www3.nd.edu/~rbarger/www7/soucolon.html.

Chesnut, Colleen E., Molly S. Stewart, and Anne Sera. *University Faculty Perceptions of Teacher Evaluation Law in Indiana.* Issue Brief, November 2015. Bloomington, IN: Center for Evaluation and Education Policy, Indiana University School of Education, 2015. http://ceep.indiana.edu/pdf/University_Faculty_Perceptions_CEEP_IB.pdf.

Chomsky, Noam. "Chomsky: The Corporate Assault on Public Education." *AlterNet*, March 8, 2013. https://www.alternet.org/education/chomsky-corporate-assault-public-education.

Cimarusti, Darcie. "What's Really Going on in Indiana's Public Schools." *Washington Post*, July 12, 2018. https://www.washingtonpost.com/news/answer-sheet/wp/2018/07/12/whats-really-going-on-in-indianas-public-schools/?noredirect=on&utm_term=.34b69aec7197.

Cobb, Paul. "Where is the Mind? Constructivist and Sociocultural Perspectives on Mathematical Development." *Educational Researcher* 23, no. 7 (1994): 13–20.

Cobb, Paul, and Kay McClain. "The Collective Mediation of a High Stakes Accountability Program: Communities and Networks of Practice." *Mind, Culture, and Activity* 13, no. 2 (2006): 80–100.

Cobb, Paul, Erna Yackel, and Terry Wood. "Interaction and Learning in Mathematics Classroom Situations." *Educational Studies in Mathematics* 23, no.1 (1992): 99–122.

Cobb, Paul, Marcela Perlwitz, and Diana Underwood-Gregg. "Individual Construction, Mathematical Acculturation, and the Classroom Community." In *Constructivism and Education*, edited by Marie Larochelle, Nadine Bednarz, and Jim Garrison, 63–80. New York: Cambridge University Press, 1998.

Cohen, Patricia. "A Rising Call to Promote STEM Education and Cut Liberal Arts Funding." *New York Times*, February 21, 2016. https://www.nytimes.

com/2016/02/22/business/a-rising-call-to-promote-stem-education-and-cut-liberal-arts-funding.html.

College of Education and Social Services, The University of Vermont. "A Brief Overview of Progressive Education." Retrieved August 6, 2018. https://www.uvm.edu/~dewey/articles/proged.html.

Costigan, Arthur. Review of *Teaching by Numbers: Deconstructing the Discourse of Standards and Accountability in Education*, by Peter Taubman. *Teachers College Record*, November 30, 2009. https://www.tcrecord.org/books/abstract.asp?ContentId=15851.

Counts, George S. *Dare the School Build a New Social Order?* Carbondale, IL: Southern Illinois University Press, 1978.

Cuban, Larry. "Schools as Factories: Metaphors that Stick." Posted May 8, 2014. https://larrycuban.wordpress.com/2014/05/08/schools-as-factories-metaphors-that-stick/.

Cuban, Larry. *How Teachers Taught: Constancy and Change in American Classrooms, 1890–1980*. New York: Longman, 1984.

Danziger, Richard. "In Your Opinion, What Should the Purpose of Education Be?" Message 36, December 2, 2011. https://www.ted.com/conversations/7491/in_your_opinion_what_should_t.html.

Dewey, John. *Democracy and Education*. New York: The Macmillan Company, 1916. http://www.gutenberg.org/files/852/852-h/852-h.htm#link2HCH0007.

Dewey, John. *Experience and Education*. New York: Simon and Schuster, 1938.

Dintersmith, Ted. "A Venture Capitalist Searches for the Purpose of School. Here's What He Found." *Washington Post*, November 3, 2015. https://www.washingtonpost.com/news/answer-sheet/wp/2015/11/03/a-venture-capitalist-searches-for-the-purpose-of-school-heres-what-he-found/?utm_term=.8c7e18bd30a1.

Dintersmith, Ted. "Venture Capitalist Visits 200 Schools in 50 States and Says DeVos is Wrong: 'If Choice and Competition Improve Schools, I Found No Sign of It.'" *Washington Post*, March 15, 2018. https://www.washingtonpost.com/news/answer-sheet/wp/2018/03/15/heres-what-our-secretary-of-education-needs-to-hear-by-a-venture-capitalist-who-visited-200-schools-in-all-50-states/?utm_term=.512e659329d8.

Dintersmith, Ted. *What School Could Be: Insights and Inspiration from Teachers across America*. Princeton, NJ: Princeton University Press, 2018.

Eagleton, Terry. "The Slow Death of the University." *The Chronicle of Higher Education*, April 6, 2015. https://www.chronicle.com/article/The-Slow-Death-of-the/228991.

Elmore, Richard F. "The Politics of Education Reform." *Issues in Science and Technology* 14, no. 1 (Fall 1997): 41–49.

Engel, Susan. "Teach Your Teachers Well." *New York Times*, November 1, 2009. https://www.nytimes.com/2009/11/02/opinion/02engel.html.

Erickson, Frederick, and Jeffrey Shultz. "Students' Experience of the Curriculum." In *Handbook of Research on Curriculum*, edited by Phillip W. Jackson, 465–485. New York: Macmillan, 1992.

Faber, Joy. "In Your Opinion, What Should the Purpose of Education Be?" Message 62, December 21, 2011. https://www.ted.com/conversations/7491/in_your_opinion_what_should_t.html.

Fang, Lee. "Selling Schools Out." *The Investigative Fund*, November 17, 2011. https://www.theinvestigativefund.org/investigation/2011/11/17/selling-schools/.

Fenstermacher, Gary D., and Virginia Richardson. "What's Wrong with Accountability?" *Teachers College Record*, May 26, 2010. https://www.researchgate.net/publication/325181686_What%27s_Wrong_with_Accountability.

Fiorini, Phillip. 2007. "Discovery Park Appoints Director for K–12 Science Education Efforts." *Research Review* 20, no. 8 (2007): 7. West Lafayette, IN: Purdue University Press.

Fiske, Edward B. "A Nation at a Loss." *New York Times*, April 25, 2008. https://www.nytimes.com/2008/04/25/opinion/25fiske.html.

Flanagan, Nancy. "In Your Opinion, What Should the Purpose of Education Be?" Message 8, November 30, 2011. https://www.ted.com/conversations/7491/in_your_opinion_what_should_t.html.

Florian, Meghan. "Notes from an Employed Philosopher." *The Chronicle of Higher Education*, April 1, 2013. https://www.chronicle.com/blogs/conversation/2013/04/01/notes-from-an-employed-philosopher/.

Frederick, Carl B. Review of *The Nature and Limits of Standards-Based Reform and Assessments: Defending Public Schools*, by Sandra Mathison and E. Wayne Ross, editors. *Teachers College Record*, April 22, 2009. http://www.tcrecord.org/Content.asp?ContentID=15622.

Fritzberg, Greg. "A Brief History of Education Reform." *Response* (Spring 2012). http://spu.edu/depts/uc/response/new/2012-spring/features/history-of-reform.asp.

Frykholm, Jeffrey. 2004. "Teachers' Tolerance for Discomfort: Implications for Curricular Reform in Mathematics." *Journal of Curriculum and Supervision* 19, no. 2 (2004): 125–149.

García, Oscar. "In Your Opinion, What Should the Purpose of Education Be?" Message 45, December 28, 2011. https://www.ted.com/conversations/7491/in_your_opinion_what_should_t.html.

Gelbrich, Judy. "Section II - American Education." Online course material, 1999a. http://oregonstate.edu/instruct/ed416/ae1.html.

Gelbrich, Judy. "Section II - American Education." Online course material, 1999b. http://oregonstate.edu/instruct/ed416/ae2.html.

Gelbrich, Judy. "Section II - American education." Online course material, 1999c. http://oregonstate.edu/instruct/ed416/ae3.html.

Gelbrich, Judy. "Section II - American Education." Online course material, 1999d. http://oregonstate.edu/instruct/ed416/ae4.html.

Gelbrich, Judy. "Section II - American Education." Online course material, 1999e. http://oregonstate.edu/instruct/ed416/ae7.html.

Gessner, Stephen L. 1998. "What the Want Ads Can Tell Us about the Educational Wars." *Education Week* 17, no. 42 (1998): 40.

Gibboney, Richard. A. *The Stone Trumpet: A Story of Practical School Reform, 1960–1990*. Albany, NY: State University of New York Press, 1994.

Ginsberg, Rick. "Education Reform - Reports of Historical Significance." Retrieved July 11, 2018. http://education.stateuniversity.com/pages/1944/Education-Reform.html.

Giroux, Henry A. *Theory and Resistance in Education.* South Hadley, MA: Bergin & Garvey, 1983.

Glaser, Barney G., and Anselm L. Strauss. *The Discovery of Grounded Theory.* New York: Aldine de Gruyter, 1967.

Glass, Gene V. "Why I Am No Longer a Measurement Specialist." Web log post, August 17, 2015. http://ed2worlds.blogspot.com/2015/08/why-i-am-no-longer-measurement.html?m=1.

Gonzalez, Gerardo. "Indiana Education Headed for Disaster." *The Indianapolis Star*, June 1, 2015. https://www.indystar.com/story/opinion/readers/2015/06/01/indiana-education-headed-disaster/28316527/.

Gordon, Claire. "Teacher's Epic Resignation Letter: Profession 'No Longer Exists.'" Web log post, April 10, 2013. https://www.aol.com/2013/04/10/gerald-conti-teacher-resignation/.

Gray, Peter. "A Brief History of Education." *Psychology Today*, August 20, 2008. https://www.psychologytoday.com/blog/freedom-learn/200808/brief-history-education.

Gray, Peter. "Children Educate Themselves IV: Lessons from Sudbury Valley." *Psychology Today*, August 13, 2008. https://www.psychologytoday.com/blog/freedom-learn/200808/children-educate-themselves-iv-lessons-sudbury-valley.

Gray, Peter. "Forces Against Fundamental Educational Change." *Psychology Today*, August 27, 2008. https://www.psychologytoday.com/blog/freedom-learn/200808/forces-against-fundamental-educational-change.

Gray, Peter. "Kids Learn Math Easily When They Control Their Own Learning." *Psychology Today*, April 15, 2010. https://www.psychologytoday.com/blog/freedom-learn/201004/kids-learn-math-easily-when-they-control-their-own-learning.

Gray, Peter. "What Einstein, Twain, & Forty-Eight Others Said about School." *Psychology Today*, July 26, 2011. https://www.psychologytoday.com/blog/freedom-learn/201107/what-einstein-twain-forty-eight-others-said-about-school.

Greene, Brian. "Put a Little Science in Your Life." *New York Times*, June 1, 2008. https://www.nytimes.com/2008/06/01/opinion/01greene.html.

Groves, Jonathan. "Re: Introducing . . . the Corporate Reform Action Pack!" Web log comment, October 15, 2010. http://groups.yahoo.com/group/Math-Talk/message/3167;_ylc=X3oDMTM0NDQxYmNmBF9TAzk3MzU5NzE0BGdycElkAzM0MDM0ODQEZ3Jwc3BJZAMxNzA1MDE2MDYxBG1zZ0lkAzMxODMEc2VjA2Z0cgRzbGsDdnRwYwRzdGltZQMxMjg3MTI1NjEzBHRwY0lkAzMxNjc-.

Hacker, Andrew. "The Wrong Way to Teach Math." *New York Times*, February 27, 2016. https://www.nytimes.com/2016/02/28/opinion/sunday/the-wrong-way-to-teach-math.html.

Hamilton, Laura S., Brian M. Stecher, and Kun Yuan. "Standards-Based Reform in the United States: History, Research, and Future Directions." Washington, D.C.:

Center on Education Policy, 2008. http://www.rand.org/content/dam/rand/pubs/reprints/2009/RAND_RP1384.pdf.

Hamilton, Laura S., Daniel F. McCaffrey, Brian M. Stecher, Stephen P. Klein, Abby Robyn, and Delia Bugliari. "Studying Large-Scale Reforms of Instructional Practice: An Example from Mathematics and Science." *Educational Evaluation and Policy Analysis* 25, no. 1 (2003): 1–29.

Hanford, Emily. "The Troubled History of Vocational Education." Essay derived from the American Public Media radio documentary, *Ready to Work: Reviving Vocational Ed*, September 9, 2014. http://www.americanradioworks.org/segments/the-troubled-history-of-vocational-education/.

Haug, Carolyn A. "Local Capacity and State Policies in Colorado: Obstacles to Standards-Based Mathematics Education Reform." Paper presented at the annual meeting of the American Educational Research Association, New Orleans, April 2000.

Heckman, James J. "Schools, Skills, and Synapses." *Economic Inquiry* 46, no. 3 (2008): 289–324.

Herrera, Terese A., and Douglas T. Owens. "The 'New New Math'? Two Reform Movements in Mathematics Education." *Theory into Practice* 40, no. 2 (2001): 84–92.

Hinnant-Crawford, Brandi. "Education Policy Influence Efficacy: Teachers Beliefs in Their Ability to Change Education Policy." *International Journal of Teacher Leadership* 7, no. 2 (2016): 1–27. https://files.eric.ed.gov/fulltext/EJ1137496.pdf.

Hoff, David J. "National Standards Gain Steam." *Education Week*, March 2, 2009. http://www.edweek.org/ew/articles/2009/03/04/23nga_ep.h28.html?tmp=140352705.

Holt, John. *How Children Fail*. New York: Da Capo Press, 1982.

Hornby, Pat, and Gillian Symon. "Tracer Studies." In *Qualitative Methods in Organizational Research: A Practical Guide*, edited by Catherine Cassell and Gillian Symon, 167–186. London: Sage Publications, 1994.

Hostetler, Lukas. "In Your Opinion, What Should the Purpose of Education Be?" Message 14, December 6, 2011. https://www.ted.com/conversations/7491/in_your_opinion_what_should_t.html.

Howey, Brian A. "A 'Revolution' Begins . . . Next Week." *Howey Politics Indiana* 14, no. 44 (2009): 1, 4–5. http://www.in.gov/library/files/HPR14z44.pdf.

Huddle, Les, Scott Hanback, and Rocky Killion. "Op-ed: The Bad News Coming on ISTEP." *Journal and Courier*, June 4, 2015. http://on.jconline.com/1ImqeFm.

Hunt, Thomas C. 2005. "Education Reforms: Lessons from History. *Phi Delta Kappan* 87, no. 1 (2005): 84–89.

Iorio, Sharon H., and M. E. Yeager. "School Reform: Past, Present, and Future." Paper presented at the School Reform Strategies symposium held at Harris Manchester College, Oxford University, Oxford, England, July 2011. http://webs.wichita.edu/depttools/depttoolsmemberfiles/COEdDEAN/School%20Reform%20Past%20Present%20and%20Future.pdf.

Indiana Department of Education. *Indiana's Academic Standards*. Indianapolis, IN: Indiana Department of Education, 2000. http://www.math.iupui.edu/~jwatt/m457/forms/INMATHStandards.pdf.

Jones, Kim. "What is the Purpose of Education?" *Forbes*, August 15, 2012. https://www.forbes.com/sites/sap/2012/08/15/what-is-the-purpose-of-education/#466dcc207795.

Kaag, John, and David O'Hara. "Big Brains, Small Minds." *The Chronicle of Higher Education*, May 13, 2016. https://www.chronicle.com/article/Big-Brains-Small-Minds/236480.

Kamii, Constance. *Young Children Reinvent Arithmetic: Implications of Piaget's Theory.* New York: Teachers College Press, 1985.

Keep, William W. "The Worrisome Ascendance of Business in Higher Education." *The Chronicle of Higher Education*, June 21, 2012. https://www.chronicle.com/article/The-Worrisome-Ascendance-of/132501.

Kennedy, Mary. *Inside Teaching: How Classroom Life Undermines Reform.* Cambridge, MA: Harvard University Press, 2005.

Kirp, David L. "Teaching is Not a Business." *New York Times*, August 16, 2014. https://www.nytimes.com/2014/08/17/opinion/sunday/teaching-is-not-a-business.html.

Klein, Rebecca. "Voucher Schools Championed by Betsy DeVos Can Teach Whatever They Want. Turns Out They Teach Lies." *Huffington Post*, December 7, 2017. https://www.huffingtonpost.com/entry/school-voucher-evangelical-education-betsy-devos_us_5a021962e4b04e96f0c6093c.

Kliebard, Herbert M. 1995. "Why history of education?" *Journal of Educational Research* 88, no. 4 (1995): 194–199.

Klinenberg, Eric. "What Trump's Win Compels Scholars to Do." *The Chronicle of Higher Education*, November 11, 2016. https://www.chronicle.com/article/What-Trump-s-Win-Compels/238389.

Kohl, Herbert. "The Educational Panopticon. *Teachers College Record*, January 8, 2009. http://www.tcrecord.org ID Number: 15477.

Kohn, Alfie. "Encouraging Educator Courage." *Education Week*, September 16, 2013. https://www.edweek.org/ew/articles/2013/09/18/04kohn.h33.html.

Kristof, Nicholas. "Starving for Wisdom." *New York Times*, April 16, 2015. https://www.nytimes.com/2015/04/16/opinion/nicholas-kristof-starving-for-wisdom.html.

Labaree, David F. "School Syndrome: Understanding the USA's Magical Belief that Schooling Can Somehow Improve Society, Promote Access, and Preserve Advantage." *Journal of Curriculum Studies* 44, no. 2 (2012): 143–163. https://doi.org/10.1080/00220272.2012.675358.

Labaree, David F. "The Chronic Failure of Curriculum Reform." *Education Week* 18, no. 36 (1999): 42–44.

Lagemann, Ellen C. "Contested Terrain: A History of Education Research in the United States, 1890–1990." *Educational Researcher* 26, no. 9 (1997): 5–17.

Layton, Lyndsey. "How Bill Gates Pulled Off the Swift Common Core Revolution." *Washington Post*, June7, 2014. https://www.washingtonpost.com/politics/how-bill-gates-pulled-off-the-swift-common-core-revolution/2014/06/07/a830e32e-ec34-11e3-9f5c-9075d5508f0a_story.html?utm_term=.509ce44b971d.

Lenzo, Kate. "Validity and Self-Reflexivity Meet Poststructuralism: Scientific Ethos and the Transgressive Self." *Educational Researcher* 24, no. 4 (1995): 17–23, 45.

Lonsbury, Justin, and Michael W. Apple. "Understanding the Limits and Possibilities of School Reform." *Educational Policy* 26, no. 5 (2012): 759–773.

Malone, Peggy. "Purpose, Processes, and Change." In *Real School Issues: Case Studies for Educators*, edited by Laura Trujillo-Jenks and Rebecca Ratliff Frederickson, 145–156. Lanham, MD: Rowman and Littlefield, 2017.

Martin, Hannah. "In Your Opinion, What Should the Purpose of Education Be?" Message 57, December 23, 2011. https://www.ted.com/conversations/7491/in_your_opinion_what_should_t.html.

Mathis, William. "Losing Our Purpose, Measuring the Wrong Things." Web log comment, September 1, 2017. https://dianeravitch.net/2017/09/01/william-mathis-what-is-the-purpose-of-school-and-what-do-we-measure/.

Medansky, C. "In Your Opinion, What Should the Purpose of Education Be?" Message 2, December 27, 2011a. https://www.ted.com/conversations/7491/in_your_opinion_what_should_t.html.

Medansky, C. "In Your Opinion, What Should the Purpose of Education Be?" Reply to Message 2, December 28, 2011b. https://www.ted.com/conversations/7491/in_your_opinion_what_should_t.html.

Michigan State University College of Education. "Professor's Analysis Reveals 'Individualistic Conception' of Public Education." *New Educator* 5, no. 1 (Spring 1999). http://www.educ.msu.edu/neweducator/spring99/analysis.htm.

Mitchell, Richard. "The Gingham Dog and the Calico Cat." *The Underground Grammarian* 6, no. 6 (September 1982). http://www.sourcetext.com/grammarian/.

National Academy of Education. *Standards, Assessment, and Accountability*. Washington, D.C.: National Academy of Education, 2009.

National Commission on Excellence in Education. *A Nation at Risk: The Imperative for Educational Reform*. Washington, DC: U.S. Government Printing Office, 1983.

National Council of Teachers of Mathematics. *Curriculum and Evaluation Standards for School Mathematics*. Reston, VA: National Council of Teachers of Mathematics, 1989.

National Park Service, U.S. Department of the Interior. "William Holmes McGuffey and His Readers." *The Museum Gazette* (January 1993). https://www.nps.gov/jeff/learn/historyculture/upload/mcguffey.pdf.

Nicholls, John G., and Susan P. Hazzard. *Education as Adventure: Lessons from the Second Grade*. New York: Teachers College Press, 1993.

Nietz, John A. "Horace Mann's Ideas on General Methods in Education." *The Elementary School Journal* 37, no. 10 (1937): 742–751.

Niose, David. "Anti-Intellectualism is Killing America." *Psychology Today*, June 23, 2015. https://www.psychologytoday.com/us/blog/our-humanity-naturally/201506/anti-intellectualism-is-killing-america.

Noddings, Nel. *The Challenge to Care in Schools: An Alternative Approach to Education*. New York: Teachers College Press, 1992.

Noguchi, Yuki. "Yay, It's Time for My Performance Review! (Said No One Ever)." Web article accompanying report on NPR's *All Things Considered*, September

28, 2016. https://www.npr.org/2016/09/28/495795876/yay-its-time-for-my-performance-review-said-no-one-ever.

Noyes, William. "Overwork, Idleness or Industrial Education." *The Child Labor Bulletin* 1, no. 4 (1913): 75–87. https://books.google.com/books?id=UcllAAAAYAAJ&pg=PA75&source=gbs_toc_r&cad=3#v=onepage&q&f=false.

Null, J. Wesley. "Curriculum Development in Historical Perspective." In *The SAGE Handbook of Curriculum and Instruction*, edited by F. Michael Connelly, 478–490. Thousand Oaks, CA: Sage Publications, Inc., 2008.

Phillips, Christopher J. "The Politics of Math Education." *New York Times*, December 3, 2015. https://www.nytimes.com/2015/12/03/opinion/the-politics-of-math-education.html.

Pinker, Susan. "Can Students Have Too Much Tech?" *New York Times*, January 30, 2015. https://www.nytimes.com/2015/01/30/opinion/can-students-have-too-much-tech.html.

Popeti, Mihai. "In Your Opinion, What Should the Purpose of Education Be?" Message 18, December 28, 2011. https://www.ted.com/conversations/7491/in_your_opinion_what_should_t.html.

Postman, Neil. *The End of Education: Redefining the Value of School*. New York: Vintage Books, 1995.

Prosen, Kevin. "'The Teacher Shortage' is No Accident—It's the Result of Corporate Education Reform Policies." *In These Times*, August 25, 2015. http://inthesitimes.com/working/entry/18344/the_teacher_shortage_isnt_an_accidentits_the_result_of_corporate_education.

Public Agenda. *The Purposes of Education: A Public Agenda Citizen Choicework Guide*. New York: Public Agenda, 2005.

Ravitch, Diane. "Andrea Gabor: Will One of the Nation's Most Innovative Districts Survive a Change in Leadership?" Web log post, May 15, 2019. http://dianeravitch.net/2019/05/15/andrea-gabor-will-one-of-the-nations-most-innovative-districts-survive-a-change-in-leadership/.

Ravitch, Diane. "How Choice May Kill Public Education." Web log post, June 24, 2012. http://dianeravitch.net/2012/06/24/how-choice-may-kill-public-education/.

Ravitch, Diane. "Mike Petrilli: In the Face of So Many Setbacks, Where Does Reform Go from Here?" Web log post, July 20, 2018. https://dianeravitch.net/2018/07/20/mike-petrilli-in-the-face-of-so-many-setbacks-where-does-reform-go-from-here/.

Ravitch, Diane. "The STEM 'Shortage' is a Scam." Web log post, September 4, 2017. http://dianeravitch.net/2017/09/04/the-stem-shortage-is-a-scam/.

Rawlings III, Hunter R. "Stop Defending the Liberal Arts." *The Chronicle of Higher Education*, December 21, 2017. https://www.chronicle.com/article/Stop-Defending-the-Liberal/242080.

Reys, Robert E. "Curricular Controversy in the Math Wars: A Battle Without Winners." *Phi Delta Kappan* 83, no. 3 (2001): 255–258.

Richardson, Joan. "Equity and Mathematics: An Interview with Deborah Ball and Bob Moses." *Phi Delta Kappan* 91, no. 2 (2009): 54–59.

Robinson, Ken. "Bring on the Learning Revolution!" Transcript of TED talk, February 2010. https://www.ted.com/talks/sir_ken_robinson_bring_on_the_revolution/transcript.

Robinson, Ken. "Do Schools Kill Creativity?" Transcript of TED talk, February 2006. https://www.ted.com/talks/ken_robinson_says_schools_kill_creativity/transcript.

Romberg, Thomas A. "The Scholarly Basis of the School Mathematics Reform Movement in the United States." *International Journal of Educational Research* 17, no. 5 (1992): 419–437. https://doi.org/10.1016/S0883-0355(05)80003-5.

Romberg, Thomas A., and Thomas P. Carpenter. "Research on Teaching and Learning Mathematics: Two Disciplines of Scientific Inquiry." In *The Handbook of Research on Teaching*, 3rd ed., edited by Merlin C. Wittrock, 850–873. New York: MacMillan, 1986.

Roosevelt, Eleanor. "Good Citizenship: The Purpose of Education." *Yearbook of the National Society for the Study of Education* 107, no. 2 (2008): 312–320. https://doi.org./10.1111/j.1744-7984.2008.00228.x.

Rose, Mike. *Why School? Reclaiming Education for All of Us*. New York: The New Press, 2014.

Ross, John A., Douglas McDougall, and Anne Hogaboam-Gray. "A Survey Measuring Elementary Teachers' Implementation of Standards-Based Mathematics Teaching." *Journal for Research in Mathematics Education* 34, no. 4 (2003): 344–363.

Russakoff, Dale. *The Prize: Who's in Charge of America's Schools?* New York: Houghton Mifflin Harcourt, 2015.

Rutter, David. "State Politicians Played Expensive ISTEP Joke on Schools." *Post-Tribune*, January 9, 2016. http://www.chicagotribune.com/suburbs/post-tribune/opinion/ct-ptb-rutter-on-istep-st-0110-20160108-story.html.

Salisbury, Mark. "Big Hopes, Scant Evidence." *The Chronicle of Higher Education*, April 9, 2017. https://www.chronicle.com/article/Big-Hopes-Scant-Evidence/239710.

Sarason, Seymour B. *School Change: The Personal Development of a Point of View*. New York: Teachers College Press, 1995.

Sarason, Seymour B. *The Predictable Failure of Educational Reform*. San Francisco: Jossey-Bass, 1990.

Sass, Edmund. "American Educational History: A Hypertext Timeline." Retrieved July 6, 2018. http://www.eds-resources.com/educationhistorytimeline.html.

Saunders, Darleen. "In Your Opinion, What Should the Purpose of Education Be?" Message 6, December 2, 2011. https://www.ted.com/conversations/7491/in_your_opinion_what_should_t.html.

Schuessler, Jennifer. "Humanities Committee Sounds an Alarm." *New York Times*, June 18, 2013. https://www.nytimes.com/2013/06/19/arts/humanities-committee-sounds-an-alarm.html.

Schwartz, Barry. "What 'Learning How to Think' Really Means." *The Chronicle of Higher Education*, June 18, 2015. https://www.chronicle.com/article/What-Learning-How-to-Think/230965.

Secada, Walter G. "Introduction." *International Journal of Educational Research* 17, no. 5 (1992): 403–406. https://doi.org/10.1016/S0883-0355(05)80001-1.

Shenoy, Amrish L. "Stephen Byrn—Outstanding Commercialization Award Winner." *Research Review* 22, no. 1 (2009): 3. West Lafayette, IN: Purdue University Press.

Singer, Alan. "Pearson Caught Cheating, Says Sorry, But Will Pay." *Huffington Post*, December 13, 2013. https://www.huffingtonpost.com/alan-singer/pearson-caught-cheating-s_b_4439043.html.

Sirota, David. "The Bait and Switch of School 'Reform.'" *Salon*, September 12, 2011. https://www.salon.com/2011/09/12/reformmoney/.

Sirotnik, Kenneth A. "What You See is What You Get—Consistency, Persistency, and Mediocrity in Classrooms." *Harvard Educational Review* 53, no. 1 (1983): 16–31.

Soll, Jacob. "The Economic Logic of the Humanities." *The Chronicle of Higher Education*, February 24, 2014. https://www.chronicle.com/article/The-Economic-Logic-of-the/144813.

Spector, Alan. "Re: (OpenForum) From Daniels' Testimony—Students for Sale?" Message posted to OpenForum@lists.purduecal.edu, March 19, 2015.

Smith, Thomas M. "Curricular Reform in Mathematics and Science Since *A Nation at Risk*." *Peabody Journal of Education* 79, no. 1 (2004): 105–129.

Sreenivasan, Sivaprasad. "In Your Opinion, What Should the Purpose of Education Be?" Message 44, December 28, 2011. https://www.ted.com/conversations/7491/in_your_opinion_what_should_t.html.

Stanic, George M. A., and Jeremy Kilpatrick. "Mathematics Curriculum Reform in the United States: A Historical Perspective." *International Journal of Educational Research* 17, no. 5 (1992): 407–417. https://doi.org/10.1016/S0883-0355(05)80002-3.

Sternberg, Robert J. "Giving Employers What They Don't Really Want." *The Chronicle of Higher Education*, June 17, 2013. https://www.chronicle.com/article/Giving-Employers-What-They/139877.

Strauss, Valerie. "Bill Gates Spent Hundreds of Millions of Dollars to Improve Teaching. New Report Says It Was a Bust." *Washington Post*, June 29, 2018. https://www.washingtonpost.com/news/answer-sheet/wp/2018/06/29/bill-gates-spent-hundreds-of-millions-of-dollars-to-improve-teaching-new-report-says-it-was-a-bust/?utm_term=.bf18bd9765b2.

Strauss, Valerie. "Statisticians Slam Popular Teacher Evaluation Method." *Washington Post*, April 13, 2014. https://www.washingtonpost.com/news/answer-sheet/wp/2014/04/13/statisticians-slam-popular-teacher-evaluation-method/?utm_term=.24cb73bde112.

Strauss, Valerie. "What's Really Going on in Indiana's Public Schools." *Washington Post*, July 12, 2018. https://www.washingtonpost.com/news/answer-sheet/wp/2018/07/12/whats-really-going-on-in-indianas-public-schools/?noredirect=on&utm_term=.34b69aec7197.

T., Mary. "In Your Opinion, What Should the Purpose of Education Be?" Message 21, December 26, 2011. https://www.ted.com/conversations/7491/in_your_opinion_what_should_t.html.

Tanner, Laurel N. "Curriculum History and Educational Leadership." *Educational Leadership* 41, no. 3 (1983): 38–39, 42.

Tarr, James E., Robert E. Reys, Barbara J. Reys, Oscar Chavez, Jeffrey Shih, and Steven J. Osterlind. "The Impact of Middle Grades Mathematics Curricula and the

Classroom Learning Environment on Student Achievement." *Journal for Research in Mathematics Education* 39, no. 3 (2008): 247–280.

Terkel, Amanda. "How Betsy DeVos Became the Most Hated Cabinet Secretary." *Huffington Post*, October 24, 2017. https://www.huffingtonpost.com/entry/betsy-devos-most-hated-secretary_us_59ee3d3be4b003385ac13c9b.

Thompson, Alba. G. "Teachers' Beliefs and Conceptions: A Synthesis of the Research." In *Handbook of Research on Mathematics Teaching and Learning*, edited by Douglas Grouws, 127–146. New York: MacMillan, 1992.

Tienken, Christopher. "Students' Test Scores Tell Us More about the Community They Live in Than What They Know." *The Conversation*, July 5, 2017. http://theconversation.com/students-test-scores-tell-us-more-about-the-community-they-live-in-than-what-they-know-77934.

Tsui, Keith. "In Your Opinion, What Should the Purpose of Education Be?" Message 30, December 10, 2011. https://www.ted.com/conversations/7491/in_your_opinion_what_should_t.html.

Turpin, Ruth. "Re: (OpenForum) What Colleges Will Teach in 2025." Message posted to OpenForum@lists.purduecal.edu, September 29, 2013.

Tyack, David, and Larry Cuban. *Tinkering toward Utopia: A Century of Public School Reform*. Cambridge, MA: Harvard University Press, 1995.

Ultican, Thomas. "Destroy Public Education (DPE) for Dummies." Web log post, February 22, 2018. https://tultican.com/2018/02/22/destroy-public-education-dpe-for-dummies/.

Walsh, Steve. "Next Goal: Full-Day Kindergarten." *Post-Tribune*, March 20, 2006. https://www.chicagotribune.com/suburbs/post-tribune/.

Warde, W. F. "John Dewey's Theories of Education." *International Socialist Review* 21, no. 1 (Winter 1960). https://www.marxists.org/archive/novack/works/1960/x03.htm.

Warde, W. F. "The Fate of Dewey's Theories." *International Socialist Review* 21, no. 2 (Spring 1960): 54–57, 61. https://www.marxists.org/archive/novack/works/1960/x04.htm.

Welner, Kevin G. "Obama's Dalliance with Truthiness." *Teachers College Record*, July 30, 2009. http://www.tcrecord.org/Content.asp?ContentID=15731.

Whitehead, Alfred North. "The Aims of Education." *Daedalus* 88, no.1 (1959): 192–205.

Wolk, Steven. "Why Go to School?" *Phi Delta Kappan* 88, no. 9 (2007): 648–658.

Woodward, John. "Mathematics Education in the United States: Past to Present." *Journal of Learning Disabilities* 37, no. 1 (2004): 16–31.

Wraga, William G. "The Progressive Vision of General Education and the American Common School Ideal: Implications for Curriculum Policy, Practice, and Theory." *Journal of Curriculum Studies* 31, no. 5 (1999): 523–544.

Yuan, Augustus. "In Your Opinion, What Should the Purpose of Education Be?" Message 43, December 28, 2011. https://www.ted.com/conversations/7491/in_your_opinion_what_should_t.html.

Zuniga, Rebecca. "In Your Opinion, What Should the Purpose of Education Be?" Reply to Message 31, December 10, 2011. https://www.ted.com/conversations/7491/in_your_opinion_what_should_t.html.

Index

About the Author

Jeff Gregg maintains an antagonistic relationship with academia, which is to say he plays the role of an academic, but often wishes he didn't. He has conducted research in elementary and secondary school classrooms, interviewed children to understand how they think about mathematics, and tried to help prospective elementary school teachers appreciate children's thinking and deepen their own understanding of the mathematics they will be teaching. Currently, he enjoys teaching multivariate calculus at a regional university. In a previous lifetime, he had a brief stint as a sportswriter and a longer stint as a freelance technical writer. In a future lifetime, he hopes to spend much time outdoors on the golf course and going for walks with his wife. He lives near Chicago with his wife, two children, four dogs, and, for some reason, a cat.